Welsh Legends

ISBN 978-1-291-98527-6

'King Arthur and the Afanc'

Painted

by

Jasmijn Evans

Introduction

Dark winter nights and a vivid imagination have created a long tradition of story telling amongst Celtic people and the Welsh are no exception. Like the Irish and the Scots, we love a good story. There are literally hundreds of Welsh legends and tales that have been passed down through the centuries. Many of them are based on factual events. Some have mythical roots, but all are entertaining.

In this book you will find a collection of eighty Welsh legends, gathered from across Wales. Previously published in five volumes as 'Legends and Myths from Wales'.Learn how the Temptress of Cilgerran tricked her husband, the truth of the French invasion, why there is a Prince sleeping in caves deep beneath Carreg Cennen, the secret of Culver Hole and why Twm Shon Cati is known as the Welsh Robin hood. Discover the story of Dafydd Gam and how he got his name, why the Men of Harlech were so valiant and the reason King Tewdrig wanted to save his kingdom. Learn the incredible story of Merthyr and its Iron Masters. These are just a few of the stories told in these pages.

Many pieces of Welsh folklore are repeated and there are variations of the same story relating to different places. At the same time, some places are associated with several legends. To avoid confusion and repetition, where legends are similar, I have used the story I liked best and omitted the rest. No offence is intended to partisan interests. One advantage I found of rewriting the more ancient legends is the licence to embroider. That is what storytellers have done for centuries. Nothing changes and I admit that I had a lot of fun adding my own interpretation to some of the tales.

The legends I have included are a diverse mixture. There are love stories, tales of heroic deeds, foolishness, greed, fables and humour. The cast includes fair maidens, evil barons, mermaids, smugglers, kings and ordinary folk quietly going about their business. Some of the stories I have included relate to more recent history; the Rebecca Riots is one example. Whilst retelling these legends I have tried to stay close to the facts.

I hope you enjoy these legends and, if you do, you may want to explore the locations where the events took place. To help you learn more, a series of five books titled 'Walking with Welsh Legends' has been published by Carreg Gwalch and are available from www.carreg-gwalch.com. More details of my books are at the back of this publication. Wales is a beautiful and diverse country filled with stunning waterfalls, mysterious lakes, imposing castles, towering mountains and golden seductive beaches. What better way can there be to explore such exciting places than by discovering the sources of these legends and myths.

Graham Watkins

Garnlwyd

2012

Table of Contents

Introduction

Part One   South-western Wales

Part Two   North Wales

Part Three   Central Wales

Part Four   South-eastern Wales

Part Five   North-eastern Wales

Part One South-western Wales

Chapter 1   The Lady of Llyn-Y-Fan

Many years ago in the village of Llanddeusant in the county of Carmarthenshire a young man lived with his mother. Their home was Blaensawdde Farm on the bank of the River Sawdde. The young man dreamt of finding a wife but Blaensawdde was a lonely place which no one ever visited. The youth never had an opportunity to meet or woo a girl. This made his mother sad. She worried that one-day she would be too old to run the house. She knew that they both needed a younger woman to live with them.

Each day the youth's mother would send him up the valley to tend the animals as they grazed. As he watched the animals he would dream of meeting a girl to make his wife. At the top of the valley, hidden below the high cliffs and known to all as the Black Mountain, there was a small lake and it was here that he would lay on the soft grass as the days passed.

One bright summer day when the sun was high in the sky and the skylarks were singing the young man heard a noise. He looked around, and there across the lake, he saw a beautiful girl. She was singing and combing her long black hair. At once he stood up and ran around the lake towards her. The girl saw him coming but she was not afraid and let him run right up to her.

'Good Sir. Why do you run here so fast?' she asked, looking at him. The young man was entranced by her beauty and resolved at once that he should marry her. It was love at first sight.

'You are the most beautiful girl I have ever seen. Will you marry me?' he exclaimed without embarrassment. The girl laughed.

'What token of love will you give me?' she asked. The young man thought hard. All he had was his lunch of stale bread and cheese. He reached into his pocket and presented the girl with the small loaf his mother had prepared. The girl saw the bread and turned away, saying.

'Cras dy fara. Nid hawdd fy nala.'

'Hard baked is thy bread. I will not have thee.' Having spoken, she walked into the lake and vanished. The following day, eager to see the girl again, he took the bread from the oven before it was completely baked and ran up the valley to the lake. The young woman was again seated on a rock by the lake. He offered her the bread but again she turned away, saying.

'Llaith dy fara. Ti ny fynna.'

'Unbaked is thy bread. I will not have thee.' One again she disappeared into the lake.

The young man told his mother what had happened and, wanting to help, she used all her skill to mix some dough for another loaf. She added fresh yeast and left the dough to rise overnight in the warm kitchen. The next day, the young man raced to the lake with the loaf his mother had just taken from the oven. It was wrapped in a towel, still warm, and had the smell of the hearth. The girl was by the lake waiting for him. He handed her the bread. She took a bite and smiled at him.

'I will be your wife. But hit me three times without cause and we will part forever.' As she spoke, sheep, cows, oxen and chickens started to come out of the lake. Overjoyed the young man picked up his new fiancé and carried her down the valley. They laughed as they went and the animals, which were her dowry, followed the happy pair. They married and the farm prospered. The girl was a good wife and bore him three sons. One day the man, for he was no longer young, scolded his wife for being slow to get ready for a family wedding. Irritated he pushed her lightly towards the door. His wife spoke sharply. 'You had no cause to hit me.'

At the wedding he tapped her lightly on the arm, in jest, to remind her of their own wedding. Again she spoke sharply. 'You had no cause to hit me.' On the way home she reminded him of her warning and never to hit her again or she would leave. The man promised faithfully that he would not.

Years passed until one cold November day, at his mother's funeral, the wife started to laugh. The man was upset by his wife's rude behaviour and, forgetting his promise, he prodded her.

10

'Be quiet,' he hissed. Without speaking a word, his wife marched out of the little church in Llanddeusant and up the valley. She walked quickly and behind her followed all the animals from the farm including a team of plough oxen. They were still pulling the plough as they went. They all walked into the lake and the man never saw them again. If you look carefully you can still see the furrow made by the plough as the oxen returned to the lake.

Distraught the man searched the lake every day for a year until, broken hearted, his health failed and he sat at home crying. The three sons also missed their mother and visited the lake often in the hope of seeing her. One day, as they drew nearer the lake, they saw her sitting on the same rock where their father had first seen her. She called out and they approached. She handed Rhiwallon, who was the eldest, a bag.

'In this bag are the secrets of healing from the Underworld. Take them and heal your father's broken heart,' she said and, without saying goodbye, slid into the lake and vanished for the last time. The boys took the bag of herbal remedies home but they were too late. Their father had already passed away. This however is not the end of the story. The brothers moved to Myddfai, near Llandovery and all became famous doctors known as 'The Physicians of Myddfai.' Their descendants continued for centuries as medical men and some say the last known Physicians of Myddfai was Doctor Charles Rice Williams who had his practice at Aberystwyth in 1881.

Chapter 2....The Tale of Twm Sion Cati

The story of Twm Sion Cati is a well-documented legend told and retold by the Welsh over the years. Twm Sion Cati was a robber and an outlaw. Like the English Robin Hood he was hated by those he stole from and loved by those who enjoyed hearing about his adventures. While there is no hard evidence that Robin Hood ever lived, Twm Sion Cati was no myth. He was a real outlaw.

Thomas Jones was born in 1530 at Porth y Ffynnon or Fountain Gate near Tregaron in Cardiganshire. His mother was Catherine, daughter of Meredydd ap Ieuen and his father John, son of David ap Madog ap Howel Motheu. These were lawless and violent times. Henry VIII was subjugating the Welsh and struggling to dominate Wales. A policy of terror was being used designed to destroy Welsh tradition and language. To complicate matters two legal systems were operating, one English and one Welsh, making it possible for robbers and thieves to live openly in different communities.

As he grew up, Thomas Jones learned quickly. With his good looks he could blend in with the English gentry. At the same time he was able to mix freely and unnoticed with the common people. With no patron to encourage his promotion and coming from a poor family Thomas, like so many young men, looked for an easy way and turned to thieving and robbing. Banditry was a common occupation but unlike most of his contemporaries Thomas Jones was not a violent man. He relied on his wits and cunning to trick his victims. His reputation soon spread and he became known throughout Wales and Twm Sion Cati or 'Cathy's son Tom' in English.

Because of his height and good looks, most Welsh at that time were short and stocky, and the courtesy he showed when robbing people it was suggested that his real father was the noble Sir John Wynn of Gwydir. How else, they argued, would a poor boy have such manners and be so learned. It was true that Twm was educated so perhaps, as an act of repentance for a wrong done to Catherine, Sir John had the boy tutored at an early age. Twm enjoyed acting the part of a gentleman. He was a showman and probably encouraged the idea that he had a highborn father. He may even have based himself on the legend of the noble outlaw Robin Hood. Twm however was not robbing the rich to give to the poor. His motives were less altruistic.

One morning Twm rode into Llandovery to buy a new iron pot for cooking porridge. He was not amused when the ironmonger showed him a poorly made pot and demanded a high price. He was the only ironmonger in Llandovery and expected a good profit from his well-dressed customer. Twm held the pot up and examined it carefully.

'Look here. There is a hole in your pot,' he exclaimed.

'Where?' asked the shopkeeper squinting up at the pot. Twm pulled the iron pot down and jammed it over the shopkeeper's head. As the man staggered about, Twm selected several items including a more expensive cooking pot and went to the door.

'If there's no hole in your pot how did your greedy head fit into it?' he asked and went on his way.

On another occasion Twm set out, dressed as a poor farmer riding an old nag, to settle a score with a highwayman new to the area. Sure enough the highwayman holds him up armed with two pistols. Appearing to panic, Twm throws two bulk bags into a pond by the track. Hearing the clinking of coins, the highwayman quickly dismounts and wades into the pond to save the sinking bags. Quick as a flash, Twm grabs the highwayman's stallion by the reins and sneaks away. The highwayman retrieves the bags only to find them full of seashells while Twm has escaped with a good horse and a pannier containing all the gold and jewels stolen by the highwayman.

Later, Twm steals the prize bull of a wealthy yeoman farmer, known locally as a bully. He disguises the animal with dye and a false tail and takes it to the local market where he dupes the

13

same farmer into buy his own animal. On the way home, it rains and as the dye washes off the farmer realises what has happened. Armed with a pistol and sword he gallops to Twm's house in Tregaron. There is a beggar sitting outside the house. Dismounting, the farmer thrust his reins and silver-riding crop at the beggar.

'Hold these he commanded,' cocked his pistol and ran into the house to take his revenge. The beggar leapt onto the horse and raced away throwing off his shabby clothes as he went. It was Twm and he had been waiting for the farmer. He rode to his attacker's farm and banged on the door. The farmer's wife, a timid woman, answers the door.

'Quick, there is no time to lose,' exclaims Twm. 'The farmer told me to fetch fifty guineas and take it to him. He leant me his horse and silver riding crop and told me to hurry.'

The farmer's wife always obeyed her husband and did not want to anger him. Without questioning Twm she handed over a purse with fifty gold coins in it. Twm knew that after this he had to get away. Every magistrate and justice would be after him so he took the horse, the silver handled riding crop and the fifty guineas and rode to London where he lived like a gentleman until his reputation started to catch up with him. To escape the law, Twm moved to Geneva where he lived for several years.

By the time he returned to Wales, Twm was tired of living by his wits. He wanted to settle down but he was still a wanted outlaw. On the run, he met and instantly fell in love with Joan, daughter of Sir John Price and being very rich, Joan was also known as the heiress of Ystradffin. Sadly, she did not return his affections.

Determined to win her, Twm hid in a cave high on Dinas Hill not far from Ystradffin. Every night he visited her and called to her until, one night, she opened the window and told him to go away and never bother her again.

'Put out your hand and I will kiss you goodbye,' he whispered.

Foolishly Joan did so and Twm grabbed hold of it. 'Promise to marry me or I will hold your hand forever.'

At first, Joan refused but when Twm took out his dagger and threatened to cut her hand off and keep it she began to think again. When he drew blood from her arm with the end of the dagger, Joan knew his point was made and agreed to Twm's demand. Joan kept her promise and, after they were married, she used her wealth to buy a pardon for Twm. She never allowed him to go thieving again and, with her help, Twm, or Thomas as he was now known became a leading member of society and a justice of the peace, passing sentence on all the rascals and robbers bought before him. He never went back to his cave on Dinas Hill again.

Elizabeth I gave Thomas Jones a royal pardon on the 15th January 1559, when he was 29 years old. After being pardoned he became a historian and studied heraldry drawing up the lineage of many noble families. Some of his heraldry work still survives. Thomas also wrote poetry and there are examples of his work at the British library. It is said that he was a bard at the 1564 Llandaff Eisteddfod.

According to research, Thomas married Joan in 1607 and would have been 77 at the time, rather old to be hiding in a cold damp cave and going wooing every night. It is more likely that he used the cave years earlier, when he was an active outlaw and on the run. He died in 1609 aged 79 leaving behind a mixture of legend and truth, a complex man of his time. I leave you to separate the fact from the fiction.

Chapter 3...The Ruin of Pennard Castle

In ancient times when the strong took what they wanted with a sword and the weak hid in terror there was a Baron so fierce and ruthless that everyone feared him. His strength and bravery in battle was known throughout Wales and women scolded their children by whispering his name. Even his own men at arms cowered when he looked at them and his enemies never dared venture near his Castle on the remote peninsular called 'Gower'. It was here that he passed his time in debauchery and drunkenness.

War was in the land and fearing defeat, the King of Gwynedd, Lord of Snowdonia, sent a messenger to the Baron pleading for help. Eager for a fight, but shrewd enough to see an opportunity for profit, the Baron sent the messenger back to the King demanding to know what his reward would be. The King was desperate. His enemies were collecting a large army in the east and he knew that his throne would soon be lost. The messenger quickly returned to the Baron's Castle.

'Well,' bellowed the Baron. 'What does your Lord and Master offer that I may take his side in this matter?'

'My master commands me to give you this,' he replied, handing the Baron a scroll with a royal seal. It was the King's guarantee to reward the Baron with anything he desired if they won the battle. The Baron tucked the scroll inside his shirt and called his men to arms. They rode swiftly to the north and joined the King. The army of Gwynedd was small and outnumbered many times over. Some were ready to turn and run but not the Baron. He charged straight at the enemy, hacking and slashing with his sword. No one could stand against his strength. As he cut and thrust, men fell right and left leaving a swathe through the ranks like a scythe through corn. The Baron's charge continued until he reached the battle flags of the invaders. Here stood the Dukes and Princes that led the invading army. The Baron cut them down, seized the flags and threw them to the ground.

Seeing their leaders slain the attackers turned and fled. The battle was won. The victors rode to Caernarfon castle and there were great celebrations. The King was determined to reward his mighty warrior.

'What prize shall you have?' he asked the Baron, ready to empty his treasury. 'Name it and it is yours.'

'You have a beautiful daughter, Sire. She will be my reward,' answered the Baron. The King was dismayed. This was not the bargain he expected but he had given his word and a King's word is not broken lightly. The King's daughter was beautiful but she was also a bit simple and impressionable. She was certainly lonely and seldom had visitors. Some claimed that her friends were fairies and that she spent her days talking to them. The Baron's demand flattered her. This hulk of a man was a mighty warrior and she liked the idea that he wanted her. Despite being a little afraid, the princess agreed to wed the Baron. With a sad heart, the King bade her farewell.

As they journeyed south to Pennard Castle the Baron boasted about his bravery and strength. As he bragged, her thoughts slowly turned from flattery and curiosity to doubt. She realised the Baron was a brute and wondered if she had done the right thing. Reaching Pennard Castle, the Baron ordered a great feast. The feasting soon turned to drunkenness with men and women engaged in lewd behaviour never witnesses by the Princess before. Drunk and full of lust, the Baron grabbed the Princess and carried her to his chambers, intent on having her. There was no talk of a wedding ceremony first. Intoxicated and overwhelmed by the Baron's strength she submitted. Suddenly, there was a cry from the guards.

'An army comes to Pennard.' The Baron ran to the battlements and saw a horde, carrying lanterns, advancing toward his Castle. He grabbed his sword and ran out to meet the attackers. He cut right and left, slashing and swinging as he ran through the invaders. The lights swarmed around him and he drove on, hacking and chopping. As he fought, his sword grew heavy and his arms burned with pain, from the exertion, until he could fight no more.

17

The Baron slumped to his knees, exhausted. His sword slid from his weary hands. Sober now, he looked up at the twinkling lights dancing around him and imagined he saw the faint glimmer of gossamer wings. This was no army but a host of fairies coming to share in the wedding celebrations.

As he watched, the wind blew the fairies away and a violent storm started to batter the Castle. The same night a mountain of sand blew in from the sea. The Castle, the Baron and the Princess vanished. The ruin you see today is all that is left from that fateful night.

Chapter 4...The Ladies of Kidwelly

Princess Gwenllian

In the time of the Norman conquests the Welsh chieftain that ruled South Wales was Gruffydd ap Rhys. He had a beautiful wife named Princess Gwenllian and they had two sons, Morgan and Maelgwn. Princess Gwenllian was an educated and cultured woman. She wrote part of the ancient book of stories 'The Mabinogion' and was the earliest known female writer. Throughout Wales, the Norman conquerors subjugated the population imposing their rule with an iron hand. In Kidwelly they built a castle to project their power. First as a simple wooden structure and then an imposing stone one dominating the town that grew beneath its ramparts.

In December 1135, following the death of Henry I, the Welsh unrest developed into rebellion and men were called to arms. A battle was fought near Swansea where the Anglo Norman army was defeated and over 500 Norman knights were killed. The time had come to throw out the invaders once and for all. Anxious to take advantage of the victory, Gruffydd ap Rhys travelled north to find reinforcements for his army.

At Kidwelly Maurice de Londres, the Norman Lord of Kidwelly, raised his battle flag. His plan to utterly crush the rebellion before Gruffydd ap Rhys could return with more men. Princess Gwenllian had no choice, if she wanted to protect her people, other than to collect what men she could muster and face de Londres in battle. They met in a field a mile north of Kidwelly. The battle itself was a short one. Although Princess Gwenllian fought like a she devil her small band was no match for the well-trained Norman garrison from Kidwelly. She was quickly defeated. Morgan was killed and Maelgwn was led away in chains like a common criminal. Princess Gwenllian also died that day. Some claim that she was killed in the battle and others that, capturing her alive, the Normans cut her head off.

The place where she fought was named after Princess Gwenllian 'Maes Gwenllian'. For years after the battle a headless body could sometimes be seen wandering the battlefield until Princess Gwenllian's skull was found in the castle and returned to her grave. Even today, after 900 years, Welsh patriots remember 'Gwenllian's Field' with pride.

The Dear Old Lady of Kidwelly

Every Schoolchild in Wales will have heard this nursery rhyme.
Hen fenyw fach Cydweli Yn gwerthu losin du, Yn rhifo deg am ddimai Ond unarddeg i mi. O dyna'r newydd gorau ddaeth i mi, i mi Yn rhifo deg am ddimai Ond unarddeg i mi.
It translates as:
The dear old lady of Kidwelly. A seller of sweets is she, Counts out ten for a halfpenny. But always eleven for me. That was very good news for me, for me. Counts out ten for a halfpenny. But always eleven for me.

By the 13th Century Kidwelly Castle had passed down through the family to Lady Hawise de Londres. She was the Castellan or Constable of the castle. Although she was a Norman, Lady Hawise was sympathetic to her Welsh tenants and, unusually for someone in her position, spoke fluent Welsh. Lady Hawise had lived at Kidwelly all her life but that was soon to change. Welsh rebels led by Meredydd ap Rhys attacked the castle and captured it. During the final hours of the siege Lady Hawise escaped down the river in a small boat leaving her home and everything she owned. These were troubles times and Wales was a dangerous place for a Norman Lady without protection. Robbers and vagrants of all types roamed the land. There was hatred and fear. A Welshman could be executed for minor crimes and taking revenge on the Normans was common practice. Meredydd ap Rhys, for one, had sworn revenge on all Normans and to kill every Norman he saw.

Lady Hawise went to her old friend Angharrad the sweet seller. She borrowed some clothes, disguised herself as the old lady, travelled to Dryslwyn Castle and, still in disguise, bluffed her way in. Dryslwyn Castle, the home of Llywelyn ap Iorwerth. Prince Llywelyn was a Welshman who had married Joan, the King of England's sister. Meredydd ap Rhys was Llewelyn's feudal vassal. In the great hall, Lady Hawise revealed her true identity and pleaded her case. Impressed with her determination and persuaded by his wife, Prince Llywelyn agreed to help Lady Hawise regain Kidwelly Castle. He gave her a parchment with his royal seal commanding Meredydd ap Rhys to return the castle to its true owner.

Returning to Kidwelly Lady Hawise once again needed her disguise to get into the castle. She approached Meredydd ap Rhys as he ate with his men at arms and placed her basket of sweets containing the royal parchment in front of him. Startled, he picked up the scroll and broke the seal. As he read Lady Hawise straightened up, cast off the old woman's clothes and spoke loudly in welsh.

'I am Lady Hawise de Londres. I am Castellan of Kidwelly and I command you to leave and remove your men.' Meredydd ap Rhys threw aside the royal parchment, sprang up and drew his dagger.

'No man or woman commands me.' He held the blade to her throat but hesitated. Lady Hawise did not flinch as the cold steel pressed against her skin. Slowly, he lowered the dagger.

'Lady Hawise, the decree you bring from Prince Llywelyn is of no consequence to me but your courage cannot be ignored. You shall have your castle. My men and I will be gone within the hour.' Meredydd ap Rhys kept his word and left Carmarthenshire forever. Lady Hawise de Londres remained as Castellan of Kidwelly for many years, kept company by her Welsh friend Angharrad, the old sweet lady.

Chapter 5...The Sleeping Prince of Carreg Cennen

Beneath a rocky outcrop, topped by Carreg Cennen Castle, there is a cave that reaches deep into the bowels of the earth. Within this cold damp dungeon lies a band of men dressed in ancient armour. Each man has his sword and shield close at hand, ready for the call to arms. Their chests slowly rise and fall and there is the quiet rasp of snoring. These ancient warriors are in a deep, trance like, sleep. The leader, like his men, has lain here undisturbed for 600 years; the most fearful and bloody warrior of all, his name is Owain of The Red Hand. Hold up your lamp and look closely at his shield. In the dim light you will see the 'Four Lions of Gwynedd', the coat of arms of a Prince. In front of you lies the last in a long and noble line of Princes.

Here slumbers Owain of The Red Hand, the last truly Welsh Prince of Wales. As he sleeps can you see his eyes are moving beneath the lids? His face is twitching. There are small sudden jerks in his arms and legs. Owain of the Red Hand is a man of action even now as he sleeps in this dark place. Owain dreams of battles fought and battles soon to come. This phalanx of warriors and their Prince have fought in wars from Switzerland to Spain. They invaded Guernsey, learned the secrets of the French Royal Court and were favoured by kings. But now they sleep and wait for the clarion call of trumpets and the clash of arms, when as one, they will seize their weapons, pour from the cave at Carreg Cennen and drive the Saxons from their land. Leave quietly, taking care that you do not wake them.

The legend of the sleeping prince has been retold many times but Owain of the Red Hand was no legend. He was born Owain ap Thomas ap Rhodri (Owain son of Thomas and grandson of Rhodri) in 14th century Wales. His lineage reaches back to Llewelyn and he could legitimately claim the title 'Prince of Wales'. The French government recognised his claim and endeavoured to help him regain his throne. Owain grew up in France and, being a gentleman with limited choices for a profession, it was either army or church, he became a soldier in the French army.

His ability and ruthless character bought swift promotion. Owain developed into a formidable leader of men and Welsh mercenaries were soon joining him. He led successful French campaigns into Switzerland then Spain and recovered Guernsey from the English. As with his reputation, the stories of his violence too became exaggerated and his followers adopted the name Owain of The Red Hand (Owain Lawgoch). Realising how effective Owain had become the French began to groom him. They made him a Captain General of France and started to make plans for him to lead an invasion of England. Owain was paid 300,000 francs (£240m in today's money) to build an invasion force. This was a serious, very well funded, invasion attempt and Owain was only delayed by bad weather.

News reached the English who realised that the threat needed dealing with quickly. One day in 1378 Owain was outside the castle at Mortagne-sur-Gironde preparing to attack the English defenders. His servant, a Welshman named John Lambe, entered Owain's tent, crept up behind him and drove a short shafted spear into his back, killing him. According to official letters from the time, now in the public records office at Kew, the English paid the assassin £20 to murder Owain. The pay for an archer during that period was just 4 pence a day. John Lambe escaped and lived in England into old age.

Owain of The Red Hand is a legend in Wales. However, as a man he has been largely forgotten; but not in France. In Montagne-sur-Gironde, 40 miles north of Bordeaux, on the 15th August 2003 a statue was unveiled with great pomp by the French Minister of Defence in honour of Owain of the Red Hand, Owain Lawgoch, Yvain de Galles, legitimate Prince of Wales and Captain General of France. The 8ft stone statue, carved by French stonemasons, is of a hand holding a disc of welsh slate. The disc, carved by a Welshman, shows the four lions of Gwynedd, the sign of a Welsh Prince.

Chapter 6...The Treasure of Craig y Ddinas

It had been a long walk but the drover was finally in London. The geese and sheep had been sold and it was time to begin the trek back to his homeland, Wales. The drover strode across London Bridge. He felt the silver coins in his purse and made sure they were well hidden. He knew the dangers for the unwary and grasped his hazel staff, prepared to defend himself. His eyes darted to and fro looking for any sign of the robbers which he knew loitered in every shadow and who might waylay him. A tall thin man stepped out of an alleyway and approached him. The drover's grip tightened on his staff.

'You have walked a long way. What country are you from?' asked the stranger. The drover looked at the thin man with suspicion.

'He may have accomplices,' he thought. 'I come from my own country,' replied the drover curtly and walked on, increasing his stride as he went. The thin man fell in alongside and easily kept pace. The drover marched on, trying to escape his unwelcome inquisitor.

'Why the hurry friend? I mean you no harm,' said the stranger. The drover ignored him. 'Your hazel stick caught my eye. Do you know where it came from?' asked the thin man. By now the drover and his follower were in the open. Confident that they were alone he stopped and turned to confront the stranger.

'What do you want of me?' he demanded, standing close to his follower.

'Do not be afraid. It is your stick I am interested in.'

The drover held up his staff as if to strike the stranger.

'Be off before I break your stupid skull with my staff,' he threatened, but the stranger did not flinch. They stared at each other for a few moments until, unwilling to strike an unarmed man, the drover lowered his staff.

'Tell me, did you cut the hazel yourself? Can you remember where it came from?' asked the stranger.

24

'Where did I cut my staff from? What nonsense is this?' asked the drover.

'Your hazel stick is from a rock near a river. Am I right?' demanded the stranger. The drover considered the question for a moment before replying.

'It's true enough. I pulled it from Craig y Ddinas and there is a river. How did you know?' he asked the stranger.

'Tell me, does it snow every day of the year where you come from?' said the thin man. The drover stepped back in astonishment.

'There is such a place at Sgwd yr Eira but how do you know? Are you a wizard?' he asked. The thin man smiled and gently put his hand on the drover's staff.

'You see the shape of the handle. It is the root. See how it curves and twists. Your staff is the key to a great fortune.' The drover looked at the handle. It was a strange shape but had always served him well on his long walks. 'Take me to the rock where the staff grew and great wealth will be yours. All I ask in return is that you show me the falling snow in summer,' said the stranger. They travelled back to Wales together and the drover showed the stranger the crevice where he had pulled his staff from the rocks. The stranger took the staff and pushed it back into the crack. Slowly the rock parted until a narrow stone stairway was revealed. The two men lit torches and clambered down into the damp cave. Half way down the steps, hung a large bronze bell. They squeezed past and continued down into a huge cavern. Gold and silver glistened in the flickering light from the torches. Coins and jewels covered the floor. The drover stared in wonder at the treasure and was about to speak when the thin man touched his arm and held his fingers to his lips.

'Shhh,' he whispered and pointed to the far side of the cave. The drover peered through the gloom and saw the men. They were asleep but dressed for war and one had a crown on the helmet by his side.

'Who are they,' he hissed quietly.

'There lies Arthur and his knights waiting for the day when the bronze bell tolls and the giant eagles of good and bad fight. When that day comes, all wrongs will be avenged. Do not wake them,' answered the thin man.

'Whose is the treasure?' asked the drover. His eyes were filled with greed.

'I have no use for it. All that you can carry away is yours,' replied the thin man. He helped the drover fill his pockets with coins and rubies and together they crept up the stairs. The thin man passed the bell easily but the drover, laden with booty, brushed against it. The bell tilted and there was a dull clang. They froze.

'Is it the day?' came a voice from behind them.

'No. Sleep on,' answered the thin man and they scurried out, into the daylight. The thin man pulled the staff from the rock and the stairway vanished. 'You can return as many times as you wish but if the knights stir and ask 'Is it the day? You must answer. No. Sleep on,' and leave quickly,' he warned and handed the staff to the drover.

'Now show me the snow at Sgwd yr Eira,' demanded the thin man.

'I will take you there,' said the drover. They began to walk up the valley. The thin man walked quickly, impatient to see the snow he had been promised. It was a hot day and the drover, laden with treasure, was soon sweating as he tried to keep up with the thin man. After climbing for some time, the two men came to a large boulder and the exhausted drover sat down.

'Your snow is down there,' he pointed down a steep slope. The thin man started down the slope. The drover, eager to see, stumbled behind. He saw the thin man, far ahead; reach the bottom of the valley and the river. The air was damp. They had reached Sgwd yr Eira, the sacred waterfall. Water cascaded down the cliff like a curtain of falling snow. The thin man strode into the waterfall and vanished, never to be seen again.

The years passed. The drover's days of herding animals along dusty tracks were over. He built a fine house and married.

His new wife, eager to impress her friends, spent his money quickly. Soon, every penny was gone and the drover took his hazel staff and returned to the cave for more treasure. They lived a good life and he made many visits to Craig y Ddinas, returning laden with gold and silver. Each time he visited the cave he was careful not to wake the sleeping warriors.

One day his wife asked him to take her to London. He agreed and, checking his purse, decided to make another visit to the treasure cave. The drover took his staff from the barn and returned to the rock. He pushed his hazel staff into the crack and the stairs appeared. Once more he went down the steps and past the bell. The knights were sleeping. He pulled a sack from his tunic and started to fill it with gold and silver. When the sack could hold no more, he dragged it across the floor to the steps. He was so intent on his haul that he forgot the bell above him. He strained and puffed as the sack moved slowly up from step to step. He slipped and fell backwards. His shoulder hit the bell. A loud clang boomed through the cave. Startled, the drover let go of the sack. It tumbled down the stairs, banging and crashing as it went. Then, there was silence.

'Is it the day?' called a voice from the cavern below. The drover had forgotten the words the thin man used. Frantically, he tried to collect the scattered treasure and stuff it into the sack. He started to run up the steps. The knights were awake. With clanking armour, they swarmed up the stairs. They caught the drover, thrashed him until he was unconscious and threw him from the cave.

He woke cold and wet. It was dark and the rain was pouring down. There was a searing pain in his leg. It was broken. He crept about, feeling for the cave and his hazel staff but they had gone. The Drover crawled slowly home and lived the rest of his life a lame pauper. Although he searched for years, he never found the cave or his hazel walking stick again.

Chapter 7...The Martyr of Llandovery

The start of the 15th Century saw an uprising against the
English that resulted in the first and only Welsh-speaking
parliament. The leader of the rebellion, Owain Glyndwr, was
descended from the princes of Powys and Cyfeiliog in the north
and, on his mother's side, the kingdom of Deheubarth in the south.
  Glyndwr was educated in England, trained as a soldier,
serving with distinction for the English King before returning to
Wales wealthy and ready to marry. The Wales he came back to was
in turmoil. The Welsh people were cowed and there was no justice
in the law. They wanted a leader and charismatic Glyndwr was the
man of the hour. He found himself drawn into a quarrel with
Reginald de Grey, Lord of Ruthin who had stolen some land. De
Grey was close to the King and things quickly developed.
  Glyndwr gathered loyal supporters around him, established
an army at Ruthin, raise his battle flag and started to drive out the
English. Ruthin fell and Glyndwr followed up with attacks
throughout north Wales. He claimed the title Prince of Wales and
Welshmen, throughout the British Isles threw, down their tools and
hurried home to join him.
  The English response was brutal and effective. They levied
a large army and marched across north Wales sacking and burning
everything. Glyndwr and his men hid in the mountains for the
winter, emerging the following year with a renewed campaign.
They seized castles including Harlech, Conwy and Aberystwyth.
By 1403, the rebels operated freely through most of Wales. A
Parliament was established at Machynlleth, treaties made with
France and Spain and plans made to invade England.
  The English had other ideas. The English army was the
largest and most effective in Europe as the French discovered two
years later at Agincourt. The Castles were retaken and Glyndwr
became an outlaw. The English army, led by Henry IV, arrived in
Llandovery, pursuing Glyndwr.

They seized local land owner Llywelyn ap Gruffydd Fychan and tried to cajole him into disclosing the whereabouts of Glyndwr's camp. Llywelyn was an elderly man from the village of Caeo. He had two sons fighting with Glyndwr, was a patriot and understood what he had to do. For weeks, he led the English around south Wales as they hunted for Glyndwr. Each day they rode out to a possible hideout that Llywelyn told them about. Each night they returned having found nothing.

Eventually the King began to lose his patience. He saw where Llywelyn's loyalties lay and resorted to harder tactics. The torturers began their grizzly work to get the information needed to capture Glyndwr and end the uprising. Despite being tortured, Llywelyn ap Gruffydd said nothing that might hurt his Prince.

King Henry lost interest in Llywelyn and decided to make an example of him by executing him for high treason. There were clear instructions for the execution, designed to strike fear into the hearts of the King's enemies, Glyndwr's supporters.

'He shall be strangled, being hanged up by the Neck between Heaven and Earth, as deemed unworthy of both, or either; as likewise, that the Eyes of Men may behold, and their Hearts condemn him. Then he is to be cut down alive, and to have his Privy Parts cut off and burnt before his Face, as being unworthily begotten, and unfit to leave any Generation after him. His Bowels and inlay'd Parts taken out and burnt, who inwardly had conceived and harboured in his heart such horrible Treason. After, to have his Head cut off, which had imagined the Mischief. And lastly, his Body to be quartered, and the Quarters set up in high and eminent Places, to the View and Detestation of Men, and to become a Prey for the Fowls of the Air.' sic

Llywelyn was dragged to the centre of Llandovery and publicly executed, in the same manner as William Wallace and Guy Fawkes. His dismembered body was salted and displayed throughout Wales. Glyndwr was never betrayed by his people and quietly disappeared into obscurity. Today, he remains a symbol of

Welsh independence and patriotism with, his loyal follower, Llewelyn.

Chapter 8...The Mermaid of Cemaes Head

Peregrine was a fisherman, like his father and his
grandfather before him, a hard workingman used to the harsh life of
working the nets and braving the elements. He was not an educated
man but he was a good fisherman. He understood the ways of the
sea and its moods and he knew the best places to fish. Peregrine
lived in St. Dogmaels, a small fishing village near the mouth of the
River Teifi. Each day he would set sail in his boat using the tide to
take him over the bar in the mouth of the river and out to sea. In the
summer the fishing was good and with fair weather Peregrine
returned each evening with his boat, low in the water, laden with
fish. In the winter when the wind blew from the west and the tides
ran fast, fishing was difficult and dangerous. Despite the bad
weather Peregrine and his friends had no choice but to set sail and
trust in God to bring them home safely. Rarely would these stout
fishermen stay home mending nets. Hungry children, empty bellies
and faith made sure they were out in all weathers.

One beautiful August morning Peregrine left early before
any of the other fishermen had risen from their beds. He set sail for
Cemaes Head and started to drift with his nets almost under the
jagged cliffs. He knew the herring would be running inshore
around the headland. They did the same at this time every year. As
the boat drifted he watched choughs mobbing herring gull nests on
the cliff. Further out to sea, bottlenose dolphins were jumping and
Peregrine wondered why they continually leapt out of the water
flipping and twisting in the air.

Suddenly his nets went taught. Peregrine stopped
daydreaming. There was serious work to do. The boat changed
direction and started to move against the current. Carefully and
very slowly Peregrine began to pull the net into the boat. He did not
want to lose such a fine fish or damage his net. The fish was
putting up a good fight and the boat started to shake as it sped
through the water. Peregrine was soon soaked with spray and sweat

as he eased the wet ropes into the boat. He could feel each tug from the fish; it was getting closer to the boat.

The battle between man and fish went on for hours until, with the sun high in the sky, the net slackened as the fish tired. With a final heave Peregrine pulled his catch into the boat. What he saw took his breath away. The tail was large with two fins covered with silver scales, gleaming in the sunlight; the body was that of a woman with a peach complexion and a head crowned with long golden hair.

Peregrine sat down in the stern of the boat to consider things. This is a fine catch he thought. Be she fish or woman, someone would pay a good price for such a creature. He looked around. During the struggle the boat had drifted far out to sea. There was no time to waste. Peregrine checked that his catch was secure, hoisted the sail and set a course taking him past Cardigan Island and home.

'Please let me go Peregrine,' whispered the creature, quietly. Peregrine hardly heard her. 'Please let me go Peregrine,' she whispered again. Peregrine stared at the creature.

'Why should I?' he asked.

'My mouth is dry and my scales are cracking. Please let me go Peregrine or I will die,' she said. Peregrine looked at the creature trussed up in his nets. She was limp and forlorn. Suddenly, he felt sorry for her. A wave of guilt and revulsion for what he was doing swept over him. Peregrine pulled out his knife, cut the nets and eased the creature gently over the side of the boat. She disappeared beneath the water and he sat there confused. Was it all a dream? He collected his thoughts, tidied the nets and reset the sail to catch the wind. As the boat slowly got under way the mermaid suddenly emerged and pulled herself up on the gunwale.

'Peregrine, you are a good man and one day I will repay your kindness,' she said then submerged and, with a flash of silver, swam away. Back in St. Dogmaels Peregrine told no one about his encounter with the mermaid. Who would believe such a fisherman's tall tale?

The months passed and Peregrine, eager to see the mermaid again, often fished at Cemaes Head. By October the weather had deteriorated and the Head, with its strong winds and winter tides, was no place to be. The fishing boats from St. Dogmaels stayed closer together now and looked for calmer water to cast their nets in. One fateful morning the boats were just leaving the protection of the lee shore of Carreg Aderyn when Peregrine felt a jerk and his boat listed to starboard. A head crowned with long golden hair appeared over the gunwale.

'Peregrine, you must turn back. Peregrine, you must turn back. Peregrine, you must turn back,' she said three times and without waiting for an answer or a question, vanished back into the water. Peregrine started to wave to the fishermen in the nearest boat.

'Turn about. We must go back,' he yelled, but they ignored him. He tried again. 'We must not fish today,' he cried but the others, now further out to sea, did not hear his cries and sailed on into open water.

Peregrine pushed the tiller over and, running before the wind, was soon back in the estuary and safely tied up in St. Dogmaels. The fishing fleet sailed out past Cemaes Head where, without land to protect them, a storm hit with its full force and many brave fishermen lost their lives.

The legend of Peregrine and the mermaid is based on events that took place in the 18th Century which are recorded in St. Dogmaels Parish Church. On the 30th September 1789 the fishing fleet was close inshore near Allt y Coed Farm and sheltering from a strong, steady southwesterly wind. Nets had been raised and the boats had a good catch of herring on board. They were waiting for the rising tide to carry them over the bar and into St. Dogmaels. Without warning the wind started to blow from the northwest so that the fishing boats had no land to offer protection from the full force of the gale. The sea quickly grew mountainous and many of the fishing boats were wrecked on the rocks. Others floundered and sank.

One fisherman however, who lived at Cwmmins, St. Dogmaels, read the weather signs correctly that day and did not put to sea. He stayed home, safe and warm in his cottage that day. His name was Peregrine. Altogether, 27 local fishermen died in the storm, a devastating calamity for such a small and tight knit community.

Chapter 9...The Temptress of Cilgerran

Rhys ap Tewdwr was the King of Deheubarth (South Wales). He lived at Dinefwr Castle near Llandeilo from where he ruled his kingdom. There were other claims to the throne and Rhys sought help from William the Conqueror to defend his kingdom. He paid William £40 a year and became the Norman King's vassal in return for his protection. Rhys had a daughter. Nest, Princess of Deheubarth, was famous for her beauty and, wishing to strengthen his grip on his throne, Rhys planned to arrange a marriage to create an alliance with his Norman masters. However, before he had the opportunity to put his plan into action events overtook him.

There were jealous princes on all his borders and Rhys fought many wars to keep them out. In1081 he defeated Caradog ap Gruffydd at the famous Battle of Mynydd Cam. In 1088 Rhys escaped to Ireland after an attack, returning with Danish mercenaries to reclaim his lands. In1091, Carmarthenshire men rose up and were defeated by Rhys at Llandudoch. Seeing the deteriorating situation in South Wales, the Normans decided to take action. All acts of patronage were forgotten and a Norman army set about re-invading Wales. The Welsh squabbling stopped and they turned to face the Norman threat together. Rhys ap Tewdwr died opposing the Norman advance at Brecon and his kingdom was seized by the Normans.

By now, William had died and Henry I was King. He saw Nest and, seeing her beauty, became her protector. As well as being beautiful, Nest was headstrong and ambitious. She soon became the King's mistress. It gave her power and prestige. She bore the King a son and named him Henry. However, King Henry was starting to tire of Nest and married her to Gerrald de Windsor. Gerrald was appointed Constable of Pembroke and despatched from court with his new bride. Nest accepted her reduced circumstances reluctantly but fulfilled her responsibilities producing five children. Unhappy with being a brood mare, Nest longed for a way out of the trap her life had become.

The Christmas of 1109 was bitterly cold. The snow had come early and the roads were treacherous with ice. People did not travel in the winter so the visitors to Cilgerran Castle were not expected but Gerald was a hospitable man and welcomed the small group of horsemen. It was Owain ap Cadwgan, Prince of Powys and his retainers travelling back from Ireland. The lamps were lit and logs stacked in the grates to warm the rooms. Owain was handsome with boyish features, a quick smile and a twinkle in his eye. As they feasted Nest laughed at his jokes and massaged his vanity with praise. Owain saw her beauty and the desire in her eyes. He wanted her. Gerrald, enjoying the lively company, drank well and retired to his bed early.

That night, after all in the castle had retired, Owain quietly collected his men together. He led them to the East Tower where Nest lay with her husband and began banging on the bedchamber door. They yelled and struck their weapons as if there was a great fight. Nest sprang up.

'Quick husband!' she cried, 'You must escape.' Confused, with sleep and ale, Gerrald stumbled from the bed. 'This way,' said Nest and, leading her husband by the hand, took him out the rear door of their chamber to the guardrobe (toilet). 'Climb down my love before they break the door down and kill you,' she pleaded. Fearing for his life, Gerrald kissed his wife, squeezed through the narrow hole into the cold stone funnel that led to the river. Nest ran back to the bedchamber, opened the door to admit Owain and they made their escape from the castle taking the children with them.

Owain and Nest lived happily together and had two children before she was recaptured and returned to her husband. She always claimed that she had been kidnapped and had been Owain's unwilling prisoner. Owain's family had their lands confiscated and Owain escaped abroad to hide. When he returned years later, thinking it was safe, Gerrald tracked him down and murdered him. After Gerrald's death, Nest went on to become the mistress of Stephen of Cardigain and have another son, but she will always be remembered, in particular, for her adventure at Cilgerran.

36

Chapter 10…David the Water Drinker

In the 6th Century a child was born in the small town of
Menevia. Nonnita was a Royal Princess. Her mother was Anne;
daughter of Uther Pendragon and her father, Cynys, was Chieftain
of Menevia. The name they gave the baby meant nurse or priestess
in ancient tongues, for her mother Anne had decided this was to be
her calling.

The child grew into a pious and devout young woman and,
loyal to her mother's wishes, she learned the sacred arts of healing
and worship. Menevia had always been a wild, mystical place,
filled with gods and goddesses. In the Mabinogion, our earliest
written collection of Welsh folk legends, this land was known as
'gwlad hud a lledrith' - 'the land of magic and enchantment'. The
very name Menevia means 'Way of the Moon'. But these were
times of change. The ancient gods were being usurped. There was a
new religion with only one god. Christianity had established a
foothold on this small corner of Wales. Nonnita embraced the new
religion with the fervour of an excited convert. She showed no
interest in men and chose instead a life of celibacy and devotion to
her one true god.

As she matured, Nonnita's reputation as a holy woman
spread and people travelled great distances to consult her and listen
to her wise words. Sant, King of Ceredigion, was one. On seeing
Nonnita's contentment and radiance he was overcome with desire
and, despite her resistance, took her and violated her. That selfish
act by Sant changed Christianity in Wales forever. Nonnita became
pregnant.

When her waters broke, Nonnita crept out of the town
towards the sea. She stopped at a small spring near the cliff,
washed herself and lay down in the mud to wait the birth of her
child. It was late in the afternoon. The sky darkened as storm
clouds gathered. Torrential rain poured down on the exposed
woman. She shook with cold. Slowly, the labour pains intensified
until Nonnita could barely stand the pain. As the child arrived the

clouds parted and a single ray of sunshine appeared from the west, danced across the angry sea and settled, illuminating the mother and her child.

Nonnita bathed the child in the cold spring and wrapped him in her cloak.

'I shall call you Dewi Sant', she said quietly as she carried the small bundle back to her home. Like his mother, Dewi, or David in English, was destined to serve the Christian Church. Shortly after the birth, Nonnita left David in Menevia and went to Brittany where she established several religious sites located by holy wells. Most of these are dedicated to 'Our Lady and St. Anne – her mother'. The name Anne originates from of the ancient name Ana/Inanna, who was the Universal Goddess of Cosmic Waters, and of Childbirth. Nonnita's tomb is at Dirion in Brittany where the well and a chapel are dedicated to her.

David continued to live at Menevia and two devout priests undertook his education. Saint Columba and Saint Finnegan both recognised that David was intelligent and a hard worker. They encouraged him and schooled him in basic theology, languages and history. The priests engaged a blind tutor, Paulinius, to continue his studies. It was Paulinius, who benefited from David's first miracle. David splashed water into his tutor's eyes and the old man's sight was restored. When David told him to open his eyes, the first thing the tutor saw was a bunch of daffodils.

As he grew, David developed his own religious ideas. He became a strong orator and rose quickly through the ranks of the clergy. David made it a rule never to drink anything but water, unusual, when it was safer to drink beer or wine. He soon became known as 'David Aquaticus' – 'David the Water Drinker'.

David was a strict vegetarian and frequently immersed himself in freezing water as an act of piety. He travelled throughout Britain preaching to the different pagan tribes. On one occasion, while giving an open-air sermon at Llanddewi Brefi near Tregaron, the crowd grew very large. The people at the back complained that they could not see David or hear what he was saying. David stopped preaching, took a handkerchief from his cassock and placed it on the ground. He then stood on it. As he did so, the ground rose up creating a small hill, giving everyone a good view and enabling them all to hear his sermon. As he continued to preach, a dove landed on his shoulder.

Wishing to learn more about his faith, David undertook a long and dangerous pilgrimage to Jerusalem, returning to establish his own monastery and church at Menevia.

Throughout his life, David's teachings were always aimed at the ordinary people. He taught that people should 'do the little things' in life - in Welsh, 'gwnewch y pethau bychain'. Eventually, he was declared the Bishop of Wales and became the most influential leader of the Celtic Church in Britain. He was killed during a Viking raid on the 1st March 589 having foretold his own death and, on his deathbed, once again imploring his followers to 'do the little things' in life.

In 1120 Pope Calistus II Canonized David and declared that two pilgrimages to David's tomb equalled one to Rome. Dewi Sant had become Saint David, the only Welsh Saint recognised by the Catholic Church. The people of Menevia honoured David by changing the name of their city to St. David's and his shrine became a very popular attraction in the Middle Ages attracting many notable visitors. The English Kings William I and Henry II both made pilgrimages to St. David's.

Today Nonnita is known as St. Non. Her well is still used for its healing properties. Nearby is the ruin of an ancient chapel. In 1951 the Roman Catholic Church built a shrine at the well dedicated to 'Our Blessed Lady'. They have also constructed a spiritual retreat there which is popular today and is sometimes fully booked years in advance.

St. Non's son, David is the Patron Saint of Wales. We remember him on the 1st March each year, the anniversary of his death, when Welshmen wear a daffodil to celebrate the life of a remarkable man.

Chapter 11...The French Invasion

It was early in the morning and the frost was thick on the ground. The horseman frantically drove his animal on. He was frightened of slipping on the ice but there was no choice. He had to get to the big house with the fearful news quickly. The French had landed. Napoleon's invasion of Britain had begun.

The squire was at breakfast when the messenger burst in. He listened to the garbled story. Thousands of French soldiers had landed at Carregwastad Point. Right now they were unloading cannon and powder. It was the Black Legion, the most feared of Bonaparte's troops, battle hardened conquerors of Europe and they were here in Pembrokeshire.

The squire summoned his son, Colonel Knox the commander of the local volunteer militia. They considered the problem. What could a few farmers and tradesmen armed with blunderbusses and farm implements do against such a fearsome and powerful enemy? The squire was cautious and counselled patience.

'Let the regular army deal with the French.' he suggested. His son, who had no military experience, was more reckless.

'I'm not afraid of a few Frenchies. We can soon give them a bloody nose,' he boasted. The headstrong Knox persuaded his father that the time for action was now. This was the opportunity for glory and to show that stout men were afraid of no one. Messengers were sent to rally the volunteers.

'Come quickly and bring any weapons you have.' They met at the fort in Fishguard and assembled into ranks. The squire's son, now a Lieutenant Colonel of the Fishguard and Newport Volunteer Infantry, sat on his horse and looked proudly at his command. Boys and men, they totalled 250. Some armed with muskets, others with pitchforks and most with clubs, hurriedly cut from the hedges. The orders were given and the heroic band marched out of the town, towards Goodwick and the enemy.

By now French troops had established a base at Llanwnda, a short distance from where they had landed. Provisions and munitions were still being brought ashore and cannons were being remounted on their carriages after being manhandled from the ships. It was a hive of activity. They were professional soldiers and every man knew his duty. The French fleet sat anchored off the point as small boats went back and forth with supplies.

News had spread quickly that the French had landed and there was going to be a battle. As the Squire's son led his men, a crowd gathered and started to follow them. Women left their kitchens, pensioners their rocking chairs and children their lessons. Soon the little band of reluctant heroes was being followed by hundreds of supporters. All wanted to see the excitement and be there to cheer when the French got a hiding.

Unsure where the French were, Knox marched his men along the coast path. The sailors aboard the French ships saw the advancing men and looked up in horror. There on the cliff stretching from Penfathach to Aber Felin was a long line of red coat soldiers. It looked like the entire British Army had arrived and was ready to do battle. They despatched a picket boat with a hurried warning to the soldiers at Llanwnda, cut their anchor cables and set sail for France.

Colonel Knox looked back at his men as they trudged along the cliff. He saw the long line of women in their red cloaks and old men following behind and, having seen the size of the French fleet, finally realised how hopeless his position was. Besides, he did not want the blood of innocent women and old men on his hands. His father was right. This was a job for regular soldiers. He wheeled his horse and the relieved volunteers marched back to Fishguard.

The invasion plan was to ferment rebellion before the Redcoats arrived and let the Welsh fight the English. When the French commander received the news that a large force of British Redcoats had cut off his retreat and that his fleet had fled, he panicked. He sent his chief of staff to Fishguard under a flag of truce and offered to surrender.

The surrender took place the next day and it was only then that the French learned that there were no Redcoats. Their invasion had failed because of an army of Welsh women dressed to keep warm on that cold February day. Thus ends the legend of the last invasion of Britain. The real reason for the French surrender is unclear but the events leading up to the surrender and the people involved well documented.

Colonel William Tate an Irish-American soldier of fortune led the invading force. He had fought the British during the American War of Independence and had escaped to Paris after being involved in a failed revolution in New Orleans. He hated the British and was given command of the force that was to invade Britain and incite rebellion in order to take over the country.

The French navy provided four of their largest and most modern warships including the frigates Vengeance and Resistance for the project. The force Tate commanded included 600 regular soldiers from Napoleon's Italian army, some of whom were grenadiers together with an assortment of 800 convicts, royalists and pressed men. Altogether he had 1400 soldiers and they were well equipped with modern weapons. The uniforms they wore were captured British army clothing that had been dyed black - hence the name 'The Black Legion'.

The invading fleet sailed flying the red ensign and headed for England. Tate's original plan was to attack Bristol and let his men plunder and rape at will but the invasion fleet could not navigate the strong tides in the Severn Estuary and retreated. They then attacked shipping and lost the element of surprise. The British posted lookouts and, on the 22nd February 1797, Thomas Williams, a retired seafarer, spotted the French fleet sailing near Strumble Head and raised the alarm.

The frigate Resistance sailed into Fishguard harbour and was fired upon by a 9lb cannon in the fort whereupon she withdrew, unaware that the fort only had 3 round of shot in its magazine. The French Fleet anchored at Carregwastad Point and disembarked men and arms including 40 barrels of gunpowder and several thousand rifles. At least one boat capsized and all the invaders' 4-pound cannon were lost. Having unloaded, the French fleet withdrew.

Colonel Knox, commander of the local militia was returning from a social engagement at Tregwynt Mansion and was riding across Goodwick sands when he met a junior officer leading some locals, intent of attacking the French. He stopped the men and ordered them back to Fishguard. His order almost certainly saved their lives, since the French had set up well-prepared ambush points in strong defensive positions. Knox decided to evacuate his forces from Fishguard to Haverford West but was met on route by Lord Cawdor with reinforcements including the Pembroke Yeomanry. Cawdor, with military experience, took command and they returned to Fishguard.

At the same time, French discipline was deteriorating. The pressed men were deserting and stealing food from the local farms. A Portuguese merchantman had recently floundered and its cargo of wine was looted and drunk. Several violent incidents took place where French soldiers and locals were killed. Llanwnda church was desecrated and the mutinous soldiers lit fires in it to keep warm, using the bible as kindling and pews as firewood.

Cawdor arrived in Fishguard late in the afternoon and elected to wait until the next day before attacking. News of Cawdor's advance reached Tate. Aware of the collapse of his army as a fighting force and the lack of any possible retreat he decided to surrender. Two French officers were sent to Fishguard under a flag of truce to negotiate terms. Lord Cawdor received them in the Royal Oak public house where he had set up his headquarters. Despite being heavily outnumbered he refused to negotiate and sent them back to Tate with an ultimatum. He demanded that the French surrender unconditionally or he would attack and destroy them the following morning. The Irish American Tate prevaricated and it was only when Cawdor's men were drawn up in battle order on the beach at Goodwick that the French capitulated. They marched into captivity with drums beating and the formal surrender document, now lost, was signed at the Royal Oak.

In 1798 Tate and his men were repatriated to France as part of a prisoner exchange. After the invasion, a subscription of £25 was made to replace the pews in Llanwnda Church and, in 1853, the Pembroke Yeomanry were awarded a battle honour for the 'Battle of Fishguard'. It is the only battle honour ever awarded to a British Army Regiment for an engagement on British soil. The French ship Resistance was captured, refitted and commissioned into the British Navy as HMS Fishguard. Her sister ship, the Vengeance, returned safely to France.

The colour of the shawls worn by Welsh women was achieved using a dye called crottal made from lichen. Crottal was also used to dye the red tunics of the British army. The women also wore tall black hats that might be mistaken for helmets so, from a distance, they would have looked like soldiers. One woman who did create fear amongst the French was Jemima Nicholas, a 47-year-old cobbler from Fishguard known to all as Jemima Fawr (Big Jemima). She took it upon herself to take a pitchfork, rounded up 12 French deserters and locked them in St. Mary's Church. With her help and the boldness of the Welsh people the last invasion of Britain ended.

Chapter 12...The Wreckers of Cefn Sidan

The Captain of the La Jeune Emma peered through the mist, desperate for a sighting of land. It had been two days since he had glimpsed the lighthouse at Ushant, or so he thought. That mistake was to cost him dearly. Since then, because of the storms and fog, he had seen nothing. Surely they were somewhere near the French coast. Cherbourg and a safe end to the voyage from Martinique must be near at hand but where were the beacons marking the entrance to the harbour? He turned to the First Mate.

'Keep her course steady North-East-by-East. Reef the outer jib and foresail and keep a good lookout.' The First Mate checked the compass.

'Aye Captain.'

'We are in shallow water. I can feel it in the swell. Call me immediately when you sight land.' The Captain turned and left the poop deck. He was exhausted. He had to get a few hours rest before they reached port. There would be work enough to do then. Below deck, Adeline Coquelin sat in the owner's saloon, her geography book lay open on the table but she was not looking at it. Her father, Lieutenant Colonel Coquelin, had just told her they would be landing in France within the day. Adeline's eyes flashed with excitement.

'Will Aunt Josephine and Emperor Bonaparte be there to meet us?' she asked.

'No child. The Emperor is a busy man but we may see them later.'

'Land ho,' cried the lookout. The Captain had not undressed. He heaved himself up from his bunk, pulled on his boots and was quickly on deck.

'Where away?' he called. The mate pointed to the signal beacons off the starboard bow.

'At last. Steer between the lights Mr. Mate. Bosun, reef the main royal. I want to lose speed before we reach the harbour mouth,' ordered the Captain. The La Jeune Emma turned to starboard and her new heading. The crew reduced sail, desperately trying to slow the vessel without losing steerage. Relentlessly the wind pushed the ship forward. A sudden squall hit the vessel from behind and she lifted, propelled faster through the darkness, towards the lights. Adeline had prepared for bed and was saying her prayers when the ship ran aground. The force of the impact threw her across the cabin. The ship lay at a strange angle. Her father ran in and helped her dress. Together they went on deck.

The La Jeune Emma was stuck fast and the sea was breaking across the deck. Screaming crewmen were being washed into the sea and disappearing into the darkness. The Lieutenant Colonel gripped his daughter by the arm and pulled her towards the bow of the ship looking for shelter or a way to escape from the vessel before it broke up.

On the shore, men stood watching the stricken ship being buffeted by the waves. They laughed and congratulated each other. It had been a good night's work. Tomorrow the proper work would begin. Then, in the light of day, when the sea had died down, they would return and collect their prize. The men turned away from the doomed vessel and walked across the beach past the bonfires they had lit earlier that evening. These men were the 'Wreckers' of Cefn Sidan and wrecking ships was their evil trade. Will Manney had been a notorious wrecker, working as a domestic servant by day and wrecking ships by night. The magistrate sentenced him for murder and Manney was left dangling on a gibbet on the top of Pembrey Mountain. Even this stark warning did not stop the wreckers. Enticing ships onto the beach and looting the vessels was a lucrative occupation and the beach Cefn Sidan the ideal place for this heinous crime. Inhabitants came from miles around to prosper by means of loot stolen from vessels stranded on the shore. Ships returning to Europe often mistook the Lundy lighthouse for the fixed light at Ushant causing them to sail far off course and into Carmarthen Bay, where they were driven by unfavourable tides and winds onto Cefn Sidan. It was a natural trap and many ships ended their final voyage here. On one occasion sixteen vessels were

46

smashed on the coast during a violent northeasterly storm. Nearly all of the crews were drowned. The wreckers, eager for plunder, often helped them to their doom with misleading signal beacons. Locals called the robbers – 'Gwyr-y-Bwelli Bach' – 'People with Little Hatchets' after the tools they used to plunder the ships. Marker buoys had been placed in the bay to warn of the peril but many of these had mysteriously vanished. The wreckers intended to protect their interests.

By eleven o'clock, the crew of the La Jeune Emma had launched a makeshift raft, in an attempt to reach the shore. It overturned tossing everyone aboard into the sea. Only four people thrown from the raft reached the beach. The few sailors still on board the ship climbed into the rigging where they clung on desperately.

At first light sympathetic villagers reached the La Jeune Emma. She was stuck in shallow water close to the beach and was listing. Valiant attempts were made to rescue the survivors. Two were bought ashore alive. At the same time the wreckers began their work. The cargo of sugar, sherry, spices, coffee, cotton, rum and ginger was swiftly carted away. Valuable lumber was stripped from the vessel.

Eventually the militia arrived from Carmarthen to take charge of the wreck. All that was left of the cargo was three hundred gallons of rum. Everything else had been plundered.

The bodies of the Captain, four crewmembers, the Lieutenant Colonel and his daughter - the 12-year-old niece of Napoleon Bonaparte - were found and buried in the graveyard at St. Illtud's Church in Pembrey. They lie alongside many other seafarers that perished in the same way. There were only six survivors from the nineteen people on board when the La Jeune Emma struck Cefn Sidan, that evening, on the 21st November 1829.

A strange footnote to the story is that several of the drowned sailors were recovered from the sea, further along the coast, and buried at Laugharne. Later, when another body was discovered and the grave was reopened to inter the corpse with the other sailors, a gruesome discovery was made. One of the coffins had been opened and the body removed. It was never found. All that was left in the coffin was a sailor's blue shirt.

Chapter 13...The Daughters of Rebecca

*'And they blessed Rebecca and said unto her, Thou art our
sister, be thou the mother of thousands of millions and let thy seed
possess the gates of those who hate them.'*
(Genesis, chapter 24, verse 60.)

In 1813, an auction took place at the George Inn, Llandeilo,
Carmarthenshire where the rights to collect tolls at several tollgates
in the county were offered to the highest bidders. These included
gates on the turnpike roads at Ffairfach, Llandybie and Llanedy
Forest. Ffairfach and Llandybie together collected £640 per annum
while, the quieter; Llanedy Forest Gate generated £21 each year.

Since most gates came with a house for the gatekeeper and
his family, there was keen interest in all the lots at the auction. At
the time Lord Dynevor paid his servants just seven shillings a week
(£18 per annum). The toll roads generated handsome incomes and
were much sought after. Many tollgate owners lived a comfortable
life in London and employed gatekeepers to collect the money from
the passing travellers.

The original idea of charging tolls had been to improve the
transport system and the money was intended for the upkeep of the
road surface. Most of the money, however, went straight into the
pockets of the owners who made little or no attempt to carry out
repairs. Tollgates proliferated. At one point it was estimated that
there was a tollgate for every three miles of road in
Carmarthenshire, many of which had been erected illegally. The
effect on the ordinary people was devastating. They were being
taxed every time they moved. Resentment against the system built
up. Something had to be done.

On the 13th May 1839 a group of men disguised themselves
as women and attacked the tollgate at Efail Wen, Narberth. It was
destroyed. The owner, an Englishman named Thomas Bullin, who
owned tollgates throughout England and Wales, had it rebuilt but
gave up after two further attacks. He ordered that the gatehouse be
demolished and for a while nothing more was heard of the culprits.

49

Attacks started again in 1842 and it soon became apparent to the authorities that this was a serious threat that had to be dealt with. Bands of men, disguised as women and calling themselves 'Daughters of Rebecca', started attacking tollgates throughout Carmarthenshire, frequently burning the gatehouse to the ground. The Daughters of Rebecca were mainly small scale farmers. Farm rents had been steadily increasing for years while poor harvests and depressed prices left many farmers living in poverty. These subsistence farmers were particularly badly affected by the toll charges.

The attacks became more violent and spread though South Wales. In one attack near Pontarddulais, the gatekeeper Sarah Williams was shot and killed. During the inquest doctors confirmed that there were two bullets lodged in her lung. Despite this evidence the jury returned a strange verdict, 'that the deceased died from effusion of blood into the chest occasioned, suffocation, but from what cause is to this jury unknown.' (sic) There was considerable public support for the Daughters of Rebecca.

Realising there was little chance of convicting the attackers locally, the trial was moved to Cardiff, where the High Sheriff selected his own jury, and five rioters were sentenced to be transported for life.

Back in Carmarthenshire, Colonel Trevor, Vice Lieutenant of the County, had returned home to the family estate at Dinefwr to help his ailing father deal with the rioters. He watched, dismayed, at the Carmarthen Assizes as Rebecca Leader, David Evans, was cleared of destroying tollgates on two different occasions. Each time the jury failed to reach a verdict, forcing the judge to release the prisoner. By now the Daughters of Rebecca had widened their activities and were attacking other symbols of authority. In June 1829 they attacked the workhouse in Carmarthen. The Colonel realised that stronger methods would be needed to crush the Daughters of Rebecca.

A new force, the Metropolitan Police, had been formed in 1829 to suppress political unrest. The Metropolitan Police had already seen action in the Industrial Midlands and Yorkshire. They were effective at riot control and were the first to develop the 'baton charge' as a crowd control tool. Colonel Trevor summoned them to Carmarthenshire. In addition to these specialist policemen, a large contingent of soldiers, complete with cannon, were garrisoned in Carmarthen. The 4th Regiment of Light Dragoons established their headquarters at the Cawdor Arms Hotel, Llandeilo and the vicarage was taken over by the 41st Regiment of Infantry. The influx of money and men into Llandeilo had one major benefit. It turned the once quiet backwater into a boom town. Nearly everyone was making money and local traders were happy that Llandeilo remained occupied by the military for two years.

On August 9th 1843, the tollgate on Carmarthen Road, between the town centre and the White Hart Public House, was attacked and the gatehouse destroyed. The audacity of the attack, so close to the town and almost outside Colonel Trevor's country house was breathtaking.

After recommending that the Metropolitan Police be armed, Colonel Trevor then announced publicly that, if it was appropriate, he would order the troops to open fire on The Daughters of Rebecca. His comments caused further polarisation in the increasingly bitter confrontation.

One morning in September 1843 Colonel, The Honourable George Rice Trevor MP, Vice Lieutenant for the County of Carmarthen was woken from his bed at Newton House. During the night a grave had been dug in the grounds of the house and a notice posted declaring that the Colonel would be buried in it by the 10th October. The Daughters of Rebecca had given him their answer; it was to be a fight to the death.

Each night, mounted dragoons scoured Carmarthenshire searching for the Daughters of Rebecca while the Metropolitan Police were spread across the county guarding tollgates and a contingent of soldiers guarded Colonel Trevor. A letter was sent to the Duke of Wellington requesting more troops be stationed in Carmarthenshire. He dispatched two thousand additional infantrymen commanded by Colonel Love, a man experienced in crushing rebellion. Love had seen action at Waterloo, had crushed the striking mineworkers in Merthyr and successfully suppressed a riot in Bristol.

Colonel Love quickly assessed the situation and found he had some sympathy for the Daughters of Rebecca's complaints. He wrote accordingly to the Home Secretary proposing that an inquiry be set up to examine the facts. As a result of his intervention a Royal Commission was formed.

Colonel Trevor's troop patrols and police guards were making little difference. During the whole conflict the soldiers failed to capture a single Daughter of Rebecca. The dragoons usually arrived long after the attackers were long gone and safely home in bed. The Metropolitan Police were equally ineffective. Without local knowledge or intelligence they were always in the wrong place to stop the attacks.

Then Colonel Trevor began to offer rewards for information and immunity from prosecution. Queen Victoria personally signed the proclamation announcing the rewards. A reward of up to £1,500 (£30,000 in today's money) and the promise of a pardon for information leading to a conviction produced immediate results. At a time when many farm workers were employed on a casual basis for a shilling a day and out of work for the winter, the lure of such a large sum of money was understandable. Now, Daughters of Rebecca were no longer sisters in arms. They were betraying each other. At Carmarthen Quarter Sessions £1500 was paid in rewards on one day alone.

The Royal Commission reported within 5 months of being set up and it supported most of the complaints against the tollgate system. A new 'Road Bill for South Wales' was hurriedly passed, sweeping away many of the iniquities and dealing with the complaints of the Daughters of Rebecca. Private Turnpike Trusts were abolished and replaced by elected County Road Boards. The toll on lime, essential for farmers working poor quality land, was halved and the number of tollgates reduced so they only occurred every seven miles. The Daughters of Rebecca had won their demands and the organisation quietly faded away. The conflict was over.

Several thousand Daughters of Rebecca were active during the four-year struggle. Over two hundred and fifty tollgates were destroyed in South West Wales, many of them several times. One consequence of the Rebecca Riots was that the first regular Carmarthenshire Police Force was established in 1843 comprising a Chief Constable, six Assistants, ten Sergeants and twenty Constables.

On 13th July 1844 Colonel Trevor, having survived the threats on his life, wrote supporting the new system of road management and proposed that bridges in the county should be bought under the same type of administration. In 1852 he became the 4th Baron Dynevor and continued to live at Newton House, Llandeilo.

Chapter 14...Paxton's Folly

William Paxton was born in Edinburgh in 1745. He joined the Royal Navy as a young man but, on arrival in India, realised that the new colony was a place of adventure and a land of opportunity. This was the place for an ambitious young fellow to make his fortune. Seizing his chance, Paxton resigned from the Navy and became a banker. He had a sharp mind and quickly won promotion. Within a few years he became the Master of the Calcutta Mint and, like other Nabobs of the time, amassed a huge fortune for himself.

In 1785 Paxton returned from India rich, and intent on becoming a country gentleman. He purchased Middleton Hall, a rundown estate in the Towy Valley, and started to improve it. Samuel Peyps Cockerell, a leading architect of the day, was commissioned to design a new country house. A country park was laid out and the house, described as the most perfect in the country, was completed in 1795.

Paxton was intent on winning respectability and used his great wealth to demonstrate his importance. Despite his grandeur, he had difficulty becoming accepted. The noble families, comfortable with their old money, thought him conceited and vulgar. The poor were afraid of him and distrusted him.

Despite his unpopularity, Paxton saw politics as a means to fulfil his ambition. He knew that his money and patronage would create the support he needed. These were the days of rotten boroughs when votes were bought and bribery common. Paxton used his money to good effect and was soon knighted. Local elections took place and Paxton was elected Mayor of Carmarthen. In this capacity he entertained Admiral Nelson who was visiting the town.

Paxton soon realised that local politics would not satisfy his aspirations. He wanted a bigger stage to perform on and decided to stand for Parliament. He started campaigning during the 1802 general election, spending money to win votes. He made promises and bought beer for the voters. One particular pledge made by Paxton was that, if elected, he would pay for a bridge over the River Towy. Despite his grand promises and a vast sum spent on bribes, the voters rejected Paxton and he failed to win the seat.

The reason Paxton failed to get elected was that someone, possibly his opponent, had started a rumour that he was insolvent and unfit to represent the people in Parliament. Determined to prove that the rumour was a lie but unwilling to build a bridge for the ungrateful electors, Paxton chose instead to spend the £15,000, that the bridge would have cost, on a tower to celebrate the victories of Admiral Nelson.

It was to be a sweet and very prominent revenge. The architect Cockerell was summoned and a site high on Bryn y Bigwrn Hill selected as suitable. Cockerell proposed a 500-foot tall gothic style structure that would dominate the countryside. Work began using limestone quarried locally and the Scottish stonemasons that he employed gave the tower a character that reminded Paxton of his birthplace, Edinburgh.

Apart from making a statement to the people of Carmarthenshire, the tower had a second purpose. It was designed so that carriages could arrive from Middleton Hall and drive inside the three cornered base, allowing passengers to alight in the dry and to climb up stairways to a grand dining room with superb views over the Towy Valley. It was here that Paxton entertained his guests and impressed his visitors. From the top of the tower you could see seven different counties. The walls of the rooms were clad in marble and there were three fabulous stained glass windows depicting Lord Nelson, his victories and his heroic death at Trafalgar. Nelson died in 1805, six years before the tower was completed.

If the tower was a snub, the people failed to understand its meaning and Paxton succeeded in winning election to Westminster at his second attempt in 1806. He lived to the age of 80, passing away in 1824. The estate was put up for sale the same year and the catalogue described the tower thus;

A Gothic Tower, Erected by the late liberal-minded Possessor, in Commemoration of our Noble Hero, Lord Nelson; A grand Ornament and Land Mark in the County. On the Ground Floor, Three Spacious Lofty Arches for the Admission of Carriages, On the Principal Story, A Banqueting Room, with Gothic Ceiling; A Boudoir and Closet, over which A Prospect Room or Observatory, with Turrets, Three of the Windows are fitted with Stained Glass, One Window representing his Lordship, the others emblematical of his Fate, From which there is a Panoramic View, of a grandeur and extent that may justly be said to stand unrivalled. On the upper Part a Lead Flat, and Two Entrance Lodges. William Paxton never did build the bridge across the River Towy.

Chapter 15...The Secret of Culver Hole

The boy stood quietly and watched as the pigeon circled above. Eventually it settled and entered the roost. Suddenly, the boy pulled the cord closing the trap and ran over to retrieve the message. He knew his uncle would want the news quickly. The boy unfastened the ribbon and ran across the beach to the Salt House, calling out as he went. John Lucas was already at the door of his home as his nephew arrived. He read the message. It was the news he was expecting. He smiled at the boy.

'Go and find George. Tell him to meet me here and bring the men. We have work to do this night,' he commanded. The boy turned and ran towards Port Eynon, eager to complete his mission.

Lucas' lieutenant, George ap Eynon, returned with four men. They were all armed and looked a villainous party of cut-throats. The gang sat in the kitchen talking and smoking.

'The message has come from Robert. He lands tonight with a load of brandy and tobacco,' said Lucas. Robert de Skurlege was also a member of the gang, as violent and dangerous as the others, but it was Lucas who had the brains and was the leader. He lowered his voice, drawing the others closer.

'We must take care tonight. The revenue men from Swansea are about. There will be no lights and no talking,' he whispered.

It was late when the men left the Salt House. There was no moon and a damp mist was drifting in from the sea. They waited for their eyes to become accustomed to the gloom and then, without a word, followed the track down to the cove. A string of mules plodded silently along behind the men. It was past midnight when the boat landed. The gang ran along the shore and began to unload the cargo. Casks of brandy and rum, crates of tobacco and parcels of fine French lace were loaded onto the mules and driven away. It was slow, heavy work and took several trips to get the cargo to the safety of the cave.

There was just one last load when one of the smugglers cried out.

'It's the revenue,'

There were lights moving along the beach towards them. Several shots rang out but the range was too great. The smugglers drove the mules around the point, away from the pursuing customs men. There were more shots and Robert de Skurlege, who had been trying to push away the boat but failed, fell dead in the water, shot through the head.

The smugglers reached the headland. Lucas stopped them and together they fired a volley at the advancing revenue men. The revenue men, happy that they had captured the boat but unwilling to risk their lives further stopped the pursuit. Lewis and his men hid the last of their booty in Culver Hole, the cave they always used. Then, to avoid the revenue men, they returned from the cave to the Salt House along a secret passageway, inside the cliff. From there the smugglers quietly dispersed to their homes. It had been a busy night's work and Lucas knew the revenue men would be back.

The following day, a squad of customs officers arrived in Port Eynon and visited the Inn where they asked for directions to the Salt House. The landlord, realising their intent, delayed them with an offer of grog and sent a message to Lucas warning him of the danger. By the time they arrived, Lucas was ready and, despite a thorough search, they found nothing to incriminate their suspect. There was no contraband and the revenue men knew nothing of the secret passage or the cave it led to.

During the next few days Port Eynon was searched several times and eventually their efforts produced a find. A cask of fine brandy was discovered in the loft of a barn. A trap was set. Two customs men waited, guarding the brandy, ready to arrest the unsuspecting owner when he returned.

Hearing the news, Lucas collected a party of locals together and, giving the impression that they were unaware of the King's men hiding above them, had a loud gathering in the barn with dancing and revelry. In the morning, one of the customs men went to move the cask and, to his surprise, found that it was empty. During the night someone had drilled a hole up, through the floor

58

and into the barrel, collecting the brandy into flasks as it drained away.

John Lucas could be a violent man but he was also a realist. He knew that to keep his secrets, he needed the support of the local community and they were well rewarded for their silence. At different times there was so much contraband arriving that more hiding places were needed. Kegs were hidden in the church altar. The cellar of the Inn was used with more barrels arriving than leaving and contraband was even hidden, buried in holes dug on the beach.

Aware of the increasing smuggling activity, the Revenue men tried harder to catch the culprits. Eight armed vessels, known as 'Sea Fencibles', were stationed along the coast, near Port Eynon, to apprehend the incoming boats and shore patrols were stepped up.

Eventually, the Revenue had a breakthrough when, in 1804, a cache of loot was discovered on Oxwich Beach and 420 kegs of brandy seized. Orders were given for the contraband to be taken to Swansea, but not all of it arrived. A horde of several hundred people surrounded the troop and mobbed them. They were only persuaded to leave when offered some of the drink. The fifty soldiers guarding the brandy then began to complain that they were being unfairly treated and they too were allowed to help themselves.

Despite some successes by the Revenue, John Lucas continued smuggling and the secret contraband hidden deep in the cliffs at Culver Hole, was never discovered.

Chapter 16...Sir Owain's Lake

Mynydd Mawr, the mountain above Gorslas, was a barren mountain with little water and hardly any grazing for livestock. The shepherds tending their animals on the mountain found it hard to make a living but they had nowhere else to go. One day, a young boy walking on the top of the mountain saw something strange glinting in the sunlight. It was a slab of rock, damp and bright, that had caught his eye. The rock was rectangular and its surface was polished. There were strange symbols carved on the face of the slab. The boy had never seen anything like it in his life.

'Look at this,' he called to the other shepherds. Soon a group of men gathered around the slab.

'Is it a grave?' asked one.

'It's the doorway to hell,' suggested another.

'Maybe there is treasure hidden beneath,' added a third. Eventually, their curiosity overcame their fear and, fetching branches to use as levers, they prised the slab up, eager to discover what lay concealed below.

As the slab began to lift there was a gurgling sound. It grew louder and then water gushed up from under the stone, defying gravity and soaking the men. Shocked, the shepherds dropped the heavy slab and jumped back. The water had stopped. All was quiet.

The shepherds debated what to do next. They agreed that this strange and magical spring was a good thing. The mountain needed water to make the grass grow and their animals thrive.

Each morning the shepherds would visit the spring and raise the slab, allowing water to gurgle up from the ground. Then, once they felt the right amount of water was released, the slab was lowered and the spring sealed again. The shepherds wanted to irrigate the land, not to flood it. Ditches were dug to spread the water across the mountain. As they carefully watered the barren mountain it became fertile, the grass turned green and lush. The animals grew fat and content. Trees began to grow and flowers sprang up in their dappled shade.

Far away from Mynydd Mawr, in the court of King Arthur at Caerleon on Usk, a mighty quest was being planned. The King selected his bravest and best knights to leave the court and scour the kingdom. The prize they sought was the Holy Grail, the cup used by Jesus at the last supper.

The Knights of the Round Table accepted their challenge, bade farewell to the King and left the castle. Sir Owain travelled west, searching the great valleys of South Wales. After many days, Sir Owain found himself in a valley where the road separated. Ahead of him was the crossroad and, blocking it, sat astride a large warhorse, was a knight. The crest on the knight's shield heralded crossed hands. This was the evil knight of Cross Hands. Sir Owain drew closer.

'Give way Sir Knight and let me pass. I am on the King's business,' demanded Sir Owain.

'This highway is mine. Yield to me and pay a tribute or you shall not pass this way,' replied the robber knight, standing his ground. No ruffian had the right to demand money for travelling on the King's highway. It was a challenge Sir Owain could not refuse.

'You are a villain Sir. Let us settle the matter,' cried Sir Owain. He pulled down his visor, lowered his lance in salute and urged his horse forward.

The battle was long and bloody. Both men were unhorsed and the fight continued on foot. Sword blows rained down on Sir Owain and he was wounded several times. The evil knight was no coward and expected no quarter, nor did he offer it. Even when Sir Owain fell to the ground, exhausted from the heavy work; he stood above the wounded man, raised his sword and was about to kill Sir Owain when, with a short dagger thrust upwards into the evil knight's belly, Sir Owain won the day. Never again would the evil knight extort money from passing travellers.

Sir Owain lay on the ground until his horse, which had been waiting patiently nearby, snorted loudly. Slowly and in great pain, Sir Owain roused himself, mounted the animal and slumped forward in the saddle.

'Find us some water,' he whispered in the horse's ear and fainted. The faithful horse, sensing that his master was not in control, walked slowly away in search of water.

It was late in the afternoon when Sir Owain awoke with a jolt. He had fallen from the horse. Sir Owain looked around. He was on the top of a mountain. Next to him on the ground was a stone slab. He read the ancient text engraved on the rock. 'The Magic Well of Gorslas'. Slowly, and with great difficulty, Sir Owain dragged aside the slab, revealing the spring and releasing the water. He drank greedily and, as his horse drank, Sir Owain crawled to a clump of heather where he fell into a deep sleep.

As he slept, Sir Owain dreamt of tumbling rivers and lakes. The following morning he woke early, feeling refreshed and revived. His wounds had healed in the night. Sir Owain sat up and found himself on a small island, surrounded by water. The island was in the middle of a lake and the water level was rising. He had failed to replace the slab over the spring and it had created the lake. Soon the small island supporting him would be submerged.

Sir Owain swam to the shore where his horse was grazing on the lush grass. Just as he got to dry land, the shepherds returned, ready to open the spring and water their mountain. They saw the lake and realised what had happened. Angrily, they confronted the knight.

'Good sirs, I admit that it was I that let the water escape and make this lake. After battling with the knight of Cross Hands, a great thirst and weariness overcame me. I forgot to replace the slab over your spring,' explained Sir Owain.

The Shepherds had heard of the battle and were relieved that the evil knight, who had frequently mistreated them, was no more. Sir Owain, they realised, had done them a great service.

'Consider things thus,' continued the knight. 'You might have lost a spring but you have gained a great lake that will soon be teaming with fine fish and waterfowl for the table.'

The shepherds were content for Sir Owain had done them a second great service. Sir Owain bade them farewell and went on his way, refreshed and eager to continue his quest for the Holy Grail.

From that day, they called the lake on the top of Mynydd Mawr, Llyn Llech Owain - The 'Lake of Owain's Stone Slab'.

Part Two North Wales

Chapter 17...Myfanwy the Beautiful

High above the little town of Llangollen, on the top of a great mountain, sits Castell Dinas Bran or Crow City Castle, named after the crows and ravens that lurk amid its towering battlements. In the 13th Century an Earl and his family lived at Castell Dinas Bran. The Earl was a wealthy man and owned much of Powys. He had a daughter named Myfanwy, which means beloved in English and he loved her very much. Myfanwy was spoiled as a child. Her father showered her with gifts of every kind. He surprised her with fine dresses of silk and damask. He had succulent foods bought to the castle for her and gave her servants orders to carry out her every wish.

Myfanwy quickly learned how to get her own way. A sly tear, a scowl or a scream would strike fear into the hearts of her servants; they knew the power of her wrath and the strength of her sulks. The years passed and Myfanwy grew into womanhood. As she grew she changed from a pretty girl into a woman of beauty. Her long black hair and dark piercing eyes enchanted all who saw her.

News of her great beauty spread and suitors travelled from across the land to woo her, eager to win her hand and, some said, to inherit her father's wealth. A brave knight climbed the mountain to the castle and sang in praise of her loveliness but she sneered at his songs and chatted loudly while he sang. Crushed by her rudeness, the knight retreated down the mountain.

A famous scholar journeyed to Castell Dinas Bran and recited a fine poem flattering her beauty. Myfanwy scoffed at his sonnet and left the castle hall while the bard was still speaking. The frustrated poet left the castle and returned to the town below. Others tried to win Myfanwy but all were treated with the same contempt. No flattery of song or verse could satisfy Myfanwy. She vainly knew she was more beautiful than any man could describe in tune or rhyme.

Disappointed suitors filled the alehouses of Llangollen exchanging tales of woe and drowning their sorrows. They sang to each other mournfully of Myfanwy's beauty and her conceited vanity.

Hywell ap Einion was a dreamer of a man. Night after night he listened to the songs and the poems. He had never seen Myfanwy but the descriptions of her beauty thrilled him. He fell in love with her long black hair, her dark piercing eyes and her soft white cheeks. His romantic mind searched for a way to win her for himself, but how, for Hywell was a penniless youth. Would the beautiful daughter of an Earl ever look on him as an equal, worthy of marriage?

The years passed and Hywell grew tall and strong. His upright frame and easy smile made him popular with the girls but there was only one vision that filled his heart, the dream that he had never seen, Myfanwy.

Myfanwy had never married and still lived in the castle high above the town. No man had flattered her enough to win her heart. Each evening, after work, Hywell would look up at the castle, longing for a glimpse of Myfanwy.

One summer night, as he watched the mountain and the castle, he heard the sound of sweet music coming from the river. He went down to the water where he found an old man playing a lute and singing. The melody danced and toyed with the noise of the tumbling water. The song entranced Hywell, as it teased and thrilled, with sensations that aroused his emotions.

The old man stopped playing and placed the lute on the ground.

'Old man, will you teach me how to play the lute and sing?' asked Hywell. The old man looked at Hywell.

'Why do you want to play and sing like an old man?' asked the old man.

'Old man, your music has no age. It speaks of love and happiness, of bravery and beauty. These things are timeless. I see now that with such music I can win my love,' replied Hywell.

'You speak of love, which is good. I will teach you to play the lute and sing but the song you use to win your love must be your own,' said the old man. They agreed and each evening the two men would sit by the river. The old man was a good teacher and Hywell an eager pupil. He quickly mastered the lute and, as he sang, his voice grew strong and confident.

Each day, while he worked, his mind was busy. He thought of the beauty of Myfanwy, of his love for her and hers for him. The words in his mind formed into couplets and verses. The song grew longer and his heart filled with pleasure.

'You are ready,' said the old man, one evening, 'Is your song ready?' Hywell picked up the lute and began to play. He sang softly at first and then louder as his emotions took hold. Towards the end of the song, his voice grew quiet, as if his love was close by his side. He stopped and looked at the old man, wanting his approval. Tears of joy ran down the old man's face.

'You are ready. Go now, tonight, and win Myfanwy,' he said, pointing at the castle. Hywell took his lute and climbed the mountain. The castle gate was open. There was a feast in the great hall. Sir Ralph, a knight from a distant land, was visiting. Hywell entered the hall and saw Myfanwy for the first time. His heart filled with joy. She was more beautiful than he had imagined. He strode nervously across the hall and stood before the high table. The Earl looked down at him and saw the lute.

'Come, play a merry tune for us,' he commanded. The guests ignored Hywell and continued to laugh and talk. Hywell lifted his lute and began to sing, quietly at first and then more loudly as his courage grew. The crowd fell silent as he sang. He looked at Myfanwy. Her dark clear eyes returned his gaze without blinking. He sang of her beauty and she smiled. He praised her pale cheeks and she blushed. His words fell like caresses on her long black hair and she laughed, but still her dark clear eyes returned his steady gaze.

Hywells' song ended quietly, like a conspiracy between two lovers. Myfanwy stood and applauded and the guests cheered. Hywell bowed and advanced towards Myfanwy. She offered her hand and he kissed it, confident that he had won her heart. Hywell was invited to sit at the top table, by the Earl and the feasting continued late into the night.

Next morning Hywell returned to the castle but Myfanwy had gone.

'Where is Myfanwy?' asked Hywell. The Earl looked at the impudent serf before him.

'She is promised in marriage to another far more noble than you,' replied the Earl.

'But she loves me,' said Hywell.

'You're a fool. Myfanwy enjoyed your adulation but will never marry a peasant like you. She has gone with Sir Ralph. The marriage contract was signed yesterday,' said the Earl.

Hywell stumbled down the mountain, broken hearted. According to the legend, he wrote one last poem for Myfanwy and never spoke of her again.

The real author of the love poem, Myfannwy was the Welsh poet Richard Davies. It was set to music by Joseph Parry was published in 1875. The song is a favourite with Welsh male voice choirs. It ends in farewell.

> *I ddawnsio ganmlwydd ar dy rudd.*
> *Anghofia'r oll o'th addewidion*
> *A wnest i rywun, 'ngeneth ddel,*
> *A dyro'th law, Myfanwy dirion*
> *I ddim ond dweud y gair 'Ffarwél'.*

> *Dance for a hundred years or so.*
> *Forget now all the words of promise*
> *You made to one who loved you well,*

Give me your hand, my sweet Myfanwy,
But one last time, to say 'farewell'.

Chapter 18…The Men of Harlech

March ye men of Harlech bold, Unfurl your banners in the field,
Be brave as were your sires of old, And like them never yield!
What tho' evry hill and dale, Echoes now with war's alarms,
Celtic hearts can never quail, When Cambria calls to arms.
1860 English lyrics by W.H. Baker.

King Edward I built Harlech Castle as part of his steel ring of castles, designed to subdue the Welsh. The concentric design and its location, which enabled it to be re-supplied from the sea, made Harlech a formidable stronghold.

In 1404, Owain Glyndwr starved the English garrison until only 21 men were left and they surrendered. Glyndwr then used Harlech as his base for the next four years until the English set out to recapture the Castle. It took them 8 months and 1000 men to retake the fortress. Glyndwr vanished, Welsh nationalism was crushed and the English re-occupied Wales.

Most of North Wales, Gloucestershire and Cheshire became part of the Duchy of Lancaster and Welsh fighting men were recruited as Lancastrian soldiers. When Edward IV came to the throne of England on the 4th March 1461 the Civil War, known as the 'Wars of The Roses', had been an on and off affair for several years. The war between the Lancastrian and Yorkist sides of the Plantagenet dynasty was a running fight for the English throne.

Edward was a Yorkist but there was another claim for the English throne, the Lancastrian, Henry Tudor, 2nd Earl of Richmond was just four years old. Young Henry, a Welshman born in Pembroke from an illegitimate line, had a weak claim to the crown but Edward could not ignore the young pretender. Henry and his supporters fled the country in fear for their lives.

They travelled to Harlech Castle where the constable, a Welshman named Dafydd ap Ieuan, helped the party escape to Scotland. Henry Tudor then went on to France where he lived and grew to manhood under the protection of the French King. With Henry gone from Wales, Edward quickly overran the country, confiscating Lancastrian property and executing his enemies. Harlech was besieged but refused to surrender to the Yorkist army. The garrison continued to hold out and was re-supplied from the sea using the fortified stairway that reached 61m (200ft) down from the castle to the water. The castle continued to resist whilst the war raged across the kingdom. In 1465 the garrison was reinforced when Lancastrian, Sir Richard Tunstall, arrived with fresh soldiers. They held out for another three years until, in 1468 when, thinking that the Lancastrians had lost, they finally surrendered the Castle. The siege had lasted seven years. It was the longest siege in British history and Harlech was the last Lancastrian stronghold to capitulate.

Henry Tudor returned to the British Isles, landing in Pembrokshire in 1485. He gathered an army of 5000 men and marched east to attack the Yorkist King, Richard III at Bosworth Field. Richard was killed and Henry crowned himself Henry VII on the battlefield.

According to Shakespeare's play Henry III part 1, describing the start of the 'Wars of The Roses', the two sides of the war met in Temple Church, London where they chose red and white roses for their emblems. This is, actually, fiction since as late as 1485 when the Lancastrians, led by Henry Tudor, fought at Bosworth, they fought under a Red Dragon standard while the Yorkist's flag depicted a White Boar.

Only later, did the rose emblems gain significance when Lancastrian King Henry VII came to the throne. He married Princess Elizabeth of York to cement his position as King and end the war. Henry then combined the red rose of Lancashire with the white rose of Yorkshire creating a red and white 'Tudor' rose to demonstrate the unity of his kingdom.

The Welshman, Henry Tudor, was an able administrator who went on to establish a peaceful and stable society, which grew prosperous during his reign. The dynasty he started included Henry

VIII and Queen Elizabeth I, both of whom became powerful Monarchs.

Harlech Castle and the courage of its garrison, withholding a siege for seven long years, are celebrated in the stirring marching song 'Men of Harlech'. It has been the regimental tune for several Welsh Regiments and has been adopted by Canadian and Australian forces. There are a number of versions of the lyrics including one especially written for the 1964 film 'Zulu'. The battle at Rourke's Drift, South Africa, depicted in the film, was an action that took place in 1879 when 139 soldiers of the '24th Regiment of Foot', later renamed the 'South Wales Borderers' fought off an estimated 4000 Zulu warriors. Eleven Victoria Crosses were awarded, the highest number ever presented for a single action.

Visit Harlech today and you will see the Red Dragon still flying high and proud above the ramparts of the stronghold that is Harlech Castle.

Men of Harlech, stop your dreaming
Can't you see their spearpoints gleaming
See their warrior pennants streaming
To this battle field
As sung in the 1964 film 'Zulu'.

Chapter 19...The Red Hand of Chirk

Lord Myddleton became a proud man when he learned that his beautiful young wife was with child. He had married late and needed to sire an heir to inherit his castle and estate before his ardour declined into old age. Lord Myddleton was a popular baron and the news of his wife's confinement was greeted with celebration in the towns and villages of the Marcher Lands. His castle at Chirk was a happy place with noble visitors arriving each day to offer their congratulations to the old man and his pregnant wife.

The weeks passed and the baroness started to show. Her belly grew quickly and her anxious husband, for this was his first child, summoned the doctors. They prodded and pushed the young baroness and consulted at length.

'My Lord. There is nothing to fear. Your wife has healthy lungs and a strong heart. She will bear your sons and be a fine mother,' they reported.

'My sons?' cried the Baron.

'Aye my Lord,' replied the doctors. 'Your wife is with twins.' The baron was overjoyed with the news. But would they both be sons he wondered. If there were two sons which one would inherit his estate?' the baron asked his friends.

'Don't worry,' they said. 'One is sure to be a girl, then you can marry her off.' The baron started to worry. He needed to be sure.

'Perhaps the midwife can advise you,' suggested a squire.

'Fetch her at once,' commanded the baron. The midwife was a common woman, stout in frame and calm in nature. She listened quietly while the baron explained his problem.

'If there are two sons how will I know which should inherit my lands and title?' asked the baron. 'They cannot both be Baron of Chirk.' The midwife considered her lordship's question carefully before she replied.

'My Lord. Have no fear. The answer to your problem is plain enough. Is it not true that the first born son should inherit?' asked the woman.

'That is so,' replied the baron.

'Then, when the time comes I will tie a ribbon to the first baby that emerges to identify your first born child,' said the midwife. The baron liked the midwife's simple suggestion and agreed to her plan. The baroness continued to grow bigger as the months went by until; at last, the time arrived for the birth. A room was prepared and the baroness withdrew. The midwife issued instructions to the women of the castle. The fires were built up to keep the birthing room hot. Boiling water and towels were fetched. The baron and his squires waited for news in the great hall.

The contractions started. Slowly the top of a head began to emerge and then a tiny arm appeared. The midwife swiftly tied on a red ribbon. Her hands were slippery with blood.

'Push now, with all your might,' cried the Midwife. The baroness screamed and pushed. Then she stopped, tired and wanting it to end.

'Baroness. You have a son,' yelled the midwife and held the baby up by its legs. The child spluttered and began to cry. Its lungs were hearty. Hearing the sound, the baron ran to his wife's chambers.

'Keep out, my Lord. Our work is not yet done,' called the midwife.

'Do I have a son?' demanded the baron, through the closed door.

'Aye, you do my Lord,' replied the midwife, returning to her work. She saw a tiny leg and a head appearing. The second baby was twisted and needed help. The midwife took her knife and cut the baroness. The second baby was delivered. It was a boy. The little body was covered in blood and on its arm was the tiny red ribbon. The midwife did not see the ribbon as she wrapped the child in a towel.

The baron could contain himself no longer. He burst into the room.

'Well. Is it done?' he cried.

'It is my Lord. You have two fine sons,' replied the midwife and handed him the little bundles.

'Which is first born?' asked the baron as he gazed at the babies.

'The one with the red ribbon on his arm,' replied the midwife, content with her reply.

As the boys grew, no one, not even their mother, could tell them apart. They were identical in size and feature. To tell the difference the baroness sewed ribbons into the sleeves of one of her son's clothes. It was he that was to become the next Baron of Chirk.

The years passed and the old baron grew frail and weak. His sons grew strong and fit, competing in everything they did. They became clever and ambitious men but one was more ruthless than the other. As the old baron's health failed he took to his bed. Feeling his life slipping away, he sent for his sons. He turned to the eldest.

'You are first born and my rightful heir. When I am dead you will be Baron of Chirk,' he said.

'How can this be so father for we are twins?' said the second son.

'The ribbon on your brother's sleeve shows he was born before you. There cannot be two barons. You must leave and make your own way in the world,' said the baron, feebly.

The first son was pleased but his brother grew angry. This was unfair. Why should his brother get everything while he has to slink away with nothing but the clothes on his back? Slowly, a plan took shape in his head. The next morning the second son woke early, dressed in his brother's clothes and went to his father's rooms. The old baron was dozing as his son entered.

'My Lord. I must speak with you,' said the son, rousing his father. The baron stirred.

'We cannot send my brother away with nothing. He is your blood. You must change your will to provide for him,' said the son. The baron smiled at his son.

'I cannot change the will. It is the law. You are the first son. The title and my wealth will pass to you,' whispered the baron.

'Very well father,' said the son. 'I will obey your dying wish.' At that moment, the other son burst into the room.

'Why are you dressed in my clothes?' he demanded.

'They are my clothes. Look here is my ribbon,' replied the son that had woken the baron.

'Usurper. You have stolen my clothes,' cried the other. The argument grew loud and the baron's servant came, drawn by the raised voices. They separated the sons and held them. The baron lay back weary. He looked at his sons through misty eyes, dilated with death. He knew he was passing away. His time had come.

'You must decide my Lord. Which of us is your true heir,' shouted one of the sons. The baron beckoned his squire to come closer.

'Carry my bed to the gardens,' he whispered. The squire ordered the servants to lift the baron's bed and take it to the garden. They propped the dying man up with pillows. The sons stood by their father's bed.

'My sons, truly I do not know which of you is my heir but there can only be one. I cannot decide so you will race around the castle. The first to return and touch my bed will be the next baron,' said the old man softly. Without a word, the sons ran from the baron to the corner of the castle. One was just ahead as they turned the corner but his brother tripped him and he fell. The second son ran on but his brother recovered and chased after him. They pushed and shoved as they ran, both determined to win the fateful race. As they entered the garden, one brother pushed the other into a yew tree. The fallen son, seeing that the race was lost, snatched a sword from a nearby guard and with a mighty blow cut off his own hand. He seized the bloody hand and threw it towards the baron's bed where it landed and won him the race.

From that day the coat of arms of the Baron of Chirk has included a bloody red hand.

Chapter 20…Dwynwen The Blessed

'Dwynwen deigr ariendegwch, Da y gwyr dy gor fflamgwyr
fflwch.'
'Dwynwen your beauty is like a silver tear, your choir is
ablaze with candlelight'.
From a 13th Century poem by Dafydd ap Gwilym
Dwynwen was a Princess, one of twenty-four children sired
by King Brychan Brycheiniog in the 5th Century. She lived on the
Island of Anglesey and was loved and cherished as a child.
Dwynwen, which translates as 'To lead a white or blessed life,'
grew to be a beautiful and clever young woman.

Her Father, King Brychan, enjoyed the good things of life
and his palace was a merry place where dancing and feasting often
continued far into the night. Many young men would visit the court
of King Brychan eager to win the hand of the beautiful Princess.
Dwynwen would flirt and tease her suitors with gay chatter. She
would listen to their proud boasts of bravery and dance with them
until her legs ached. But, when the feasting and dancing were over,
she would quickly lose interest in each new admirer.

One day a messenger arrived at the castle.

'The King of Gwynedd is to visit you, My Lord. It is a great
honour,' said the messenger.

'And so it is,' replied the King. 'Tell your master we shall
have a royal banquet to celebrate his coming to my kingdom,' he
added. Plans were made for the great day when the two Kings
would feast together. The finest cattle were slaughtered, poultry
plucked and suckling pigs prepared for roasting. Sweet fruits were
gathered and fine cheeses matured. The King commanded that his
best wines were fetched from the cellars. Beer was brewed and the
great hall made ready. Tables were laden until they groaned with
the weight of the fine delicacies.

The King of Gwynedd and his entourage were greeted with
pomp and ceremony. The banquet began. The King of Gwynedd
had a son with him; Prince Maelon, who some called Maelon

Dafodrill. Prince Maelon saw Princess Dwynwen and admired her beauty. He heard her gay laughter and resolved, at once, that he would marry her. The Princess was quickly aware of his interest and toyed with his emotions. At first, she pretended to ignore his advances. Then, she encouraged him with broad smiles and direct gazes into his eyes. Maelon became a lovesick puppy as she teased him. They danced together and, seizing the moment, he spoke. He whispered as he held her.

'Dwynwen my Princess. I worship and love you like a goddess and I can feel your love burning for me. Shall I speak with your Father? Tell me you will be mine.' Princess Dwynwen stiffened in his arms.

'Do not tease me Prince Maelon. We cannot marry. You have only known me for a few hours. Let us enjoy the evening and have no talk of love or marriage,' she replied. The Prince refused to accept her answer and the following day he visited King Brychan.

'King Brychan, I wish to marry your daughter. We are in love and I ask you for her hand,' he said.

'But does she love you?' enquired the King.

'I am sure of it, My Lord. I saw the love in her eyes as we danced last night,' replied the Prince. Princess Dwynwen was summoned and the question put to her.

'Do you love Prince Maelon?' asked the King.

'I do not,' answered the defiant Princess.

'There is your answer. Tomorrow you shall return to your own kingdom,' said the King, turning to Prince Maelon. Bewildered and angry, the Prince withdrew but that night, his last chance to see Princess Dwynwen, he visited her in her chambers. True to her nature, she began to tease him once more and because they were alone Maelon responded to her flirting, like a man. The next morning, the King of Gwynedd and his followers left. Prince Maelon had gone.

The young Princess felt ashamed and confused. She dare not tell her Father she had been raped: it would mean war. Dwynwen left the palace and wandered into the forest. She found a sunny glade with a small river where she lay down and fell asleep. As she slept, she dreamt that an angel appeared and asked why she was sad. In her dream, she replied that she hated Maelon and wanted him dead. She cried as she told the angel what the Prince had done. It was almost dark when she woke.

There was a great commotion when the Princess returned to the palace. News had come from Gwynedd; Prince Maelon had turned into a block of ice. Princess Dwynwen hurried to her chamber. Her heart was broken, for now she knew she loved the Prince. That night the Angel from her dream returned.

'I beg you to release Prince Maelon from his ice prison,' she cried.

'I cannot release your Prince but I grant you three wishes. Use them well,' replied the Angel.

'Release Prince Maelon and let him live a good and honest life,' whispered the Princes.

'What are your other wishes?' asked the Angel.

'I pray that God will watch over and protect all true lovers and my last wish is that, in penance for my vanity, I may never marry,' said the Princess.

'You have chosen your wishes well,' said the Angel and vanished.

Prince Maelon thawed completely, recovered from the ordeal and went on to live a good life. He married and raised a family. Princess Dwynwen left the palace and moved to a small island where she built a chapel. The Princess placed a golden statue in the chapel, kept lit with a hundred candles day and night. People travelled to the shrine in pilgrimage and to pay Princess Dwynwen to pray for their souls. Nearby, was a well where a strange eel lived. Women would come to ask Dwynwen if they had found true love. To answer their question, she sent them to the well where they threw bread on the water and covered it with their lover's handkerchief. If the surface remained smooth the love was true but when the love was false and the man a cheat, the eel would devour the bread in a flurry of anger.

The Princess never married and when she died, in 465 A.D. she was buried beneath the chapel she had built. Princess Dwynwen had paid for her vanity and lived a blessed life. She became the Welsh patron saint of lovers and her feast day is the 25th January. The chapel and the well are now in ruins but Llanddwyn, the island named after her, is still the perfect place to visit with your true love.

Chapter 21...The Gwiber of Penmachno

One day a visitor came to Penmachno and called on Rhys Ddewain.

'Tell me about the Gwiber,' said Owain Ap Gruffydd. Rhys Ddewain was an old man. He studied his inquisitive caller. Why is this brash young man interested in the Gwiber, he wondered?

'It's a foul evil beast. Have nothing to do with it,' replied the old man.

'Tell me more of this evil beast,' demanded Owain.

'The Gwiber is a giant snake with wings. Its body is covered in slime and stinks of putrid death. It slithers on the land, can fly through the air and lurks in the river where it feeds on fish and unwary animals that stray near the water,' said the old man.

'Such a beast must be killed and that is what I have come to do,' said Owain Ap Gruffydd and drew his sword. The blade glinted in the sunlight.

'You are brave but foolish. Many have tried to rid us of the Gwiber but all have perished. Put up your sword and go home. You are no match for the Gwiber,' said the old man.

'Old man, you are weak and afraid but I am not. I will kill this snake,' said Owain.

'You are right. I am afraid of the Gwiber and rightly so. If you hunt the Gwiber, I tell you now, it will kill you,' said the old man.

'If you can see my future, old man, tell me. How will I die?' demanded Owain.

'The Gwiber will bite your neck and kill you,' replied the old man.

That night, as Owain tried to sleep he considered what Rhys Ddewain had foretold. If it was true he would indeed be foolish to hunt the Gwiber. As he tossed and turned he resolved to test the truth of the old man's prophecy. The following morning Owain dressed as a vagrant and, so disguised, called once more on Rhys Ddewain.

'They tell me old man that you can see the future,' said Owain.

'That is true,' replied the old man.

'Then pray tell me, when my time comes, how will I die?' asked Owain.

'Your death will be violent, painful and very soon. You will slip while you are out walking and the fall will break your neck,' replied Rhys Ddewain.

The following day Owain put on a millers apron, covered his face with flour and returned to the old man's house for a third time.

'Good morning Master Miller. What can I do for you?' asked the old man.

'Can you tell me the nature of my death?' asked Owain.

'Master Miller, I am sorry to tell you that your time is short and when your end comes it will be by drowning,' replied the old man.

Owain threw off the miller's apron and wiped the flour from his face.

'Rhys Ddewain, your prophecies are false,' cried Owain. 'You have predicted three different deaths for me,' he added.

'You will see. Time will tell,' was all the old man would say.

Convinced that the old man was lying, Owain, at once, resolved to find and kill the Gwiber. He collected his armour and sword and set off along the riverbank, below the village. As he went, he prodded the water and slashed the bushes with his sword.

'Come forward Gwiber and meet your end,' he yelled. A rush of wind tore along the valley and caught Owain by surprise. It was the Gwiber. The great serpent grappled with Owain. Its wings flapped furiously. Owain tried to lift his sword but the beast trapped his arm with its coils. A foul stench began to overwhelm Owain. He felt faint. His strength was slipping away as the snake began to crush him. Suddenly, the Gwiber bit deep into Owain's neck and blood ran down his chest. The beast gave a great roar and released Owain. Owain slipped on the slimy ground and fell. His head hit a large rock. There was a loud crack as his neck snapped. Owain's body continued downward into the river where he took his last breath and drowned.

The people of Penmachno found his body floating in the water later that day and carried it back to the old man's house.

'What should we do?' they cried.

'You must kill the Gwiber,' replied the old man. The men collected their bows and spears and set out to find the great snake. They searched the valley until they found the serpent sleeping by the river. A volley of arrows and spears woke the Gwiber, inflicting many wounds. The Gwiber rose up and tried to fly but its wings were torn and twisted. The animal writhed on the ground snarling and spitting at its attackers.

A second flight of arrows hit the beast and it howled in agony. Suddenly, the Gwiber slithered towards the villagers and, arrows spent, they backed away. They watched, with horror, as the evil snake gave one last roar and slid into the river where it vanished forever.

Look closely, as you walk along the riverbank at Penmachno, for some say that the Gwiber's eyes can still be seen looking up from the deepest pools. The place is now called Wibernant, which in English means 'The Valley of the Gwiber' and in the Welsh language today a gwiber is a viper or an adder.

Chapter 22...The Demon of Cerrigydrudion

'Do you see it, over there in the window, a face?' asked the farmer. The innkeeper peered at the church and then he saw it: a hideous face staring out through the dirty glass. The eyes were sunken and cold, the cheeks white with the pallor of death itself.

'What is it?' whispered the innkeeper as the two men backed away from the apparition staring out from the little church. News spread quickly through the village of Cerrigydrudion and a small crowd gathered in the road outside the church. The priest arrived.

'What's going on?' he asked.

'There in the window. It's the Devil himself,' cried the villagers.

'The Devil, superstitious nonsense. There's no devil in my church: It's a house of God,' cried the priest and marched along the path to the door of the church. The face in the window watched him approach. The priest took hold of his cross, held it up and opened the door. The crowd watched as the priest disappeared into the church. They looked back at the window. The face had vanished. There was a muffled scream and the priest stumbled backwards out of the church. He turned and staggered through the churchyard, his face contorted with fear.

'What happened Father?' cried the crowd.

'It's Satan. He is here,' sobbed the priest and started to shake violently. The crowd looked back at the church. The evil face stared back at them from the window. Days passed. Each day, the evil face would stare out from the church. Each night, strange screams and manic laughter were heard coming from the church. A dog that wandered into the churchyard vanished. The people grew afraid and would not go near the church; not even to worship on the Sabbath. In desperation, the villagers sought out a wise man for advice.

'What can we do?' asked the farmer.

'You will need great charm to tempt the Devil from the church and great strength to drag him away,' replied the wise man.

'You must find a beautiful girl to tempt him and you must use great strength to remove him from your village,' said the wise man.

'We are not strong enough to move the Devil,' wailed the people.

'Go to the mountain and catch the oxen Dau ychain Banawg,' said the wise man. The villagers knew of the two huge oxen called Dau ychain Banawg that grazed on Waen Banawg. They listened carefully as the wise man told them what needed to be done. A beautiful young girl called Eira Wyn (Snow White) was chosen to tempt the Devil. She was dressed in silk and the women brushed her long golden hair until it shone. Men searched the mountain and found the great oxen. They tempted the beasts to return to the village with sacks of corn. The blacksmith forged stout chains and soaked the links in holy water. An enormous sledge was built using tree trunks for runners. While the villagers worked, the Devil sneered as he peered through the window of the church.

When all was ready, Eira's seven brothers bought her to the church. The Devil watched as the girl entered the churchyard. He smiled at seeing such a pretty offering. The face disappeared from the window and the door swung open but girl did not go into the church. Instead, she started to arrange flowers on the graves and began to sing. The girl's innocent beauty and her sweet voice excited the Devil. Attracted by the girl and with wicked thoughts in his mind, the Devil swaggered from the church into the daylight. The villagers were ready. They rushed into the churchyard. The Devil roared with laughter as they grappled with him.

'You puny people cannot hold me,' he cried, but he was wrong. The people flung the stout chains soaked in holy water around the Devil and pulled them tight. Still the Devil roared with laughter. The two huge oxen, known as Dau ychain Banawg, bought down from the mountain Wan Banawg, were yoked to the chains. The powerful beasts dragged the Devil from the churchyard. He lay in the road kicking and screaming.

'I will have my revenge on you,' he cried. The Devil was chained to the sledge made of tree trunks and more chains were tied to the evil demon, to make sure he was held fast. The women greased the tree trunks with pig fat to help the sledge move. Slowly, the huge beasts began to drag the Devil away. The oxen strained every sinew as the evil load shuddered and jolted along the track. The people pulled the chains and pushed the sledge to help it on its way while the Devil cursed and shouted foul insults with every step.

After hours of toil the Devil and his captors reached a lake on Hiraethog Mountain but they did not stop. The two oxen, known as Dau ychain Banawg, and the sledge with its evil load, kept on going and marched slowly into the water. They were never seen again. The people named the lake Llyn y Ddau Ychain (The Lake of the Two Oxen) in honour of the brave beasts that perished that day.

Today, the lake is part of Alwen Reservoir but, if you look closely at the track, you can still see the ruts cut as the sledge took the Devil to his watery resting place.

Chapter 23...The Death of Arthur

It was the winter of life. Camelot was no more and the high ideals of valour and courage were nothing more than tales told by old men to eager children. Arthur, King of Briton, old and tired now, had vanished. The Knights of the round-table were dispersed across Europe, searching for the Holy Grail. Darkness and evil percolated the land.

Arthur's evil son Mordred wanted the throne and, after years of searching, his spies finally located Arthur and sent word to the usurper. Arthur was at the city of Tregalan, hidden in Cwm Tregalan in the Kingdom of Gwynedd, with just a small retinue of men led by ever-faithful Sir Bedevere.

Mordred was eager to claim the crown and had no love for his father. He gathered his army and marched on Snowdonia to seize power. Errant knights and outlaws of every kind flocked to Mordred's banner, greedy for plunder and the spoils of war. As they advanced, Mordred's army pillaged and burned. Word reached Arthur of the advancing throng and, old as he was, he knew that he had to give battle. Mordred had to be stopped.

A weary Arthur gathered together his small band of warriors, mainly old knights and boys and rode out to meet Mordred in mortal combat. Expecting Arthur, Mordred sent archers to hide in the mountains with orders to let Arthur by while the rest of Mordred's army camped at Pen y Pass. His plan was to trap Arthur between Llyn Llydaw and Yr Wyddfa (Mount Snowdon) and kill every man with him. He wanted no survivors to talk of heroism or martyrs.

It was a cold damp winter morning as Arthur and his men marched down the valley past Llyn Llydaw to confront Mordred's army by the bank of Llyn Teyrn. The battle was fierce and no quarter was given. Men that fell wounded were slain. Outnumbered, Arthur's small band was forced to retreat. Slowly they fell back along the valley towards Mount Snowdon leaving a trail of dead as they went.

88

As they pressed on, Mordred's soldiers tripped and fell over their fallen comrades. Friend and foe alike sank into the slimy mud. The battle raged throughout the day until it was nearly dark and a damp mist enveloped the exhausted men. Still they fought. Now Arthur had just a few men left. They were trapped below the great mountain, Snowdon. Sensing victory, Mordred pushed his way to the front of the fight. He saw Arthur, bloody and wounded, surrounded by his enemies. Hatred and greed filled Mordred's heart and he charged at Arthur, eager to kill his own father.

Arthur raised his sword, Excalibur, and with a mighty blow cleaved Mordred's head from his body. As Mordred fell, a flight of arrows rained down on Arthur and, clutching his sword, he fell to the ground. The archers, hidden at Bwlch y Saethau (The Pass of Arrows) behind Arthur and his men, had done their evil work.

Without a leader, Mordred's army had no cause and the fighting quickly stopped. Loyal Sir Bedevere helped Arthur from the battlefield and listened as the dying King whispered his last command.

'Take Excalibur and throw it far into the lake,' croaked Arthur. Sir Bedevere took the King's sword to throw it into Llyn Llydaw, but he could not. Twice he returned to Arthur asking the King to keep the mighty blade and twice Arthur commanded him to throw it into the lake. Finally overcome with grief Sir Bedevere cast Excalibur far into the lake. As he watched, the water parted and a silky white hand emerged holding aloft the sword that had been Arthur's symbol of authority and strength since the day he had pulled it from the stone. Slowly the hand and the sword submerged into the copper green water.

Sir Bedevere looked back at his King. Arthur was dead. It was dark now and a fine rain was falling. Silently, a boat glided across the lake out of the darkness. In it sat three maidens dressed in black velvet. Torches flared and spluttered in the damp. They carefully placed Arthur's body in the funeral barge and, without a sound or a spoken word, the maidens, the boat and Arthur glided into the darkness and the otherworld.

Quietly, Sir Bedevere and the few remaining men who had fought so valiantly climbed Mount Lliwedd and vanished from history. There they remain, deep in the mountain, waiting for Arthur to return from the green waters of Llyn Llydaw, ready to lead them once again.

Chapter 24...Prince Idwal

At the beginning of the 12th Century the Kingdom of Gwynedd was ruled by Owain ap Cynan. King Owain, whose royal title was Owain Gwynedd, had nineteen sons but the fairest, by far, was Prince Idwal. The other princes raced each other, played rough games of war and grew strong. Idwal however, was not like his boisterous brothers. He would sit for hours quietly reading or listening to the court musicians as they practiced. Sometimes he would wander alone in the gardens admiring flowers and singing sweet melodies.

Owain realised that Idwal would never be a warrior and that saddened him but as the boy grew his father saw that he was intelligent and kind to all. The King admired Idwal's perfect features and placid temperament. Some called the boy weak but the King was proud of Idwal.

When the King of Powys attacked the Kingdom of Gwynedd, men were called to arms to drive off the invader. Eager to prove their strength in battle, the King's sons pleaded with their father to go to war. The king agreed since it was their duty, as royal princes, to earn their place with deeds of bravery in battle. But what, the King wondered, should he do with Idwal?

'Send him to Nefydd Hardd,' suggested a courtier. 'Nefydd is a great musician and will teach Idwal to play the harp.'

'Where does Nefydd Hardd live?' asked the King.

'High in the mountains by Llyn Ogwen. No harm will come to Idwal there,' replied the courtier. Nefydd Hardd was a 'Gentleman' and leader of one of the fifteen noble tribes of Wales. The King agreed to the plan and Idwal was sent to the house of Nefydd Hardd, high in the mountains, where he would be safe from the King's enemies. Nefydd Hardd greeted Idwal and introduced Dunawt, his son, to the royal guest.

'You will be brothers. I will educate you together,' he cried and squeezed Idwal's hand. Idwal took well to the music and poetry lessons from his new tutor. Each day the young men sat together as Nefydd Hardd instructed them. Idwal learned quickly but Dunawt, who was slow witted, struggled. Nefydd Hardd, which means 'Nefydd the Beautiful' in English, was a vain man. Often, he had boasted to his friends how clever his son, Dunawt, was and sung in praise of the boy's good looks.

'He will grow up to be as brilliant and good looking as me,' he said. But, as he watched the two boys together, he grew envious of Idwal's handsome face and resentful of Idwal's sharp mind. Only a fool could fail to see that Dunawt was a plain, stupid oaf by comparison and Nefydd Hardd was no fool.

As the weeks passed, Nefydd Hardd grew to despise the royal prince sheltering under his roof and his dull son grew jealous of their visitor. Idwal could feel the jealousy and hatred but being a kindly youth with no malice in him, responded with courtesy and compassion. Prince Idwal's good manners infuriated Nefydd Hardd and his son even more. One dark afternoon Nefydd Hardd sent for his son.

'Dunawt, you should take Prince Idwal for a walk. Show him the lake at the head of the valley,' said Nefydd Hardd.

'But Father, it will be dark soon and there are storm clouds on the mountain,' replied Dunawt.

'Take Idwal to the ridge above the lake but be careful that you don't slip. The path can be dangerous when it's wet,' said Nefydd Hardd.

Dunawt looked at his father. The old man was grinning.

'And, what if Prince Idwal slips and falls into the lake?' He asked.

'That would be a terrible accident, which would be no one's fault,' replied his father. It had started to rain as the two young men left the house. Dunawt marched ahead.

'Come on,' he cried. 'There is something I want you to see.' Price Idwal followed behind, the rain streaming down his face. They walked around the lake towards the mountain. Their legs sank deep into the soft peat. Dunawt strode on into the gathering gloom. When they reached a narrow ledge he stopped.

92

'Here it is, look,' he yelled. Prince Idwal hurried to join his companion.

'What is it?' asked the Prince looking around.

'See the lake below, it's your destiny,' laughed Dunawt and shoved the Prince off the ledge. Prince Idwal screamed as he fell into the lake but the wind snatched the sound from his lips and carried the plaintive cry up into the mountains. Dunawt walked back to the house alone.

King Owain returned from the war and searched for his son but Prince Idwal's body was never found. He suspected foul play but had no proof that Nefydd Hardd or his son Dunawt had murdered the prince. Even so, he seized Nefydd Hardd's lands and banished him and his son, Dunawt, from the kingdom.

The evil pair never admitted the crime but, in 1170, when King Owain Gwynedd died, Rhun ap Nefydd Hardd, younger brother of Dunawt, returned to Gwynedd and built a church at Llanrwst in penitence for the foul murder done by his family.

Today the lake where Prince Idwal drowned is named after him and, it is said, that no bird will fly across the water where the evil deed was done. Sometimes, when the wind blows from the west you can hear the echo of the young prince's scream as he fell into the icy water.

Chapter 25…Prince Madoc Sails to America

*In memory of Prince Madoc, a Welsh explorer, who landed
on the shores
of Mobile Bay in 1170 and left behind, with the Indians, the
Welsh language.*
Plaque erected in Mobile, Alabama, USA in 1953
Prince Madoc was the son of Owain Gwynedd, King of
Gwynedd. The King, not content with just two wives, the
maximum allowed according to Welsh law at that time, also kept
four mistresses. He sired nineteen sons many of whom, including
Madoc, were illegitimate. According to custom, all the children
were openly acknowledged as the King's. When the King died in
1169, rivalries between his sons eager to take the throne quickly
escalated into open warfare.

Being illegitimate, Prince Madoc was not a contender for
the crown and, unwilling to take sides in the increasingly bloody
fights, he resolved to escape from Wales. Two stout ships were
fitted out ready for a voyage. The Gorn Gwynant and the Pedr Sant
had been built from sturdy oak trees hewn from the forest of Nant
Gwynant. Prince Madoc had sailed in them before and was a
skilled navigator already famous for his adventures.

The prince was a popular leader and men were eager to
crew his ships. The ships departed from a jetty on the River Ganol,
now Rhos on Sea, and set sail west. They stopped at Lundy Island
where Prince Rhirid, one of Prince Madoc's brothers, joined them.
From Lundy the two vessels sailed on past Ireland, steering steadily
west heading for the edge of the known world.

The fight for the throne of Gwynedd continued. Owain's
designated son and heir, Hywel ab Owain Gwynedd, fell at the
battle of Pentraeth, killed by his half brothers Dafydd and Rhodri.
The war continued and other brothers were killed in battle or
murdered until only Dafydd and Rhodri remained strong enough to
claim the crown. Eventually, the kingdom was divided between
Dafydd and Rhodri and an uneasy peace was established. Another

generation would pass before the Kingdom of Gwynedd was finally reunified under Llyweln the Great.

Prince Madoc had almost been forgotten when, years later, he returned with a strange tale to tell. The Prince had crossed a great ocean to a distant land. A land inhabited by friendly people with dark skins who welcomed him and his crew. A land where, if you were hungry, you just had to reach up and pluck sweet fruits from the trees. He told of rivers that were full of fish and great plains covered with herds of huge beasts the natives called buffalo.

Some of the prince's crew had remained behind in the strange land and Prince Madoc announced, at once, that he would return across the great ocean to join his men. He invited others, who might want to start a new life, to come. Ten ships were prepared and quickly filled, ready for the long voyage. Once more, Prince Madoc sailed away to the west.

After a long and dangerous journey, they landed at a place we now call Mobile, Alabama. From Mobile, the ships travelled inland along mighty rivers. Mandan Indians guided the Welshmen. The settlers built forts to protect themselves against unfriendly Indians. They taught their Indian guides to speak Welsh and how to fish, using coracles. The Welshmen took native wives and, over the years, the Mandan and the Welshmen merged to become one tribe.

Prince Madoc never returned to Wales but there is ample evidence of his arrival in America. In 1608 explorer Peter Wynne discovered a tribe in Virginia calling themselves Monacan Indians and wrote that they spoke 'Welch'. In 1669 Reverend Morgan Jones was captured by a tribe called the Doeg. When he conversed with them in Welsh they understood his meaning. He stayed with the Doeg for several months before being released and returning to the British colonies. In 1799 Governor John Sevier of Tennessee reported the discovery of six skeletons wearing brass armour bearing the Welsh coat of arms.

A mound and stone fortification called the 'Devil's Backbone' exists fourteen miles unstream from Louisville, Kentucky built about the same time as Prince Madoc arrived using a design similar to castles that existed in North Wales. Cherokee Indian tradition refers to a tribe of 'fair skinned moon eyed' people, known as Modoc, who built a stone castle on Fort Mountain, Georgia. In 1832 German ethnologist, Prince Maximilian of Wied-Neuwied, travelled up the Missouri River and across the Great Plains. He studied the Mandan language and made a comparison list of common Welsh and Mandan words. In 1841, the painter George Catlin painted Mandan Indians fishing using a round boat referred to as a 'Bull Boat'. Its design was the same as the Welsh coracle.

Other evidence exists, including DNA and radio carbon dating, to support the fact that Prince Madoc discovered and settled in America more than 300 years before Christopher Columbus arrived. In 1738 French traders visited nine Mandan villages along the Heart River containing 15,000 inhabitants. The Mandan had become a great Indian nation and had prospered and spread up into the Great Plains of America.

Sadly, in 1837, the Mandan Indian tribe was infected with smallpox by the crew of a visiting boat. The disease tore through the nation and only 125 Mandan survived the epidemic. The United States government then merged the Mandan with other Indian tribes and the last full blooded Mandan died in 1971. How much of Prince Madoc's Welsh blood ran in his veins we shall never know.

The plaque commemorating the voyage of Prince Madoc was damaged by a hurricane in 1979 and removed, for safe keeping, by the US military. Since then, the Alabama Welsh Society has been campaigning for it to be replaced, in its original position, in honour of the first European to discover America.

'I have dwelt longer on the history and customs of these people than I have or shall on any other tribe... because I have found them a very peculiar people. From the striking peculiarities in their personal appearance, in their customs, traditions, and

language, I have been led conclusively to believe that they are a people of a decidedly different origin from that of any other tribe in these regions.'

George Catlin 1796 - 1872 American Artist

Chapter 26...Maelgwn Gwynedd and the Yellow Eye

'... you the last I write of but the first and greatest in evil,
more than many in ability but also in malice, more generous in
giving but also more liberal in sin, strong in war but stronger to
destroy your soul ...'.
De Excidio et Conquestu Britanniae
On the Ruin and conquest of Britain.
A sermon by St. Gildas (500-570AD)

Maelgwn Gwynedd, also known as Maelgwn Hir,
(Maelgwn the Tall) was the King of Gwynedd. He was a ruthless
and ambitious man and had seized the throne from his uncle. Even
after he became King of Gwynedd, his ambition was not satisfied,
for there were three other kingdoms in Wales. Maelgwn was a
jealous man. He wanted to be more powerful than the other kings.
He wanted them all to pay homage to him.

He invited the other kings to meet him on the sands of
Aberdovey and to bring their thrones with them. There would be
feasting and games, said the invitation. Maelgwn told them that
they would be treated as honoured guests. The kings accepted the
tempting offer and journeyed from across the land with their
retainers. A great tent, filled with carpets and tables laden with
silver platters loaded with food, was erected on the beach. Men at
arms lined the shore, their weapons sparkling in the sunshine.
Royal banners fluttered gaily in the breeze. Trumpeters welcomed
the visitors and fine words of greeting were exchanged between
them.

The thrones were carried into the tent and the feast began.
The kings chatted gaily. All agreed that the food and wines were fit
for kings. Slowly, so as not to be obvious, Maelgwn turned the
conversation to address a question. Which of the four kings was the
most senior? The kings could not agree. One said they were equal,
another claimed he was Chief King. The debate grew heated and
the kings began to argue.

'My Lords. There is a simple way we can settle the matter,' cried Maeglwn.

'How so?' asked the Kings.

'The tide is out. Let us have our thrones moved to the edge of the water where we will sit. Whichever of us remains seated for the longest shall be honoured by all as Supreme King,' suggested Maeglwn. It was agreed and the four thrones were carried to the water's edge. The tide turned and the water started to rise. Before long their feet were under water but none of the kings moved. All wanted to be Chief King. The sea level continued to rise, covering their knees but they did not move. Then, a strange thing happened. Maeglwn's throne began to lift up while the other kings slowly submerged. One by one they abandoned their thrones and waded away leaving King Maeglwn alone, floating on the water.

Concealed beneath his seat, King Maeglwn had fitted pigs bladders filled with air. The three kings had been tricked but, having given their solemn word, were obliged to honour Maeglwn and pledged their loyalty to him as their Chief King.

Maelgwn built a castle with a great tower on the twin hills of Deganwy known as the Vardre. He prayed with the monks but quickly grew bored with their piety.

'Life is for living and I shall live like a king,' he told his courtiers. Maelgwn summoned musicians to entertain him and bards to write epic stories of his courage and goodness, but the songs and poems were lies for the truth was that Maeglwn was an evil man with a violent temper.

When Maelgwyn's nephew visited Deganwy with a new bride, Maelgwn grew jealous. He wanted the woman for himself. So the king had his own wife and the nephew murdered and seduced the young bride. As time passed, Maelgwn's tyranny grew worse until all his people hated him.

'Who will rid us of this evil king,' they cried.

A wise prophet and bard, named Taleisin lived in the land.

'Tell us, wise man. Who will end Maelgwn's evil,' asked the people.

'A great beast will appear from the east. Its skin will be rotting and fetid. Its teeth and eyes will be yellow and its foul breath will whisper of death. This great putrid beast will avenge Maelgwn's evil and people will speak of the long sleep of Maelgwn in the Church of Rhos,' said Taleisin.

A plague, which had started in Europe, spread quickly across England. It reached Gwynedd in 547 bringing misery and death to the people. Their skins ran with sores, their lungs filled with blood, their teeth and eyes turned yellow and their breath stank of death. Maelgwn feared for his life and, ignoring the cries for help from his courtiers, as they died around him, he fled from the castle. The evil king locked himself alone in the church at Llanrhos and prayed for sanctuary. The few loyal guards that remained waited outside, unsure of what to do. They knocked on the door of the church.

'Sire. What are your orders,' they shouted.

'Go away,' yelled the king. That night, as Maelgwyn knelt praying, he heard a strange scratching at the door.

'Maelgwyn I have come for you,' whispered a voice from outside.

'Leave me alone,' cried the King.

'Maelgwyn. Let me in,' whispered the voice. Maelgwyn picked up his candle and moved to the door. He bent down and peered through the keyhole. A large yellow eye stared back at him. The guards returned the next morning but Maelgwyn did not answer their calls.

'The king is asleep. We dare not wake him,' said the guards and went away. Days passed before they broke down the door. The evil king's body was rotting and fetid. His teeth and eyes had turned yellow. Maelgwyn's body was taken to Ynys Seiriol and buried. Taleisin's prophecy had come true.

'Hir hun Faelgwn yn eglwys Ros.'
'The long sleep of Maelgwn in the Church of Rhos.'

Chapter 27...The Legend of Gelert

Prince Llewelyn the Great was a fine sportsman. His good
humour and high spirits were known far and wide. Llewelyn's hall
was a welcoming place, full of fun and friendship. He enjoyed his
hunting and spent his days out with his horse and hounds. The
biggest of his hounds was Gelert.

Llewelyn loved his animals and Gelert was his pride and
joy. Never had a man owned such a fine hound. Gelert was the
fastest and the bravest of his dogs and always the first at the kill.
Gelert was fierce and brave. He was loyal and attentive. It was as if
he knew his master's wishes and understood his moods. Of all the
hounds, Gelert was Llewelyn's favourite.

It was autumn and the leaves had fallen from the trees. The
woods were bare and the game easy to chase. Llewelyn took his
horn and summoned the hounds with a long blast. They clamoured
around his horse's hooves, baying with excitement. Their blood
was up. It was time to hunt.

Llewelyn waved goodbye to his young wife and their baby
then galloped out of the courtyard and away with his friends. The
hounds followed close behind. The hunt went well and Llewelyn
was pleased with the day. There would be a good table tonight with
meat for all. They continued hunting until late in the afternoon and
the light was fading when Llewelyn turned for home. Men, horses
and dogs were all weary but elated with the day's sport.

As they trotted back from hunting, the men boasted about
their brave deeds. They teased one and other and joked about the
day's sport. The dogs followed silently, eager for home and their
dinner; the reward for their effort. They did not bay now. Their
work was done. Llewelyn looked around. He felt uneasy.
Something was wrong. Who was missing he wondered.

'Where is Gelert?' he asked his friends. They stopped their
idle chatter and searched for the great hound. He was nowhere to
be seen.

'He was with us when we left the hall this morning,' said one.

'I have not seen Gelert at all today,' said another.

'He was with us a few minutes ago. I swear,' added another.

'Don't worry, he will turn up my Lord. Gelert is big enough to look after himself,' said another, cheerily. They laughed and the hunting party rode on. It was dark as they approached the great hall. The door was ajar and light shone through the doorway, illuminating the courtyard.

'This is strange' thought Llewelyn. Suddenly, a piercing scream came from inside the hall. Llewelyn leapt from his horse and sprinted inside. His wife was slumped on a bench sobbing.

'What's wrong? Tell me,' he demanded. His wife pointed to the back of the hall and their bedchamber.

'There. It's killed our baby,' she cried. Llewelyn drew his sword and ran towards the bedchamber. The room was dim but he could see the crib by the light shining from the hall behind him. It was empty. He could hear his wife weeping. His stomach turned and hate filled his heart. There was a noise near the crib. It was Gelert and the hound's jowls were red with blood. The dog sprang up to greet its master. Llewelyn raised his sword and ran the dog through.

Lord Llewelyn returned to the hall and tried to comfort his grieving wife. Their hearts were broken and they sat together hugging and weeping. There was a whine from the bedchamber. Llewelyn leapt up with his sword and returned to finish the job. Then, a baby cried out and his wife rushed into the bedchamber. Their child, hidden behind the bed, was alive and unharmed. Beside it lay the biggest wolf that had ever walked the lands of Gwynedd. The animal was dead, killed by the faithful hound Gelert. His wife took the child while Llewelyn cradled the dog's head in his arms. Gelert gave one last whimper and died.

The noble dog was buried and, as Llewelyn commanded, his grave marked with a stone to record the bravery and loyalty he had shown. Llewelyn was consumed with guilt and sorrow. The

102

great hall became a place of sadness and there were few visitors. For the rest of his life Llewelyn never hunted with the hounds and those that knew him said he never laughed again.

Chapter 28...Llyn Tegid and the Harp

Tegid Foel, or if you prefer his English name, Tegid the Bald was a warrior prince. He lived with his wife, Ceridwen, in a beautiful palace, sheltered in a valley surrounded by mountains. They had two children, a daughter, Creirwy and a son, Morfran. Creirwy was beautiful but their son, Morfran, was ugly and dim-witted. His skin was dark, like leather. The people called him Afagddu, which means utter darkness; for his appearance and manners were so repulsive he darkened any room he entered.

Ceridwen, who was a sorceress, loved her children equally and was determined to help her son. She took the ancient cauldron of wisdom and brewed a potion of herbs and poisons so strong that drinking just three drops would give incredible knowledge and intelligence. A blind servant was given the job of stirring the broth and sat labouring beside the roaring fire. As the servant stirred, three drops splashed from the giant pot onto his hand. Without thinking, the servant licked his fingers and in the blink of an eye he became a great Baird destined to write fine poetry and sing beautiful songs throughout the land.

Later, when three drops were given to Morfran nothing happened. The magic of the potion was spent and the youth remained hideous and stupid. Ceridwen cleaned out the ancient cauldron and boiled another brew but it made no difference. The ancient cauldron of wisdom had lost its magic.

As the years passed, Prince Tegid watched his son grow more gruesome and dull. Slowly the prince's unhappiness festered and his heart turned to anger. The prince began to hate. He hated his wife for failing to give the boy intelligence. He hated the people who sneered and whispered behind his back. He hated himself for failing to provide a male heir for his lands. Most of all he hated his son, Morfran, for being so ugly and stupid.

As Prince Tegid's hatred grew he became a cruel tyrant. The people began to fear him and hide whenever he rode near. The palace became a place of darkness, filled with loathing and disgust.

The bile and spite spread like some dank mist and leached into the ground. The river that once made the valley so fertile drained away leaving nothing but dust. The valley withered and the crops failed. The people blamed Prince Tegid for the famine and turned against him.

Ceridwen was sad to see such hatred and anger. She knew the valley needed laughter and happiness to thrive. It was time to end the bitterness before it destroyed them all. Princess Ceridwen invited all the villagers to the palace. She ordered food to be fetched from far away. She prepared a great feast and summoned the greatest harp player in the land. Fine food and beautiful music would, she thought, lift the gloom that was suffocating the valley.

The day of the feast arrived. As the people entered the palace, the harp player entranced them with gentle melodies that floated through the rooms. As he played, a tiny bird flew into the palace, landed on the harp and started to sing. The people ate and drank greedily, glad of the free food and wine. As they drank they became merry. Princess Ceridwen was pleased. Her plan was working.

The harp player continued to fill the air with gentle melodies but the people had stopped listening to the music. The wine they had drunk dulled their senses and made them aggressive. They scorned and sneered at the prince and his ugly son and laughed with contempt as they filled their goblets from the great vats. The feast became a drunken frenzy and the palace was filled with spite and venom. Prince Tegid leapt up and shouted at his guests, ordering them to leave, but it made no difference. The harp player stopped playing and heard a shrill voice. It was the little bird.

'Come away. Come away. Vengeance has come. Vengeance has come,' cried the little bird. The harp player wondered what the little bird meant.

'Come away. Come away. Vengeance has come. Vengeance has come,' cried the little bird for a second time and fluttered onto the man's sleeve. The tiny bird pulled at the cloth, tugging with his beak until the musician stood up. The little bird continued to pull and the harp player found himself being led from the palace. No one noticed him leaving. The man and the little bird climbed up away from the palace leaving the noise of the revellers far below. Just as they reached the top of the mountain there was a giant crashing sound. Water thundered across the land. The harp player looked back. A vast river was surging across the land, destroying everything in its path. He watched horrified as water flooded across the valley.

The harp player sat on the mountain watching as farms and villages were washed away. By the morning the thunder of water had gone. A great lake had appeared, filling the valley from end to end and drowning the evil prince with his spiteful people.

The little bird's warning had been true. Vengeance had come. The man searched for the little bird that had saved him but it was gone. Slowly, the harp player climbed back down the mountain. The surface of the lake lay still as glass, the silent water hiding its terrible secret. The man, now alone, stood on the bank. A strange gurgling sound erupted from deep within the lake. Something emerged from the gloomy depths and bubbled to the surface. It was a harp.

Today Llyn Tegid, as it is known, hides the secret of the drowned palace 150 feet beneath its waves while the teachers of Bala proudly tutor their scholars in the beauty and magic of Celtic harp music.

Chapter 29...The Curse of Nant Gwrtheyrn

Gwrtheyrn was a king who lived in Kent during the 5th Century. He was a timid man and his kingdom was weak. He employed mercenaries from Saxony to fight his enemies and paid them with gold. The Saxons, led by the brutal warrior Hengist, drove off Gwrtheyrn's foes. King Gwrtheyrn was pleased and gave Hengist the Isle of Thanet as a reward. The Saxons bought their families to Kent and settled on the fertile island. Before long, they started to take more land. Seeing the danger he had invited into his kingdom, Gwrtheyrn negotiated a wedding to protect his throne. He asked for the hand of Alys, the beautiful daughter of Hengist, the Saxon leader. Hengist agreed to the match and a great feast was prepared with Saxons and Britons sitting together. Suddenly, as one, the Saxons jumped up, drew their daggers and stabbed the Britons beside them. Gwrtheyrn had been tricked. He escaped and ran for his life, accompanied by Druid priests.

The king and his priests travelled far across the land looking for a remote part of Britain where the evil Hengist would never find them. After years of searching, they found a small valley, hidden behind a mountain on a remote peninsula. The land could be ploughed and there were fish in the sea. King Gwrtheryn had found his refuge and the little party settled in the valley. They built houses and soon a thriving village was established, a village that was so remote that it should never be discovered.

One hundred years later, three Christian monks found a tiny track leading down a steep mountain and followed it to the valley below. Near the sea, they found a village with a pagan church. The monks told the villagers to build a Catholic church but the people refused. They threw stones at the monks and drove them away. The retreating monks stopped on the track, high above the village and each monk cursed the tiny hamlet below them.

'The ground in this valley is unholy. No man shall be buried here,' yelled the first monk.

'The men of Nant Gwrtheyrn shall never marry the women of Nant Gwrtheyrn,' cried the second monk.

'Your village is doomed and will be ruined three times. The third time it falls will be forever,' bellowed the third monk. The people in the valley heard the curses and laughed at the monks.

'Words cannot hurt us,' they said. The following day the men of the village took their boats into the bay to fish. A violent storm blew up and overturned the boats, drowning the men. The bodies disappeared into the sea. With no men, the women had no choice but to leave the village and start new lives. Nant Gwrtheyrn became a deserted ruin.

As the years passed, people began to return to the valley to farm, but strange accidents happened to the men. Some fell into the sea and disappeared beneath the waves. Others vanished into the forest, never to be seen again. Slowly, the graveyard filled with headstones carved with the names of their widows. Wary of the curses, the people dared not wed each other. The men travelled away from the village to find their wives and bring them back to the valley. Small farms were started but they were so far from any market and the track out of the valley was so steep that the farmers struggled to make a living. Eventually, people gave up and drifted away until there were only three farms left at Nant Gwrtheyrn called 'Ty Hen', 'Ty Canol' and 'Ty Uchaf'.

Rhys Maredydd lived at Ty Uchaf with his sister Angharad. They were orphans. Their father had been consumed in a terrible fire that had destroyed the winter hay. Their mother had died of a broken heart. The orphans had a cousin, Meinir who lived with her father at Ty Hen. The three children were friends and would play together when their jobs were done. As the youngsters grew older, Rhys and his cousin, Meinir fell in love. They wandered, hand in hand, on Mount Eifl above the farms. A great oak tree stood on the mountain where they would sit and plan their lives together, sheltered by the giant branches. When Rhys asked Meinir for her hand in marriage, she willingly agreed and the happy couple ran down the mountain to seek her father's permission.

'You cannot marry Rhys,' said her father.
'But we love each other,' cried Meinir.
'Rhys is your cousin. You cannot marry your neighbour.
Remember the curse,' said her father. Tears ran down Meinir's face
as her father spoke and his heart melted. He relented and embraced
the young lovers, agreeing they could wed. Plans were made for the
wedding. It was agreed they would wed far away from Nant
Gwrthyren, at the church of Clynnog Fawr. Surely the curse would
not hurt them there.

The morning of the wedding arrived. It was a fine summers
day. Rhys dressed in his Sunday clothes and walked across the
fields to Meinir's farm. Her father stood in the doorway, solemnly
refusing entry. Eventually, to the merriment of the gathering
wedding guests, Meinir's father grinned and stood aside. Rhys
went inside to find his bride. Searching for the bride on the
wedding morning is an ancient custom and Rhys went from room
to room happily calling for Meinir to reveal herself but she did not
appear. Meinir, eager to make Rhys work to find her, had slipped
away to hide, long before her betrothed had arrived.

Enjoying the game, Rhys searched the barn and the cow
sheds but they were empty. Meinir had vanished. He called her
name but there was no answer. The wedding guests cheered and
encouraged Rhys as he went from field to field looking for his
bride. The morning passed and the sun beat down. Rhys grew hot
in his wedding suit. He was no longer enjoying searching for
Meinir. He called again. Still there was no answer.

'Perhaps she has gone to Clynnog Fawr and is waiting for
you at the church,' said the wedding guests.

Rhys set off along the track, leading up the mountain
towards Clynnog Fawr. The wedding guests followed behind as
quickly as they could. But Meinir was not waiting at the church.
Rhys turned and ran back towards Nant Gwrtheyrn desperate to
find his bride. Meinir's father, weary from the long walk to the
church, borrowed a horse and galloped after Rhys. The two men
searched the farm again but could not find Meinir. The dark came

but they did not stop. They cut torches and scoured the mountain through the night, calling for Meinir to reveal herself.

Rhys and Meinir's father continued to search as the months passed. Then one night Meinir's father did not return from the search. He was never seen again. Rhys was alone in the valley.

The corn went uncut and the cows grew wild as Rhys searched. Summer turned to winter but he would not stop. Each day Rhys would walk for miles called out, 'Meinir, Meinir where are you?' Each night he would sit huddled under the great oak tree on the mountain and cry softly, 'Meinir, Meinir where are you?'

Thirty years passed then, one night as Rhys sat shivering under the great tree, storm clouds gathered on the mountain. A flash of lightening struck the tree, splitting it in two. A hideous cry echoed across the valley for, in the flash of light, Meinir's hiding place had been revealed. There, wedged in the hollow trunk of the tree, stood the twisted skeleton of a young woman. All that was left of the wedding dress, that was once so pure and white, were a few grey rags hanging from the bones. Rhys was found next morning lying dead beneath the tree, with Menir's corpse in his arms.

The curse of Nant Gwrtheyrn had left the valley desolate and empty for the second time. It would be another 200 years before Nant Gwrtheyrn became ruined for the third and final time.

Chapter 30...St. Eilian and the Leaping Deer.

In the 5th Century Britain was a dark pagan country.
Following the success of Saint Patrick in Ireland, further
missionaries were sent by the Pope to Britain to bring the word of
God and return the people to the path of Christianity. The Pope sent
many good, pious men on missions to convert the heathens and
save them from damnation. One such man was St. Eilian. He sailed
from Rome, with his family, in a small boat loaded with all his
worldly possessions. Unsure of the nature of Britain and
determined to be self-sufficient, Eilian included cattle, sheep and a
deer in his cargo.

Eilian was a quiet, confident man, slow to anger but single
minded in his task. He had a way with animals. They responded
well to his soothing words and the animals became pets during the
long voyage. The deer, a handsome stag, was his favourite.

After many weeks at sea, Eilian landed at a small inlet
called Porthyrychen on the Island Anglesey and began to unload.
The ruler of the Island was Cadwallon Law Hir (Cadwallon Long
Hand), Prince of Gwynedd. Word reached him that a strange
foreigner had arrived. The Prince sent his men to investigate.
Cadwallon's men hid on the cliff and watched as the animals
waded ashore and began to climb up from the beach. They were
fine looking beasts. Eager to please their master the men decided to
ambush Eilian and steal his cows. They knew that Cadwallon
would value such prize animals.

Cadwallon's men arranged themselves on each side of the
path hidden in the bracken. After a short time Eilian passed them
followed by his cattle and sheep. The deer, sensing that something
was wrong, hung back from the rest of the animals pawing the
ground. The robbers ran from their cover knocked Eilian to the
ground and, with loud yells, drove the animals away.

That night, one of Eilian's cows was roasted over a fire pit
at Cadwallon's castle as the men celebrated with their master. Later
in the evening, when their bellies were full of meat and wine, there

was a loud bang on the outer-gate. The guard peered over the battlements and did not believe what he saw. Outside the castle was a large stag and on its back sat a man.

'Who are you and what is your business at this hour?' demanded the guard.

'I am Eilian and I have come for my animals,' replied the man on the stag. The guard ran to the great hall to tell his Prince of the strange caller. Cadwallon laughed when he heard the news.

'Fetch him in, stag and all,' he bellowed. Solemnly Eilian, still astride the stag, was led into the hall. Cadwallon studied his visitor while his men sat silently, waiting for a command from their prince. Menace filled the air.

'What can we do for Eilian?' asked Cadwallon, smirking at his guest.

'You My Lord, have something that belongs to me,' said Eilian firmly.

'And what might that be?' replied the Prince.

'My sheep and cattle. I want them back,' said Eilian.

'Eilian wants his sheep and cattle back,' scoffed Cadwallon to his men. They laughed.

'Do you own any land?' asked Cadwallon, turning back to Eilian.

'I do not,' replied Eilian.

'I see that you are a foreigner, so you have no right to graze on common land,' said the prince adding 'but I am a fair man. When I see that you own some land you can have your animals. Until then I will keep them safe here, with my cattle.'

'You see nothing but your own greed,' answered Eilian. Eilian turned his mount and the stag walked out of the great hall.

That night, as he slept, Cadwallon went blind.

Eilian returned to Porthyrychen and built a church, just to the west of the inlet, beside a small stream. He added a well beside his church and, before long, people began to visit him, to listen to his teachings and to drink the pure water from his well. The water from the well had mysterious powers, curing the sick and, some

112

said, restoring sight. Stories spread far and wide, telling the tale of St. Eilian's sacred well.

Cadwallon, the blind Prince, knew that he had been wrong to steal Eilian's cattle. His heart was full of remorse. He ordered that all of Eilian's livestock should be returned to Eilian and sent the animals back to their rightful owner with a message of repentance. Eilian replied, asking the Prince to visit him without delay. Cadwallon was led on his horse to the holy man's little church at Llaneilian. Seeing Cadwallon's humility and sorrow Elian forgave him. Eilian bathed the prince's eyes and his sight was restored.

'How may I repay you?' asked the prince.

'Let me have enough land to keep my animals on. That is all I ask,' replied the holy man.

'How much do you want?' asked Cadwallon, feeling far less humble now that his sight was restored.

'Let us settle the amount with a race,' answered Eilian.

'What sort of race? Asked the prince.

'Your hunting dogs shall chase my stag, starting from here. The place where they catch him will be the boundary of the land you shall grant me,' replied Eilian.

Cadwallon liked the idea. He owned the fastest hunting dogs in the land. They would soon catch the stag, he thought. He agreed and the race began.

Eilian's stag ran like the wind but the dogs strained to keep up. The stag thundered across the countryside with the dogs close behind. It was going to be a short race. Then, the stag leapt a huge gorge and disappeared into the distance. The dogs, unable to cross the chasm, returned dejected to their master.

The gorge the stag leapt is known today as Llam y Carw (The Deer's Leap). Prince Cadwallon kept his word, and that is how Saint Eilian became one of the most powerful and biggest landowners on Anglesey.

A religious community grew at Llaneilian and for centuries the sacred stream served the holy order well. Pilgrims travelled for miles to pay 1 groat, a sliver coin worth two pence, to drink the healing water and Llaneilian grew into one of the richest churches in Wales.

Chapter 31…Seiriol The Fair

In 494AD a baby was born to a royal family. They named him Seiriol. One of his brothers became King Cynlas of Rhos and a second, King Einion of Lleyn but Seiriol was destined for another life. He chose to go to Ynys Mon, which we know today as Anglesey and live as a hermit. Seiriol found a small spring in a cliff near Penmon Point and built a well to catch the water. Beside the well, he built a simple stone cell for himself.

News of Seiriol and the pious life he lived spread. People began to journey to Penmon to look at this holy man and to drink the water from his well. Seiriol's holy well, they said, healed the lame and cured the sick. His brothers were concerned for Seiriol and built a priory at Penmon so that he could live in more comfort. Monks came to worship with Seiriol and a community grew up around the holy well. The monks farmed the land and built ponds to provide fresh fish. They lived a frugal life and, with Seiriol's guidance, the priory prospered.

Seiriol yearned for a life of quiet prayer. He needed to get away from Penmon and decided to build a retreat where no one could bother him. He moved to the island half a mile from Penmon where he built a new cell for a bedroom. The island became known as Ynys Seiriol (Seriol's Island). The Vikings named the island Priestholm because of its religious inhabitant. There was to be no escape for Seiriol and before long his followers established themselves on the island with their spiritual leader. In 1188 Gerald of Wales recorded, 'that the settlement was inhabited by hermits, living by manual labour and serving god.'

No women were allowed on the island and this caused some friction. Sometimes the monks on the island quarrelled and when they did, a plague of rats would appear and devour all their food. Seiriol found the squabbling upsetting. He needed to escape and find somewhere to meditate, away from the island. At low tide there was a small path from the island, which led to the mainland and Penmaenmawr, 5 miles across the bay. Seiriol would walk from his island to pray at Penmaenmawr. A chapel was built for him and Seiriol regularly walked across the bay, taking care to return before the incoming tide carried him away.

As Seiriol grew older, he visited other holy men to increase his wisdom and knowledge. He became a friend of St. Cybi who lived at Holy Island, on the far side of Anglesey. Every morning, they both walked 20 miles to meet at Clorach, in the middle of Anglesey, to pray and discuss religious matters. Every evening, they both walked 20 miles back to their monasteries. In the mornings Seiriol walked west with the sun at his back and each evening he walked east, again, with the sun at his back. His face never saw the sun and his skin was as white as milk. Every morning Cybi walked east with the sun in his face and each evening he walked west, again, with the sun in his face so that his skin turned as dark as parchment. This is the reason Seiriol is known as 'St. Seiriol Gwyn' (St. Seriol the Fair) and his friend St. Cybi Felyn (St. Cybi the Tawny or Dark).

Seiriol retired as Abbot and lived to a venerable age. When he died, the monks buried him on his island. Eventually the island was abandoned and Seiriol's remains were removed to Penmon where he is now buried at the priory. Today, Seiriol's Island is also known as Puffin Island and is privately owned. Landing on the Island is not allowed unless special permission is obtained.

Chapter 32...St. Patrick's Shipwreck

In 432AD an open boat was sailing from England to Ireland when it was caught in a storm. The wind had quickly strengthened from the west during the afternoon. By the evening the little vessel was being driven east by the storm, unable to reach a safe haven. The sail had shredded in a violent gust. The crew was wet and cold. They huddled together in the bottom of the boat, exhausted from battling with the wind, helpless and afraid as the stricken craft rolled and pitched through the mountainous waves. They could hear the thunder of water crashing against cliffs, somewhere nearby in the darkness.

Only one man showed no fear on that dark night. Bishop Patrick was used to danger. His journey from Rome had been full of adventure. From the beginning, when the Holy Father Pope Celestine had given the bishop his mission to convert Ireland to the true faith, Patrick had known that it would test his devotion and his courage to the limit.

The journey to Ireland had been a long one. Surely, he thought, God would not bring him so far just to be drowned on the final sea voyage. He knelt and prayed for the vessel to survive the storm. The wind swung to larboard away from the coast and the little vessel turned, towards the open sea, away from the land, away from certain disaster on the jagged cliffs that thundered in the darkness. The bishop crossed himself and muttered a silent thanks to God for his timely intervention.

There was a flash of lightening. In that second the sailors saw the rocks ahead. The boat, lifted by a giant wave, rose above the rocks and then dropped like a stone. The keel snapped and the vessel disintegrated throwing men and cargo into the churning water.

By the first light of dawn the wind had died down. Bishop Patrick was lying on the rocks half submerged in a pool of salty water. He sat up and looked around. He was alone. As the light improved, Patrick found that he was stranded on a small barren island. He was hungry. The salt had split his lips and his throat was swollen. In the distance he could see land.

Patrick searched the island for wreckage, anything that would ease his thirst and hunger. He found a wine bladder caught up in the rocks. It was full. He pulled out the stopper and drank deeply. The wine burned as he swallowed. Nearby was a shattered basket of loaves. Its contents, soaked by the sea, lay ruined on the ground. Patrick ate greedily and drank more wine to mask the salty taste of the bread. Then he prayed and slept.

The sun was high in the sky when he woke. His head ached and he had a foul taste in his mouth. The wine and the salty bread had done their worst. He stood up and looked at the land. Somehow he thought he had to escape from his island prison. An idea came to him.

He poured the last of the wine away and blew into the bladder. When it was inflated he fitted the stopper, pushing it firmly home. He tied the bladder to his body, jumped into the sea and started to swim towards the land. The cold water cleared his head and, to start with, Patrick made good progress. As Patrick swam, the current carried him along the coast towards high cliffs where there was no chance of getting ashore. He swam until, weary, cold and thirsty, he realised that swimming against the current was hopeless. He floated exhausted, with the bladder resting under his stomach as the tide carried him along. Now the current was carrying him further out to sea.

Patrick mumbled a quiet prayer and sank into a dull torpor. As he did so, the tide turned and he began to drift back along the coast. A shrill cry above Patrick's head woke him with a start. Patrick looked up to see gulls returning to their nests and squabbling as they arrived. He was floating right below the cliffs. In front of him was a small ledge, level with the sea and a cave. Patrick swam to the ledge, pulled himself out of the water and stumbled into the cave. Inside the cave, water trickled from the roof. He tasted the water. It was fresh and pure. Patrick filled the bladder and drank his fill. His prayer had been answered.

Before continuing his journey to Ireland Patrick built a church at the top of the cliff to give thanks to God for saving him when the ship was wrecked on Middle Mouse Island. The Welsh call the island 'Ynys Badrig' (Patrick's Island). 'Llanbadrig' (St Patrick's Church) is still standing in the cliffs today, 1600 years later.

Pope Celestine I died in 431AD, before Patrick reached Ireland. Bishop Patrick's mission to Ireland was a success. He arrived in Ireland in 433AD, one year after being shipwrecked at Mouse Island and, using the shamrock to explain the holy trinity, introduced Christianity to the Irish. He also, it is believed, drove every serpent from the country.

Although Patrick has never been canonised by a pope, he is recognised as a saint by many religious orthodoxies and is the Patron Saint of Ireland, his Saint's Day being celebrated on March 17th each year. Before he died in 493AD, Patrick wrote The Declaration or 'Confessio' containing an account of his life, written in Latin.

Part Three Central Wales

Chapter 33...The Land of the Dead

Gwyn ap Nudd was King of the Underworld and the mountains of Cadair Berwyn and Moel Sych his throne. His was a cold, barren kingdom filled with foul swamps, evil vipers and devils. This was the land of the dead, a dangerous desolate place seldom visited by mortals. The gateway to this distant kingdom was Pistyll Rhaeadr and each night Gwyn ap Nudd would leave his kingdom to stalk the lands of Wales, collecting the souls of the dead.

Mortal men who were brave or foolish enough to venture into mountains of Berwyn would find the King feasting in a fine palace. The lamps would be lit. Gold and silver plate would sparkle in the shimmering light. None could resist the King's offer to join in the feast and enjoy the sumptuous food and wine that was being offered. As they ate the meats and fruits and drank the fine wines, King Nudd would steal their souls and throw them onto the mountain where they would lay tormented until time ended. None ever returned to their homes or their loved ones.

Wives cried for their husband and children mourned their lost fathers. Wary of calling out loud lest they upset King ap Nudd, people whispered about the missing souls. Slowly, the stories of how no one ever returned from the mountain above Pistyll Rhaeadr spread across the land.

In Llangollen, St. Collen listened intently as the tales of woe were repeated in hushed tones. Seeing that this was the devil's work, he at once determined to climb the mountain and put an end to the misery. Armed only with a small bottle of holy water, the saint set out on his perilous quest. As he walked, he wondered what had happened to the missing people. He arrived at the little village of Llanmaeadr ym Mochnant to find the people fearful. A dark cloud hung over the once beautiful valley and pressed up against the mountain filling the air with damp, putrid fog.

St. Collen walked on up the valley, following the river until he came to a great waterfall. The icy water poured down from the mountain with a defiant roar that chilled his blood. Slowly, the saint picked his way across the rocks and began to climb. As he climbed, the air grew colder and the damp soaked through his cloak, mixing with his hot sweat. He reached the top of the waterfall where a cold wind sliced through his wet clothing and chilled him to the bone. Exhausted by the climb, he sat and rested. The sky grew dark and rain began to fall. St. Collen began to shake violently, his frozen body aching with cold. He could feel evil in the air.

Standing up, St. Collen started to walk north towards the higher mountains. Beneath his feet the ground was fetid with decay and his legs sank into the mud. Slowly, he made his way forward, climbing as he went. After many hours trudging through the slime, exhausted, he sank down on his knees and wept. He knew he could not go on. As he knelt, the wind gusted and a voice howled across the mountain, 'Why do you weep? Come. Here is warmth and food and wine that will warm your very innards.'

St. Collen peered into the mist and saw bright light twinkling in the distance. He pulled himself to his feet and stumbled on. Getting closer, he saw a fine palace blazing with radiant illumination. The doors were open and a stream of light poured out. He could smell tempting food being cooked. He went into the palace. Inside, sat on a great throne, was a giant of a man. In one hand he held a huge golden goblet and in the other a leg of beef. Below him was a table laid to overflowing with gold and silver plates loaded with fine foods of every description.

'Who are you?' demanded St. Collen.

'Who am I, you ask. I am Gwyn ap Nudd, King of the Underworld and this is my house. Come join me. We will eat and drink together,' said the king. St. Collen crossed the floor and sat on a stool near the king. He looked at the table piled high with food.

'You must be hungry after your climb. Help yourself,' snorted the king as he chewed on his beef. But, although he was hungry, St. Collen did not eat and, although he was thirsty, he did not drink. Instead he opened his cloak and drew out the small bottle of holy water that he had bought with him and drank sparingly. Then he replaced the bottle in his pocket and sat quietly looking at the King. Gwyn ap Nudd continued to feast, pretending to ignore his visitor but watching the saint slyly as he did so. Nudd wondered why the mortal did not eat or drink. This had never happened before.

After some hours the king grew tired of eating and drinking. He wiped his mouth on his sleeve and sat back in his throne eyeing the saint with suspicion.

'Why have you come to my table and insulted me by refusing my hospitality? He yelled.

'Come, humour me by tasting a little of this fine fruit,' he said more quietly, pointing to the table.

'Why do you steal the souls of the living?' asked the Saint.

'The souls of all mortals belong to me!' answered King Nudd.

'Not before their time,' replied Saint Collen. King Nudd and Saint Collen debated and argued for days over who owned the souls of the living. The heated discussion went back and fore as the King ate and drank heartily, eagerly encouraging his opponent to join him. Saint Collen saw this was a trap. He did not eat a morsel of food or touch a drop of wine. Instead he took tiny sips of holy water to keep refreshed.

The King grew tired of the argument. He saw that he would never win against the quiet saint. As he argued he knew his grip over mortal men was slipping away. Slowly, as the King of the Underworld ran out of arguments, his palace began to fade. Before long it had vanished forever, taking the King with it.

Saint Collen found himself sat on a pile of stones on the top of the mountain. All that was left of the palace below him was a deep hollow where the Kings' throne had been. The sun was shining on Moel Sych and the birds were singing as Saint Collen trudged wearily down the mountain. His work was done.

Chapter 34...Owain Glyndwr

These signs have mark'd me extraordinary;
And all the courses of my life do show
I am not in the roll of common men.
King Henry IV - William Shakespeare

The start of the 15th Century saw an uprising against the English that resulted in the first and only Welsh-speaking parliament. The leader of the rebellion, Owain Glyndwr, was descended from the Princes of Powys and Cyfeiliog in the north and, on his mother's side, the kingdom of Deheubarth in the south. His royal lineage gave him a strong claim to the Welsh throne.

Glyndwr was educated in England, trained as a soldier, serving with distinction for the English King before returning to Wales wealthy and ready to marry. The Wales he came back to was in turmoil. The murder of Llywelyn the Last at Cilmeri and the harsh treatment of the Welsh by Edward I had left the people smouldering with resentment. The Welsh people were cowed and there was no justice in the law. They wanted a leader - and charismatic Glyndwr was the man of the hour. He found himself drawn into a quarrel with Reginald de Grey, Lord of Ruthin who had stolen some land. De Grey was close to the King and their private argument quickly developed into feudal warfare.

Glyndwr gathered loyal supporters around him and established an army at Ruthin. He raised his battle flag on the 16th September 1400 and started to drive out the English. Glyndwr was 51 years old. Ruthin fell and Glyndwr followed up with attacks throughout North Wales. He claimed the title Prince of Wales and Welshmen throughout the British Isles threw down their tools and hurried back to Wales to join him. Welsh archers deserted the English to join Glyndwr. University students abandoned their studies at Oxford and returned to Wales eager to fight.

The English response was brutal and effective. They levied a large army and marched across North Wales sacking and burning everything. The Welsh language was suppressed and penal laws were introduced to break the rebellion, the effect of which was to drive more Welshmen to take up arms.

Glyndwr and his men hid in the mountains for the winter emerging the following year with a renewed campaign. They seized castles including Harlech, Conwy and Aberystwyth. By 1403 the rebels operated freely throughout Wales. A Parliament was established at Machynlleth and Glyndwr was crowned King of Wales. Treaties were made with France and Spain whose ambassadors attended the court. Glyndwr made a triple alliance with Edmund Mortimer, The Earl of March and Thomas Percy, The Earl of Northumberland. Plans were made to invade England and divide the country between them. French troops arrived to help the revolution and Scottish privateers raided English towns on the Llyn Peninsula. French ships landed Welsh troops in Devon and attacked Dartmouth. Glyndwr petitioned Pope Benedict XIII for support.

The English quickly reacted. The English army was the largest, and most effective in Europe, as the French discovered two years later at Agincourt. Henry IV sent army after army into Wales, killing everyone as they went. Castles were lost and retaken many times but slowly the strength of the English forces wore down the Welsh. In 1408, eight years after he had raised his standard, Glyndwr suffered a major defeat when the castles at Aberystwyth and Harlech were lost. Personal tragedy followed when Henry's forces captured Glyndwr's family. His wife, Margaret, two daughters and three granddaughters were imprisoned in the Tower of London. They were all dead within seven years.

The English changed their strategy by blockading Wales. They cut off trade routes and arms supplies to squeeze the rebels and many Welshmen started to ask for terms of surrender. The revolt struggled on but the crushing superiority of the English was taking a dreadful toll and only a few rebels remained, conducting a guerrilla campaign. Glyndwr became an outlaw.

The English army seized prominent landowners and executed them, attempting to discover where Glyndwr was hiding. After more than twelve years of warfare the revolt finally petered out when pardons were offered to the last rebels. The Welsh had had enough. Having won, the English built a ring of castles across Wales to tighten their grip.

Henry V replaced his father as King in 1413 and softened the English position on Wales helping the last of the rebellion to peter out.

In 1485 English laws and customs were adopted across Wales when Henry VII was crowned King of England. He was a Welshman.

Glyndwr never surrendered to the English and was never pardoned. Instead, he quietly disappeared into obscurity, protected by the silence of the Welsh people. One of Glyndwr's daughters, Alys had married and lived in Kentchurch and there have been claims that he spent the rest of his life living with her family in Herfordshire, passing himself off as an elderly Franciscan Friar employed as the family tutor. The family kept his secret for nearly 600 years. A more fanciful claim is that he became 'Jack of Kent' a folk hero living in that part of the world.

In 1808 the Royal Navy launched the frigate HMS. Owen Glendower. She served on the West Coast of Africa, capturing slave ships and helping to end that evil trade, a fitting tribute to an extraordinary man. Today, Owain Glyndwr remains a potent symbol of Welsh independence and patriotism, invoked whenever Wales needs to remember a hero.

Chapter 35...The Lost Land of Wales

Seithennin, saf-di allan,
ac edrychwyr-di faranres
môr. Maes Gwyddnau rydöes.

Seithennin, stand out here and look at the wild sea:
It has covered Maes Gwyddno.
Black Book of Carmarthen 1250 AD.

King Gwyddno Garanhir ruled a wealthy kingdom called Cantref y Gwaelod in an area we know today as Cardigan Bay. The 'bottom hundreth' as the kingdom was known was so rich and fertile that the grain stores were always full and the people of the kingdom content. The King's palace was on a hill, surrounded by villages and farms. He spent his days hunting in the great forest while his people tilled the land.

A great dam with two giant gates protected this fine land. The guardian of the dam was a prince named Seithennin. Seithennin was a seventh son and proud of the great responsibility given to him. As the youngest son, he had no wealth but the job gave him status and the people respected him. Within the gates were giant sluices and each day, when the tide was low, Seithennin would turn the huge wheels that opened the sluices to let the water from the 'bottom hundreth' escape into the sea. Before the sea returned, he would close the sluices, keeping the land safe.

As the years passed, Seithennin grew bored with his job. He began to neglect the dam. Seithennin no longer walked the dam, each morning, checking for cracks. He stopped spending the afternoons putting grease on the gears that opened the sluice or painting pitch on the gates to protect them from the salt. Instead of doing his duty Seithennin would pass each morning drinking wine as he waited for the tide to turn. Each day, after his midday meal, Seithennin would sleep for a while and then he would drink more wine. He did not see the hinges on the gates growing rusty or notice the gears that turned the sluices slowly stiffen with age.

One day a great Prince arrived in the kingdom and King Gwyddno decreed that there would be feasting in his honour. Musicians collected from across the land. Fine wines and beers were brewed for the occasion. Beasts were slaughtered and roasted. Huge fish were prepared for the banquet and sweet dishes by the hundred set out, ready for the feast. Everyone in the kingdom was invited to the palace. Seithennin dressed in his finest clothes, mounted his horse and rode to the palace. King Gwyddno greeted Seithennin.

'This is Seithennin, the guardian of the dam,' said the king to his noble visitor.

'Tell us Seithennin. Are the gates closed?' asked the king.

'They are Sire but the tide is out so the sluices are open,' replied Seithennin.

'When will you shut them?' asked the noble visitor.

'I shall shut the sluices at midnight before the tide turns,' said Seithennin.

'Leave early Seithennin. It's a long ride from the palace to the dam,' said the king and turned to greet other guests. The feast started and musicians played loudly as the people ate. The wine flowed and the feast was devoured. The clock in the tower struck nine.

'Seithennin, the gates, you should go,' said a reveller.

'Nonsense. It's still early,' answered Seithennin and reached for another flagon of wine. The King and his guests danced and laughed, as the party grew louder. The clock on the tower struck ten.

'Seithennin, the gates, there isn't much time,' yelled King Gwyddno above the noise.

'I told you, do not worry. My horse can fly like the wind. There is plenty of time,' replied Seithennin and drank greedily. Seithennin's cheeks were red with wine, his laughter loud and raucous. The clock struck eleven.

'That's enough. You are going now. That is a royal command,' snapped the king. Seithennin got to his feet and staggered from the palace. He mounted his horse and rode away.

The wind had started to blow from the west and the rain lashed his face. It was a fearful night. Thunder crashed between the clouds and lightening flashed across the sky. The torrent quickly turned the track to mire and the horse slowed, sinking into the slimy mud. Suddenly, the horse missed its footing and slid into a ditch. Seithennin landed in the mud. Groggily he stood up and began to run towards the dam. He knew that he had to get to the gates before the tide turned. His feet slid on the mud. Brambles tore at his mud covered clothes. Sober now, he forced himself forwards. The sky cleared for a moment and the moon broke through. There, in front of Seithennin, were the gates. As he staggered forward the sea, whipped up by the wind, broke through the sluices. The force of the rushing water breached the rotten gates and smashed the rusty hinges. The sea flooded in. The water carried Seithennin away and he was never seen again.

King Gwyddno and a few of his followers managed to escape and lived the rest of their lives in poverty, but the land of Cantref y Gwaelod vanished beneath the waves. The 'bottom hundreth' was lost forever. Listen carefully. Sometimes you can still hear the bells from an ancient clock tower ringing mournfully from the bottom of the sea.

Chapter 36...Llywelyn the Last

Llywelyn the Great had united Wales. Welsh patriots called him King Llywelyn I of Wales. He ruled for 40 years but when he died in 1240 his sons began to squabble about who would replace him as ruler. It was the opportunity the English King, Henry III had been waiting for.

'We will invade and crush the Welsh while they are arguing amongst themselves,' he ordered. The English army swept across North Wales. The Welsh Princes, unprepared for a war, sued for peace.

'Lay down your arms and pay homage to me,' demanded the King. The Princes protested and Henry grew angry.

'You challenge my authority? I'll show you who is King. From this day forth, all your land east of the River Conwy will be part of England to be ruled by my son, Prince Edward. The people there are his vassals, to do with as he pleases,' said the King.

'You cannot annex half our land and make it English,' complained the Welsh Princes.

'Take care or I will take all of your land,' warned the King, and dismissed the Welsh Princes.

'Your Majesty, we do not have enough soldiers to garrison all of Wales,' warned one of the King's advisors. King Henry considered the problem. He knew the Welsh Princes would one day rise up against him if he did not do something. Then a plan came to him.

'Llywelyn has grandsons and they are his rightful heirs, are they not?' said the King.

'That is so, your Majesty,' replied an advisor.

'West Wales will be divided into three petty kingdoms. Each kingdom will pay homage to me and each will be ruled by one of Llywelyn's rightful heirs to the throne,' commanded the King. It was a final act of humiliation for the Welsh nobility. As commanded by King Henry, Llywelyn the Great's grandsons were made the rulers of West Wales and the land was divided between three young princes, Llywelyn, Owain and Dafydd.

'Your Majesty, why have you given the west of Wales to three young princes?' asked a minister.

'Watch and see. They are young and vain and will soon argue over their petty estates. They will turn on each other. Brother will battle brother and cousin, conspire against cousin,' replied the King. Henry III's strategy worked. Young Dafydd conspired with his elder brother Owain and they turned on Llywelyn. Llywelyn gathered his men and met his brothers in battle at Bryn Derwin. He defeated Owain and Dafydd and captured them. It was a brilliant victory.

'Are we not all Welshmen here? Join me. Let us unite and take back what belongs to Wales,' said Llywelyn, to his prisoners. The patriotic appeal to his countrymen, worked. The combined Welsh armies led by Llywelyn, Owain and Dafydd, turned east, crossed the River Conwy and reclaimed Welsh land, ruled by the English Prince Edward. The men cheered Llywelyn as victory followed victory. A messenger arrived at Llywelyn's camp.

'The English King wants peace,' he cried.

'What are his terms?' asked Llywelyn.

'King Henry will recognise that you are the true Prince of Wales and allow you to keep all the land that you have captured east of the River Conwy,' said the messenger.

'That is generous of him. What does the King want in return?' inquired Llywelyn.

'The king is old and sick of war. All he asks in return is your tribute and yearly payment of 3,000 marks,' answered the messenger.

'His terms are fair. Tell King Henry that we accept them,' said Llywelyn. That night many toasts were drunk to Llywelyn, Prince of Wales.

A short time later bad news reached Wales. Henry III was dead. There was a new King on the throne of England, Henry's son Edward. Edward had been humiliated by Llywelyn and wanted revenge. He sent a secret message to Dafydd with an offer to make him Prince of Wales.

'Kill Llywelyn and I will make you the Prince of Wales.' It was a tempting proposition.

The three assassins listened to Dafydd carefully.

'When the deed is done, you are to ride East and speak to no one. Do you understand,' whispered Dafydd. The men nodded. They left and rode towards Llywelyn's camp. Snow began to fall and before long a blizzard raged. The land turned white and the men's horses sank up to their flanks in the deep snow.

'We are lost,' cried the murderers and abandoned their quest. When King Edward heard the assassination had failed he vowed to deal with Prince Llywelyn himself, but he needed an excuse to invade Wales again. His chance came when Llywelyn failed to pay the yearly tribute promised to Edward's father. Once more, an English army crossed the border into Wales. Dafydd, the deceitful brother, turned against Llywelyn and sided with the English King. Llywelyn's property was seized and, realising that he could not win, Llywelyn surrendered to the King.

'Why should I let you live?' said Edward to his captor.

'My liege. I swore loyalty to your father Henry and I am an honourable man. I have not broken my pledge,' replied Llywelyn. Edward recognised that Lywelyn had spoken the truth and granted his freedom. A period of peace followed during which Llywelyn fell in love with Eleanor, grandaughter of King John of England. Llywelyn and Elanor married and the, now impoverished, Prince of Wales lived contentedly with his new bride.

'I am with child,' announced Eleanor one day. Llywelyn was overjoyed. Then, a rider bought news to Llywelyn's house.

'Your brother Dafydd has turned against King Edward,' said the rider.

'Why? He's been well rewarded by Edward,' said Lywelyn.

'My Lord. Your brother Dafydd is a greedy man. He betrayed you once, hoping to win a kingdom and even now, as lord of the land east of the River Conwy, he thirsts for more,' explained the messenger.

'Where is he?' asked Llywelyn.

'Dafydd has attacked Harwarden and massacred the English garrison. He marches on Rhuddlan. As we speak, the English King is preparing for war,' replied the messenger.

'I must help my brother,' said Llywelyn.

'My Lord, Dafydd is your enemy. He sent assassins to kill you,' said the messenger.

'I know but he is a Welshman and my brother,' replied Llywelyn. Prince Llywelyn gathered his retainers together and marched south, to raise a new army. Once more, Welshmen rallied to his banner. As the army travelled, sad news reached Llywelyn. His wife Eleanor had died giving birth to a daughter. The heartbroken Prince named the child Gwenllian. By the time Llywelyn reached Builth Wells, his army was 7000 strong. They stopped and camped at Cilmeri by the Irfon River.

An English army, led by the Marcher Lords Edward and Roger Mortimer, approached from the south. The armies lined up ready for battle. Only the River Irfon separated the opposing forces. A Herald from the English army crossed the river under a flag of truce.

'My Lords Edward and Roger Mortimer want peace and offer terms to avoid giving battle today,' cried the Herald.

'What are the terms?' called Prince Llywelyn.

'They wish to meet and talk with you,' replied the Herald. Llywelyn and eighteen of his men went forward carrying a white flag. As they reached the river a great roar went up from the English. It was a trap. English archers had forded the river and sprang upon the Welsh army. A ferocious fight began. English heavy cavalry charged across the river straight towards Llywelyn. A lance struck the Prince in the chest and he fell to the ground dead.

The Welsh soldiers fought on but, without their leader, the cause was lost and the English army won the day. After the battle

Prince Lywelyn's head was cut from his body and sent to London where it was crowned with ivy to show that Llywelyn was nothing more than the 'King of the Outlaws'. The head was then set on a spike above the Tower of London gate where it remained for the next fifteen years.

Having humiliated Llywelyn, King Edward wanted to ensure that there would be no future heir left to claim Llywelyn's legacy. He destroyed all the trappings of the Royal House of Gwynedd. Houses were looted. Royal plate was seized and melted down. Heraldic crests and royal records were destroyed. Llywelyn's treacherous brother, Dafydd, was hung drawn and quartered and his two young sons were incarcerated at Bristol Castle. Llywelyn's daughter Gwenllian was also seized and sent, together with Dafydd's daughters, to the remote Priory at Sempringham in Lincolnshire. None of the children were ever released and Gwenllian remained a prisoner, behind the high walls of the priory, for the next 55 years until she died.

King Edward I invested his son Edward as the Prince of Wales, crowning him at Caernarfon in 1301. He was the first Englishman to be crowned a Prince of Wales. It was the final act of humiliation for the Welsh. The valiant patriot, Llywelyn, Lord of Snowdon, Prince of Wales and loyal brother was the last Welshman to ever hold the title.

Chapter 37...The Drovers

'Our cattle driven and sould in most parts of England, hath bin and is the onelie support of yo'r petitioners being and livlihood, among whom be many thousand families on the mountainous part of this country, who sowing little or noe corn at all, trust merely to the sale of their cattle, wool and welch cottons for provision of bread.'
Petition asking for protection written, to Charles I, during the civil war.

Before the invention of the railway, the wealth of Wales walked slowly to England. Records show that in one year in the 18th Century 9,000 cattle swam across the Menai Straits from Anglesey and were driven to England. 6,000 left from the Lleyn Peninsula and 30,000 from Mid Wales. William Brooke in his work, The True causes of our Present Distress for Provisions, estimated that in 1798 a total of 600 million pounds of beef were consumed in England. English yeomanry ate Welsh beef while Welsh farmers lived on a meagre diet of barley and potatoes. A Pembrokeshire farm labourer's grace tells the story.

'Arglwydd annwyl ! Dyma Fwyd
Cawl sur a bara llwyd.'
[Good Lord! What a spread- Sour broth and mouldy bread]

To protect the cattle's hooves, on the long walk, they were shod with narrow metal shoes that were nailed on. A thrower, or feller, would pass a rope over each beast and loop it around the legs. Then he would topple the animal by the horns and tie it, allowing a blacksmith and his lad to shoe the animal. It needed great strength and the team of men would shoe between sixty and seventy cattle in a day. It wasn't only cattle that walked to distant markets. Flocks of geese would be walked through wet tar and sand to coat their webbed feet ready for the journey. Pigs were dressed with leather soled woollen socks.

The drovers that took the animals to the markets of England were tough men. Droving paid well but it was a dangerous job.

Wolves, robbers and cutthroats roamed the countryside. Drovers undertook financial errands on behalf of farmers, paying absentee landlords. On the 10th April 1734 a Mr. Bulkeley wrote to Thomas Lewis, a drover, instructing him to use £15, from the sale of animals in London, to pay for his sons keep as an apprentice lawyer in Chancery Lane. Travellers joined the drovers for protection. Jane Evans travelled with drovers from Pumsaint to join Florence Nightingale and travel on to the Crimea.

Drovers handled large sums of money and a banking system grew up around the business. It is recorded that, in 1806, drovers David Roberts and Griffith Jones arrived at the cattle fairs in Kent and sold their herd for the handsome sum of £6,053. Banks in Llandeilo issued their own promissory notes and Lloyds Bank began life serving the drovers of Wales. The Aberystwyth and Tregaron Bank, often called the Black Sheep Bank, started as a drover's bank. The values of its £1-£10 notes were illustrated by numbers of sheep while the 10 shilling note had a smaller picture of a single sheep. Drovers transported gold to be sold in London for the miners of Rhayader, agreeing to split profits.

The responsibilities of transporting animals to England and money back to Wales, was based largely on trust but the industry was regulated by the state. Drovers had to be over 30 years old, married and own a house before they could be licensed. When applying for a licence the drovers would always describe their work as 'An art and a mystery'. Anyone caught droving without a licence could be fined £5 and imprisoned for vagrancy. To stop drovers defaulting on their customers, Queen Anne passed a law prohibiting drovers from declaring themselves bankrupt to avoid repaying money in their care. Droving was not allowed on Sundays. In 1869 a drover was fined £1 plus 8/6p (42.5pence) costs for driving swine through Builth Wells on the Sabbath.

Drovers were the main carriers of news to the people. It was a drover that first bought news of the British victory at Waterloo in 1815 to Wales.

Using the turnpike road system was expensive. Heavy toll charges for moving the animals made them uneconomical for many drovers while others were willing to pay the tolls in order to reach the cattle fairs more quickly and with the animals in better condition so they would fetch a higher price. Mostly however, the drovers used ancient tracks and high roads where the animals could graze as they moved and the tolls avoided. Many of the drover's routes still exist while others have vanished, becoming part of our network of trunk roads.

During the civil war, landowners of North Wales wrote to the King asking for protection for the herds being moved. The war made droving a particularly dangerous business. In 1645 parliamentary soldiers seized nearly 1000 beasts from a party of 18 drovers and no compensation was paid.

Welsh black cattle are a hardy breed and ideal for droving. They can survive on poor pasture and are nimble enough to climb mountain tracks. There were frequent inns and cider houses along the drover's routes. These important places of refreshment were often signposted by three Scots pines, positioned to be visible from miles away. Each night the animals were corralled in a field for half a penny per beast. These halfpenny fields are still greener and lusher than the surrounding land because of the manure left by so many animals. Head drovers, known as Porthmon, would sleep in the inn while the junior drovers would sleep by the animals. Often the inn would have a blacksmith ready to repair broken shoes.

Travelling at a steady two miles an hour, a drive from North Wales to London would take three weeks. The cry 'Heiptrw Ho' could be heard for miles, warning the farmers ahead to secure their animals so they did not become mixed with the moving herd. Corgis were used to drive the stock. These intelligent dogs were low enough to avoid getting kicked by the cattle as they did their work. Returning after the drive, the dogs would often go ahead of their masters, arriving home a day or two before the men.

Drover Robert Jones kept accounts of bringing sheep from Carmarthenshire to London through Pinner and Edgware between

1823 and 1837. Pigs made a similar journey travelling at a steady six miles per day.

The drovers of Monmouthshire would congregate at 'Two Tumps' on the Western end of the Kerry Ridgeway with their animals, ready to start their drive along the oldest road in Wales.

While it was a tough business, some of the drovers were educated men. Edward Morus was a famous poet who continued as a drover until he was 82 when he died and was buried in Essex. Others grew wealthy from the trade. When part time drover Rowland Edmund died in 1819, his will included £963 plus sheep, cattle, pigs and horses amounting to a considerable fortune. He was buried in a cemetery near Harlech Castle.

Finally, with the coming of the railways, droving went into decline. It was easier and quicker to move the animals by train and they arrived in better condition. Droving did not die out completely though. During the 1914 - 1918 war cattle were again walked from Wales to England. One of the last drovers, Morris Roberts, finally retired in the 1930's and became a farmer, ending a proud tradition that had lasted for over a thousand years.

Chapter 38...Black Bart

In an honest service there is thin commons, low wages, and hard labour. In this, plenty and satiety, pleasure and ease, liberty and power; and who would not balance creditor on this side, when all the hazard that is run for it, at worst is only a sour look or two at choking? No, a merry life and a short one shall be my motto.
John Roberts, alias - Black Bart.

'You'll be back with your tail between your legs,' yelled George Roberts, as his teenage son walked down the road. The boy, named John, had finally rebelled against his religious father and left home. He ignored his father's shouts and kept walking. Three days later, the tired and hungry youth came over the brow of a hill. Below him the sea sparkled in the sunshine. A harbour bustling with life and filled with the rigging of tall ships beckoned him. It was Aberystwyth, the busiest port in Wales. Ships from here sailed across the seas to exciting places. Cargoes of copper, pitch and coal filled the holds. Stacks of slate and lead covered the quays. Barrels of salt and bales of wool filled the warehouses. Oakum lay in bundles, ready for loading. Strange sounds and smells intoxicated John. He picked his way along the quay, clambering over mooring ropes, unsure what to do. He felt faint with hunger. Captain Price watched as John wandering past his ship.

'Look out, boy!' cried the captain. John looked up and jumped aside. A sling loaded with casks landed heavily on the dock beside him. The captain ran down the gangplank onto the quay.

'Are you all right, boy?' he asked. He got no answer. John stumbled forward and fainted in his arms. The ship was at sea when John awoke.

'What's your name boy?' asked the crew.

'Bartholomew,' lied John, remembering the name of a famous buccaneer. The crew called him Bart; a name he would use for the rest of his life. A sailor's life suited Bart. He learned to run the rigging, splice and knot ropes and grew into a strong, confident seaman, able to navigate as well as any captain. Coal and pitch were not the only cargoes that offered profit. There was a cargo that promised richer rewards: slaves.

Years later, in 1719, the slave ship 'Princess' was anchored on the Gold Coast, loading its sad cargo. The third mate, Bart Roberts watched two vessels come into the bay. He saw the gun ports open.

'Pirates, they're going to attack!' he cried. The captain of the Princess knew they were no match for the attackers and surrendered. The crew of the slave ship were at the mercy of their captors.

'Who are you?' called the pirate captain pushing Bart with the point of his sword.

'Bart Roberts. I'm third mate,' replied Bart. He felt the plank bend under his weight and looked down at the sea beneath his feet.

'Can you navigate?' demanded the pirate captain.

'As well as any man,' answered Bart.

'I need a navigator Mr. Roberts. Join us in a life of profit and plunder or finish your walk along the plank to Davy Jones locker. Make your choice.'

'Profit and plunder you say. Then I'm your man,' cried Bart and joined the cutthroat pirate crew. Bart enjoyed life with the pirates and quickly became a popular member of the crew. Six weeks later the pirate captain was killed in an attack on a Portuguese island and the crew needed a new leader.

'Bart, you can navigate. We want you as our captain,' chorused the crew.

'Shipmates, I have dipped my hands in muddy water and must be a pirate but it's better to be a commander than a common man,' answered Bart. The crew cheered their new captain.

'We will return and avenge the death of our shipmates,' ordered Bart.

Bart returned with his crew to the island and took their revenge.

'Run up the colours,' ordered Bart.

The skull and crossbones, Bart's new flag, unfurled for the first time.

'Kill them all,' cried Bart. The attack proved his ruthless cunning and bravery. The crew became devoted to their new captain and named him Black Bart. The pirates captured more ships and sailed to Brazil where their fleet began to plunder the coast and raid shipping.

'Mr Kennedy, your cutlass is sharp. You have done well today,' said Black Bart, after one of the attacks.

'I want you to take command of the captured ship. You know what to do with the crew!'

'Aye Captain. A pirate's life or a watery grave,' replied the pirate Kennedy. The following morning, at first light, the pirates looked for the captured prize but Kennedy had deserted his comrades and the captured ship, together with its treasure, had gone. Black Bart flew into a rage.

'The scurvy dog. He's stolen our treasure. Is there no honour among shipmates?' he cried. He gathered all the pirates together. 'Each man will swear, holding a bible, to twelve rules he agrees to live by,' ordered Black Bart. 'Any man that breaks his solemn pledge will answer to all of us,' he cried when the oath was made.

The rules protected every pirate's rights to a share in the treasure and were popular with the pirate crew. The fleet moved north to Barbados and the attacks became bolder. French pirates joined Bart and captured slaves became enthusiastic pirates.

'The coast of North America, that's the place for treasure. We sail tonight,' ordered Black Bart.

Honest sailors shook with terror when they saw the black flags on the pirate ships. Many surrendered without a fight. Black Bart became fabulously wealthy. He dressed in fine clothes and jewellery taken from captured ships.

The fleet returned south to the Caribbean where their attacks brought trade to a virtual stop. In one month alone they captured ten ships. From the Caribbean the pirates then sailed east to Africa. More shipping was captured including a troop ship, taking soldiers to the Cape Coast. Faced with walking the plank many of the soldiers chose to become pirates and joined Black Bart's gang of cutthroats. The pirates attacked the African port of Ouidah, capturing eleven ships.

On the 10th February 1722, the pirates spotted another prize.

'Bring us about and run out the guns,' ordered Black Bart. Then, he went below for breakfast and to dress, ready for the battle.

'Captain, the ship has turned into the wind. She's not running away. She's coming towards us,' yelled the pirate first mate. Black Bart dressed carefully and went on deck. The pirates cheered their leader. He made a gallant figure dressed in a rich crimson waistcoat and white breeches. There was a red feather in his hat, a gold chain round his neck with a diamond cross hanging from it. His sword was in his hand and two pairs of pistols hung from his belt. Black Bart watched the approaching ship through his telescope.

'That's no merchantman. It's a man of war,' he cried. The British warship, HMS Swallow, commanded by Captain Ogle, turned to starboard and fired a broadside at Black Bart's ship. Cannon balls tore through the pirate ship's hull.

Black Bart staggered and fell. A huge wooden splinter had ripped his throat open. He was dead. The pirates threw their leader overboard and fought on valiantly for another two hours until they struck their colours and surrendered to Captain Ogle.

272 men were captured including 72 black pirates who were sold back into slavery. Many of the rest were condemned to death and some were indentured to the Royal African Company to serve out their days. Captain Ogle was knighted; the only British officer to be honoured for an action against pirates. He retired a wealthy man with the rank of Admiral; his fortune in gold plundered from Black Bart's cabin. Walter Kennedy, the deserter, returned to Britain and opened a brothel in London but was exposed as a pirate and hanged at Execution Dock in 1721.

During his short, three-year career as a pirate captain, Black Bart captured an estimated 475 ships, far more than any other pirate. It was the 'golden age' of swashbuckling buccaneers and Black Bart was one of the most feared of them all.

The pirate rules Black Bart made his men swear to obey.
1. Every man shall have an equal vote in affairs of moment. He shall have an equal title to the fresh provisions or strong liquors at any time seized and shall use them at pleasure unless a scarcity may make it necessary for the common good that a retrenchment may be voted.
2. Every man shall be called fairly in turn by the list on board of prizes, because over and above their proper share, they are allowed a shift of clothes. But if they defraud the company to the value of even one dollar in plate, jewels or money, they shall be marooned. If any man rob another he shall have his nose and ears slit, and be put ashore where he shall be sure to encounter hardships.
3. None shall game for money either with dice or cards.
4. The lights and candles should be put out at eight at night and if any of the crew desire to drink after that hour they shall sit upon the open deck without lights.
5. Each man shall keep his piece, cutlass and pistols at all times clean and ready for action.
6. No boy or woman to be allowed amongst them. If any man shall be found seducing any of the latter sex and carrying her to sea in disguise he shall suffer death.
7. He that shall desert the ship or his quarters in time of battle shall be punished by death or marooning.
8. None shall strike another on board the ship, but every man's quarrel shall be ended on shore by sword or pistol in this manner. At the word of command from the quartermaster, each man being previously placed back to back, shall walk ten paces, turn and fire immediately. If any man do not, the quartermaster shall knock the piece out of his hand. If both miss their aim they

shall take to their cutlasses, and he that draweth first blood shall be declared the victor.

9. No man shall talk of breaking up their way of living till each has a share of 1,000. Every man who shall become a cripple or lose a limb in the service shall have 800 pieces of eight from the common stock and for lesser hurts proportionately.

10. The captain and the quartermaster shall each receive two shares of a prize, the master gunner and boatswain one and one half shares, all other officers one and one quarter, and private gentlemen of fortune one share each.

11. The musicians shall have rest on the Sabbath Day only by right. On all other days by favour only.

12. If a member of the crew were to rape a woman he would be put to death or be marooned.

Chapter 39...The Robber's Grave

In the early 1800s Montgomery was a thriving market town. A plaque on Broad Street tells us that in 1840 over 50 tradesmen were based in the town including two blacksmiths, five bakers, three cobblers, three butchers, three carpenters, three coopers, eight grocers, two seedsmen, four drapers, four maltsters, two plumbers, two masons, three saddlers, two tailors, one bricklayer, one brazier, one timber merchant, one tanner, one *currier, one clockmaker, one bookseller and one *scrivener.

When John Davies, a plasterer from Wrexham found himself out of work in 1819, he travelled to Montgomery looking for work where he gained employment as a Gawas (Farm Servant) working for Mrs Morris, a widow. Mrs Morris lived with her daughter Jane and, since the death of her husband, the farm had become neglected and run down. Creditors including a local tradesman, Thomas Pearce, were watching eagerly, hoping to obtain the farm at a knock down price.

Mrs Morris was relieved to employ Davies. She knew she could not run the farm without a man to do the heavy work. John Davies was a quiet, taciturn individual of few words who kept himself to himself but he was strong and a hard worker. Robert Parker, a local quarryman, was a regular visitor to the farm and was engaged to the daughter Jane. He saw the new farm servant living at the farm as a threat and took an instant dislike to Davies.

Davies was good with the animals and he quickly improved the quality of the stock, getting good prices for them at the market. Before long Davies' hard work made a difference to the farm and Mrs Morris' fortunes started to improve. The daughter, Jane, grew to like the quiet young labourer. Sensing that he was losing her, Parker became aggressive and one evening the two men came to blows.

When Davies returned to the farm, Jane bathed his cut face but he would say nothing of how he became injured. Later, when a friend told the young woman about the fight, she realised that

Parker was a bully and that she did not want to marry him. She broke off the engagement leaving Robert Parker a bitter man, intent on revenge.

The tradesman, Pearce, was also bitter as he watched Davies' effort to improve the farm and saw his opportunity for some easy money slipping from his grasp. One evening Pearce and Parker met in the taproom of a public house and, after several drinks, hatched a plan to get rid of John Davies for good. The following day Pearce staggered into town with a bloody head.

'Help me,' he moaned. 'I've been robbed.' A crowd quickly gathered around the stricken man.

'Tell us, what happened?' they cried.

'I was riding along the road at Hendomen. When I got to the crossroads a ruffian attacked me and beat me about the head with a cudgel,' he whimpered.

'Did you see who it was that attacked you?' asked the crowd.

'No, but he stole my money, six guineas and my gold watch,' answered Pearce with a sly grin. A hue and cry began and the magistrate's men combed the countryside looking for the highway robber but there was no trace of the villain.

Later, unaware of the manhunt, John Davies came to market. It was busy on Broad Street with buyers and sellers enjoying the banter of quick business. The lambs Davies had bought from the farm sold for a good price and he went to the tavern to refresh himself before the long walk back to the farm. He saw Parker at the bar and turned to leave.

'Don't go. Come let us end our argument with a drink and behave like civil men,' called his adversary. Davies eyed his enemy with distrust.

'Why should I drink with you?' he asked.

'I want to apologise for my temper. Here take a glass of beer with me and let us be friends. Landlord, another tankard if you please,' commanded Parker and beckoned the farm servant to join him. The two men stood at the bar and drank. Davies was unaware

146

of the danger he was in. A few minutes later Parker's accomplice
Pearce arrived and, spying the pair, let out a shriek.

'That's him, the man that beat me to the ground and stole
my money and my watch,' he yelled and pointed at Davies. The
unfortunate farm servant was grabbed and searched. His drinking
companion of moments earlier thrust his bulging hand into Davies
pocket and gave a triumphant yell.

'Here, what's this in his coat pocket?' He pulled out his
hand and revealed six golden coins.

'That's my money,' cried Pearce.

'There's something else in the pocket,' said Parker with an
evil leer. He thrust his hand in once more and produced the final
proof.

'My gold watch! Fetch the constable. This villain must go
before the magistrate,' called Pearce. John Davies was taken to the
jail on Goal Street and kept in chains in the underground cell until
his trial.

The Quarter Sessions were held in the Town Hall. Davies
had no money to pay for a lawyer and conducted his own defence.
The evidence against him was strong. The tavern was crowded
when the stolen goods were found in his pocket and all swore to his
guilt, unaware that Parker had placed the money and watch into the
pocket of the unfortunate man. Davies protested his innocence
throughout but his pleas fell on deaf ears. Highway robbery was a
capital offence and he was quickly convicted of the crime he knew
he did not commit.

The day of the execution arrived. It was cold and a great
storm raged. A piercing wind blew from the north and sleet soaked
the waiting crowd as they looked up at the noose.

'Have you anything to say before sentence is carried out?'
said the hangman as the condemned man stood on the gallows with
the rope about his neck.

'I have been ill judged by man but am innocent of any
crime. I curse my enemies for this foul deed and offer my soul to
God for his honest judgement. If I am innocent in his court I tell

147

you this; no grass will grow on my grave for 100 years so people, in years to come, will remember this evil injustice against John Davies, an honest fellow,' said the condemned man.

The trap door opened and John Davies dropped to his death. He was buried in un-consecrated ground outside the churchyard at St. Nicholas Church in 1821 and, for over 100 years, no grass grew on the grave. It is still there today and, although the grass has finally started to grow back, the simple grave, marked with a wooden cross bearing the words *Robber's Grave*, still reminds us of when an honest man was unjustly hung and buried in a robber's grave.

A currier is a person that dresses and dyes tanned leather, ready for finishing by saddlers, cobblers and other leather workers. A Scrivener is a professional reader and writer employed by the illiterate to write letters and deal with legal matters: an early form of lawyer.

Chapter 40...The Drowning of Hafren

'Sabrina fair
Listen where thou art sitting
Under the glassie, cool, transluscent wave,
In twisted braids of lillies knitting
The loose train of thy amber-dripping hair,
Listen for dear honour's sake
Goddess of the silver lake'.
John Milton 1608 – 1674
English Poet

Geoffrey of Monmouth tells of a time when the Celtic nation covered the whole of Britain and there was a ruler named Locrinus. Invaders from the east were threatening the Kingdom and there were constant skirmishes. A fleet of Saxons, led by Humber the Hun, arrived and the King's brother died in the battle that followed.

When King Locrinus learned that his brother was dead he vowed revenge on Humber. His family honour demanded it and the protection of his Celtic realm made it inevitable. The Angles and Saxons had been threatening to invade for too long. Locrinus gathered his army and travelled east, to war. The two armies met near a mighty river and Locrinus killed his enemy. Humber had fought valiantly to the death and, recognising the bravery of his foe, King Locrinus named the river in honour of his enemy.

Following the battle Locrinus plundered the captured ships of his enemy, seizing gold plate, silver and prisoners. He divided the gold and silver amongst his victorious army and sold the prisoners into serfdom, all that is, except one; a great beauty named Princess Estrildis. The Princess was a noblewoman of Teutonic birth, kept for ransom by Humber.

As soon as King Locrinus saw the Princess he fell instantly in love with her. Her long golden hair and slender waist excited him and her sweet tender voice made him want to protect her from every evil, like a doting father. The King was smitten but there was

149

a problem; he was already betrothed to Princess Gwendolen. Gwendolen was from the house of Cornwall and the engagement was a political match to strengthen his throne. Gwendolen's father was a powerful man and could not be crossed. Locrinus could not have Estrildis. To take her would shatter his kingdom.

The King had Estrildis secretly taken to Trinovantum, later rebuilt and named Caer Ludd by King Ludd. Today we know the city as London. He hid Estrildis in a cave, guarded by trusted men at arms, and claimed that she had returned to her homeland.

The marriage of King Locrinus to Princess Gwendolen was a great occasion attended by nobles from across the land. The King and his new Queen toured the land, accepting tributes and homage from the people. For seven years the King deceived his queen, pretending to be a loyal husband while sneaking away to be with his lover.

The Queen gave birth to a Royal Prince and they named the child Maddan. King Locrinus despised his son and sent the boy to live with his Grandfather in Cornwall. Princess Estrildis also gave birth, to a girl. She was a fair child and they named her Sabrina, a Latin name which means Severn in English but those who saw her beauty only spoke her Welsh name; Hafren.

Queen Gwendolen grew sad without her son to nurture but she could do nothing to bring him home. Then one day, a messenger from Cornwall bought news of her father's death and her heart broke in two. King Locrinus was pleased to hear the news. He had feared the old man and knew that at last he was free to do as he pleased.

Within days, Estrildis and Hafren were taken from their underground hideaway and brought to the King's castle. The King banished Queen Gwendolen to Cornwall where she was reunited with her son but she was not happy. Her anger turned to hatred when she learned of her husband's years of deceit. The years passed and as Madden grew to manhood his mother taught him to hate his father. They plotted and planned the downfall of the King.

Madden grew into a fine warrior and, when his mother said the time was right, he marched north with an army to challenge his father. The two armies met on the bank of the River Stour and in the heat of battle, Madden pulled the King from his horse and ran him through with his sword.

Following the battle, Gwendolen, who was still the Queen, ruled in place of her dead husband. Her first command was to find Estrildis and Hafren. She wanted revenge. The King's lover and her daughter had taken refuge in Dolforwyn Castle and were quickly captured by the Queen's men. They were bound and dragged from the castle. People watched with shame as the two women were paraded through the streets like common criminals.

Then, the Queen's revenge was completed as Estrildis and Hafren were thrown into the river to drown, but a strange thing happened. As Hafren's lungs filled with water and her body sank down into the depths, she transformed into a goddess of the river and, to this day, glides under the water, peering up from her watery home. Next time you cross the Afon Hafren look down and think of her under the glassie, cool, transluscent waves.

Chapter 41...The Devil's Bridge

The widow, Marged, lived on the south bank of Afon Mynach. For company she kept a little dog and a cow. Each morning, as the sun's warming rays crept over the mountain, she would rise from her bed and milk her cow. The milk was rich and creamy and Marged would make butter and cheese. Each afternoon Marged would push a heavy barrow, loaded with butter and cheese, to the village of Ponterwyd where she would sell her produce at the crossroads. Because she could not cross the river near her house, the current being too fast, Marged had to push her simple cart along the bank of the river until it was shallow and calm enough to ford. Each evening, as the sun vanished in the west, she would trudge the long journey home along the riverbank, dragging the empty cart behind her.

'My bones ache and my legs are so stiff. If only there was a bridge; it would save me hours of walking,' she moaned, as she fell into bed. She slept a deep troubled sleep and did not hear the rain beating on her roof, nor see the lightening flashing across the sky or hear the thunder crashing as a great storm raged through the night.

Next morning, Marged woke and dressed. The dog, eager to start the day, scampered around her feet. She opened the door to the byre and called, 'I am here Malen (for that was the cows name). It is time to give your milk'.

Marged peered into the gloom but her precious cow was gone. The old woman ran outside. The dog followed and started to bark excited by her confusion.

'Where are you, Malen?' cried the old woman. Then she saw her cow. It was standing on the far bank of the river. The river was swollen with the storm, running fast and deep with a deafening roar. Next to the cow, stood a man, dressed in a monk's habit. A hood covered his head.

'Is this your cow?' yelled the monk. His voice was strangely powerful and carried easily above the thunder of the river. The old woman replied but her answer was carried away, drowned by the noise of the water. She nodded a reply.

'She must have been frightened and got lost in the night. You will have to walk miles upstream if you want to cross the river to collect her,' boomed the monk across the gorge.

'Oh dear! If only there was a bridge I could skip across the river and milk her in a moment,' wailed the old woman.

'Marged, I shall build you a bridge before noon,' cried the monk.

'A bridge before noon? That would be a miracle but how could I repay such a kindness? I have no money,' called the old woman. The monk laughed.

'Money means nothing to me. All I ask in return is the soul of the first living thing that walks over the bridge,' he cried. Marged wanted the bridge and eagerly agreed to the contract.

'Go inside your house and wait. I will call you when the bridge is finished,' yelled the monk. Marged took her dog into the house and closed the door. Outside, a great commotion started. She could hear rocks being hammered and split, trees being felled and sawn into planks, chains clanking with heavy loads and great shouts as the monk toiled to build the bridge. As time passed Marged grew hungry. She took some bread and cheese from the cupboard and started to eat. The noise outside stopped.

'It is ready,' called the monk. Marged opened the door and ran outside, still holding her breakfast in her hand. The monk and her cow were stood on the far side of the river. In front of them a fine bridge with a stone arch stretched across the ravine.

'Come across and inspect your new bridge,' invited the monk.

Just as she was about to walk onto the bridge, the old woman remembered what the monk wanted in payment for his work - the soul of the first living thing that walks over the bridge. She stopped.

'Your cow needs milking. You must come and get her,' implored the monk with a devious grin.

'How can I be sure the bridge will take my weight?' called Marged.

'Come, Marged. You can see how strong the bridge is,' coaxed the monk.

'The river runs fast. I might fall in and drown,' yelled the old woman.

'Trust me. You will be quite safe,' replied the monk. But Marged did not trust the monk.

'Here boy,' called the old woman. As the dog sprang up, Marged threw her bread and cheese right over the river. It landed by the monk's feet. The hungry dog chased across the bridge to the food and wolfed it down. The monk flew into a rage. His face grew red and his hood fell to his shoulders revealing two black horns. Marged had dealt with the Devil.

'I'm an old woman but I'm not an old fool. Our deal is done. Be on your way Satan and take your dog's soul with you,' cried Marged.

'The soul of a dog is no use to me. Keep it. You have tricked me, Marged. I won't forget this,' boomed the Devil and vanished. The old woman lived with her dog and cow for many years and people travelled from far and wide to see her fine bridge over Afon Mynach. The Devil never returned but the bridge he built in one morning stands to this day.

Chapter 42...Y-Ddraig Goch (The Red Dragon)

Ancient Welsh legends tell of the time when strange beasts walked the earth and a red dragon lived high in the Cambrian Mountains. It harmed no one and was respected by the people. The land of Wales was at peace and when Prince Ludd inherited the throne he was content to share his kingdom with the great beast. The kingdom prospered and grew larger than it is today, covering most of Britain. King Ludd built a new city called 'Caer Ludd', later to be known as London.

But an evil tribe of dwarfs, named 'The Coranaid', lived in the east. The Coranaid had ears that were so sensitive they could hear any sound whispered in the wind. They heard their neighbours in the west talking about their good fortune and grew jealous. The Coranaid invaded King Ludd's land armed with three weapons. The first of these was their hearing. Because the Coranaid could hear every word ever spoken it was impossible to plot their downfall. The Coranaid knew everything the Welsh planned and were ready for everything the desperate defenders tried.

The second weapon was a fearsome white dragon, which breathed fire and scorched everything in its path. The red dragon, woken from his peaceful dreams, rose up and the two mighty beasts became locked in a fearsome battle. They flew into the air, spitting plumes of fire. They clawed at each other with sharpened talons, ripping flesh as they fell to the earth. Their tails flailed the ground as they locked in combat. The screams of the battling dragons caused women to miscarry and animals dropped dead with fear. The battle between the giant beasts continued for years as they thundered back and fore across the land. Fertile land, trampled by the powerful dragons turned to barren rock. Plants withered and blew away.

The third weapon the invaders brought with them was a wicked magician who, each night, plundered the grain from storehouses of the kingdom. Every night, guards would lock themselves in the storehouses but always fell asleep, victims of the magician's spells. Each morning when they awoke the grain was gone. With no grain there was no flour and the bakers could bake no bread. With no bread to eat, the people began to starve but still the Coranaid advanced and the dragons battled. King Ludd left his kingdom and travelled to France where his wise brother, Llefelys, was king.

'Tell me brother. What can I do to stop the Coranaid? I fear my kingdom is lost,' he cried. The two kings spoke quietly together using a brass horn to hide their words from the Coranaid.

'I hear tell there is a poisonous oil, made from boiled insects, that will not harm your people but when sprinkled on the Coranaid, will kill them instantly,' said King Llefelys.

'But how will I catch them?' asked King Ludd.

'You must trick the invaders and trap them,' replied the wise brother.

'The dragons are destroying the land. What is to be done to stop their battle?' cried King Ludd.

'Your red dragon is a brave beast but he can never win against the evil white dragon. There is only one way to end the fight,' answered Llefelys.

'You are wise my brother but do you know how to end the dragon's battle and stop the magician stealing our food?' asked King Ludd.

'Listen carefully,' whispered King Llefelys. King Ludd moved closer to his brother and pressed the brass tube tight against his ear. King Ludd returned to Wales with a cask of oil from his brother; the poison prepared from boiled insects. He called his nobles together for a secret council.

'We cannot win this war against the Coranaid. We must surrender and show respect to our invaders. Send a messenger inviting them to the castle tomorrow to accept our homage,' he commanded. But the Coranaid did not need a messenger. They had heard his words.

The next day the people of Wales gathered to greet their new masters. The Coranaid arrived with a fanfare of trumpets. King

Ludd waited until all his enemies were together in the castle then gave a loud cry. It was the signal his warriors, on the ramparts, were waiting for. They showered poisoned oil over the throng below. It was harmless to the king's subjects but every invader was killed instantly.

That night the king locked himself inside the castle's grain-store and hid in a large barrel of icy water. As it grew dark a terrible sleepiness came over the king but the freezing water kept him awake. His arms and legs grew numb and he shook with cold as he waited. Then, a strange light appeared in the room and King Ludd saw a little man busy moving sacks of corn. The man wore a strange cloak and muttered as he worked. It was the evil magician stealing more grain. The king leapt out of the barrel and seized the man.

'Don't hurt me,' snivelled the magician.

'Promise never again to steal our food or harm my people in any way and I will let you go,' cried the king.

'I honour you, great King Ludd. The Coranaid tricked me and made me steal from you. You have my pledge,' promised the magician and swore a magic oath that he would keep his word.

The invaders were gone but their ferocious white dragon was still at war, battling with the red dragon. King Ludd gave orders for a huge pit to be dug. The men filled the pit with mead and covered it with cloth. As the two giant beasts fought they fell into the pit and, thirsty from the years of fighting, drank their fill of mead. Both dragons fell into a drunken sleep. The king's men tied them both with stout ropes and buried them in a stone vault deep beneath the mountain Dinas Emrys in Snowdonia where, according to the Mabinogion, they remain until this day.

The king, however, was proud of the red dragon of Wales that had fought so valiantly and for so long to protect his kingdom. He had the red dragon secretly removed from the vault and taken to the dark forest of Radnor, a lonely place, where it could sleep and recover from its wounds. To protect the dragon from evil, the king ordered that four churches be built surrounding the forest. The

Churches of Llanfihangel Cefnllys, Llanfihangel Rhydithon, Llanfihangel Nant Melan and Llanfihangel Cascob were all dedicated to St. Michael and, it is said, if any of the churches are ever destroyed, the red dragon of Wales will wake and rise up from its secret hiding place, ready to do battle once more.

Chapter 43...The Red Bandits of Mawddwy

Hen ddwyediad lleol – 'Tri pheth o Fawddwy a ddaw, Dyn
cas, nod cas, a glaw'.
Old local saying - Three things come from Mawddwy,
hateful men, blue earmarks and rain'.

In the 16th Century the land of Merrionnydd was a wild and
dangerous place. Gangs of robbers roamed the countryside. They
terrorized the people; stealing, cheating and murdering at will. The
most treacherous were the Red Bandits of Mawddwy, a gang so
evil that villagers shook in fear when they swaggered past. The
bandits had bright red hair, which they wore long as a mark of
allegiance to their clan.

Fearing for their safety, villagers never left home without
weapons. At night, doors were locked, windows shuttered and
barred. Some put sharpened scythes in their chimneys to stop the
robbers entering down the flue and murdering them in their beds.
The Red Bandits of Mawddwy spoke a strange language that only
they understood. People whispered that they had arrived from a
distant land in the east, exiled for their evil ways.

News of the Red Bandits of Mawddwy reached Queen
Mary. She summoned the Sheriff of Meirionnydd, Baron Lewis
Owen, and commanded him to end the reign of terror of the Red
Bandits. Baron Owen gathered together his men and attacked the
bandits while they slept in their hideout on Dinas Mawddwy. Many
bandits were slain in the fight and those that survived were led
away in chains. Baron Owen ordered a gallows to be built. Eighty
men were separated from the women and led to the scaffold.

'I will end your tyranny,' shouted the baron.

'Hang all the men,' he ordered. One by one the bandits were
placed on the scaffold and dropped with a sickening jolt as the
noose snapped their neck. The women screamed and pleaded for
mercy but the baron ignored their cries. Among the condemned
men were two young boys. Their mother, Lowri, broke away from

the other women. She fell on her knees in front of the baron and grabbed his coat.

'My Lord. They are just boys,' she wailed. 'Please be merciful. Spare their lives,' she sobbed. The baron looked down at the prostrate woman. He lifted his boot and kicked her to the ground.

'Hang the two boys next,' he commanded. When it was done, the woman stood up, a sullen look of hatred in her eyes. Lowri bared her chest and cupped her breasts with her hands.

'These yellow breasts have given suck to life and these hands will be washed in your blood,' she spat. The baron snorted at the demented woman and strode away leaving her standing by the bodies of her two children.

The tyranny of the Red Bandits of Mawddwy was broken but the red haired women wanted revenge for the murder of their men folk. They waited and plotted until one day the baron was out riding with his retainers. Suddenly, as they trotted through the valley at Bwlch Oerddrws, a hail of arrows rained down on the riders. The riders were unable to protect themselves and were cut down. More arrows followed. The baron's horse, wounded with an arrow through its neck, fell to the ground.

The baron was alone; all his men were dead or wounded. Red haired women emerged from behind rocks. They seized the baron and bound him with leather thongs. The prisoner was dragged to a camp hidden high in the forest above Dinas Mawddwy.

A woman emerged from a cave. It was Lowri, the mother of the two boys. Her face was contorted with hate. With her was an old man with red hair.

'Strip the baron and tie him to that tree,' commanded the woman. The baron struggled as hands ripped his cloak and tunic from his shoulders. His arms were pulled back and lashed to a stout tree.

'What evil is this?' he cried. The man produced a knife and walked towards the baron. Lowri stood in front of the baron and

160

cupped her hands. The baron screamed as the old man raised the knife. Then, with one quick movement, he slashed the Baron's throat. The Baron looked down, silently, and watched while the vengeful woman washed her hands in the blood spurting from the wound in his neck. Then he died.

Baron Lewis Owen, Sheriff of Meirionnydd was murdered on the 12th October 1555. The old man, known as John Goch (Red John), a relative of the young boys, was captured and charged with striking the lethal blow. His accomplice Lowri was tried at Bala in 1558. She claimed to be a spinster and attempted to avoid the gallows by announcing that she was pregnant. A jury of women confirmed the pregnancy and she was not hanged while carrying the child. No record exists to confirm whether or not she was executed after giving birth.

Chapter 44...The Beast of Llyn Barfog

It was a time when strange animals roamed the land and people stayed home, near a blazing fire, after dark. No one ventured near Llyn Barfog, (the bearded lake) for here lived the Afanc; a dreadful monster loathed by all. The Afanc spent its days hidden deep in the weeds and slime. At night it came out to hunt and fill its belly, A creature half crocodile, half beaver with teeth like razors and a scaly hide like armour. It stalked the land devouring animals and anyone foolish enough to be out when the sky was black.

Sometimes the Afanc would surprise its prey and eat it in one gulp. Sometimes it would stun its victim with a slow poison that left the mind alert while paralysing the body. Late in the night, a dog would howl or a man would scream as he was slowly dragged down into the lake, to be eaten later. Widows would find the bones of their husbands on the shore of the lake, gnawed and white. Young Arthur heard of the dreadful beast that was terrorising the land and resolved to kill it. He talked to his friend Merlin.

'How can I kill such an animal, Merlin?' he asked.

'To kill the Afanc, first you have to catch it but beware of its poison,' answered Merlin. Arthur went to the blacksmith.

'Heat your forge, blacksmith. Build me a chain strong enough and long enough to catch the Afanc,' he cried. The blacksmith forged links from the finest iron. He added carbon for strength, hammering it into the red hot metal. Link by link, the chain was made until it was long enough to catch the Afanc.

Arthur's strongest battle horse, Llanrai, was saddled. The great iron chain was loaded onto twenty carts and oxen slowly pulled the heavy loads to the lake. All was quiet. The monster was asleep somewhere in the murky depths below. Men at arms spread the chain around the lake, surrounding the tranquil water. Arthur, resplendent in shining armour, mounted Llanrai and the ends of the chain were harnessed to the noble beast.

'Come friend. There is work to be done,' cried Arthur. The great warhorse walked forward. The chains pulled tight. Llanrai leaned forward into the traces, using all his strength. Slowly, the stallion began to draw the heavy chains into the water, and then they stopped. Llanrai strained and pulled with all his might but the chains would not move.

'We are stuck,' cried Arthur. Then, the surface of the lake erupted and the Afanc burst up into the air. Its tail thrashed the water and its body writhed.

'The chain, it's wrapped around the monster's leg,' yelled Arthur.

The Afanc submerged once more and began to pull Arthur and his steed back, towards the lake.

'Hold fast, Llanrai!' cried Arthur. Hearing his master's command, Llanrai stretched every sinew as never before. The Afanc rolled and twisted as it tried to break free. It gnawed the chain with its razor sharp teeth but the carbon did its work and the links did not fail. The battle raged for hours with no sign of ending. As he strained, the great horse stamped the ground. Its hooves cut deep into the rock.

Then, without warning, the Afanc charged at speed, out of the water, straight towards Arthur and his mount. Llanrai was taken by surprise and stumbled forward. Arthur was thrown to the ground. Quickly, he sprang up and drew his sword. The Afanc advanced towards him, spitting vile poison as he came. Arthur covered his eyes to protect them from the poisonous spray. He lifted his sword and plunged it into the neck of the attacking monster with as much force as he could muster, killing it instantly and so ended the reign of terror of the Afanc.

The marks where Llanrai's hooves cut into the rock can still be seen near the shore of Llyn Barfog today.

Chapter 45...The Salt Smugglers of Mawddach

'The only thing worse than a smuggler is the excise man who tries to catch him!'
Dr. Samuel Johnson 1709 - 1784

In 1693, King William III was short of cash. 'I need more money,' he told his tax collectors.

'Tea, bibles, brandy, wine, lace, candles, linen; we are taxing everything we can think of,' they replied.

'That's not good enough,' shouted the King.

'What about a tax on windows?' said one of the tax collectors.

'That's a silly idea,' answered the King.

'I know, a tax on salt,' suggested another.

'Salt!' sneered the King.

'Your majesty, everyone in the kingdom uses salt for cooking. They must have salt to preserve fish and meat. Bakers use salt to make bread and dairies need salt to make butter,' they explained.

'A salt tax will make your Majesty lots of money,' added the tax collectors.

'It's a capital idea. I like it,' replied the King. Salt offices were set up throughout the land and the tax collectors began their unpopular work. King William was pleased but he was an extravagant monarch.

'I need more money,' he cried.

'There are still the windows. We haven't taxed them yet,' said his tax collectors.

'I agree. We will have a tax on windows,' ordered the King. The revenue men built Custom Houses across the land to collect the tax. One was built at Barmouth, at the mouth of the Afon Mawddach.

Sir William Jones lived in a grand house near the town. Each day the people saw him out riding a beautiful horse or being driven in his carriage.

164

'What a refined gentleman. He must come from a noble family,' they said as he rode past. But Sir William had a dark secret; he was the leader of a ruthless gang of smugglers. When the nights were dark, his men would quietly row down the Afon Mawddach, past the harbour entrance and out to sea where ships would anchor, waiting for the smugglers and the morning tide.

'What's the cargo,' whispered Sir William to a ship's captain on such a night.

'1000 bushels of salt from Ireland,' replied the captain.

'It will be a good pay day for the revenue men when you land at Barmouth,' smirked Sir William.

'Aye, it's a crime. The tax is more than the salt is worth,' replied the captain.

'I can take 500 bushels and pay you gold,' said Sir William and shook his purse to show he had the coins. The crew unloaded the sacks of salt into the little boats while Sir William went with the captain to his cabin and paid his debt.

'Let us toast our good fortune,' said the captain and poured two glasses of Brandy.

'To the King. Thanks for his greed, the people's hatred and our good luck,' said Sir William and took a gulp. He drained the glass.

'It's a fine brandy. Do you have any more?' he asked.

'Aye, twenty barrels hidden in the hold,' replied the captain.

'I'll buy them all,' cried Sir William. They agreed a price and the barrels of brandy were loaded into the boats.

'Look out for the revenue cutter,' called the captain as the smugglers began to row away. Sir William smiled to himself. He knew exactly where the revenue men were. He had paid them well to stay in their beds. The smugglers were safely ashore before the sun came up.

'Where shall we hide the contraband?' asked one-eyed Jack.

'Use the cave at Trwyn Glanmor,' answered Sir William. One eyed Jack was a surly fellow and as greedy as his master. He took four barrels of brandy for himself and hid them in Llanaber churchyard. The hollow, table tomb in the graveyard was his own secret hiding place. Sir William soon discovered the theft but he said nothing about it.

'We have heavy work to do tonight,' said Sir William a few nights later.

The tide carried the little boats quickly out to sea where a ship was waiting.

'We must be quick about our work. There is a new revenue officer in Barmouth who can't be bribed,' whispered Sir William. The men worked quietly while their leader paid the ships master.

'Where are you bound?' asked Sir William.

'We sail for America,' replied the captain.

'Here is an extra 100 guineas,' said Sir William.

'What's it for?' asked the skipper. 'I want you to take one-eyed Jack with you and throw him overboard when you are far out to sea,' replied Sir William.

'That's easy money,' said the captain and took the hundred guineas. The smugglers left one-eyed Jack bound and gagged in the hold of the ship.

Years passed and Sir William forgot about one-eyed Jack. The revenue men were offering rewards for information and went armed, intent on shooting smugglers on sight. Smuggling was getting dangerous and Sir William wanted to retire.

'One last trip and that's it,' he promised himself. The moon was in its first quarter and there was a light offshore breeze as the smugglers rowed downstream. They passed Barmouth harbour and were soon out to sea. The sea was choppy and the smugglers had to row hard.

'There she is, on the port side,' called Sir William pointing to a ship. As they approached the ship another vessel came into view.

The smugglers heard a cry, 'Heave to or we open fire'.

'It's the customs men. Row for your lives,' yelled Sir William. A cannon roared and one of the smugglers boats disintegrated. Sir William's boat made it to the ship. He clambered aboard leaving his men floundering below. On the deck a row of muskets were levelled at his chest.

'Move and my men will shoot you down,' said the revenue officer.

'Is this the man?' asked the revenue officer. A figure stepped out of the shadows. 'That's him. Sir William Jones, Gentleman, Murderer and Smuggler. Remember my reward and that you promised him to me,' said the man, pointing to Sir William. It was one-eyed Jack, returned from the dead.

'You'll get your reward money. As for him; I'm as good as my word,' said the revenue officer and ordered his men ashore.

'What about me,' cried Sir William.

'We are going on a little sea voyage together,' sneered one-eyed Jack and laughed. Sir William Jones, Gentleman from Barmouth, was never seen again.

Chapter 46...The Curse of Maesyfelin

Melldith Duw fo ar Maesyfelin
Dan boh carreg, dan boh gwreiddyn;
Am dafiu blodau plwyf Llanddyfri
Ar el ben i Deifi foddi.
May God with heavy curses chase
All Maesyfelin's villain race,
Since they have drowned in Teifi's tide
Llandovery's flower, Cymru's pride.

Sir Francis Lloyd, owner of the Estates of Maesyfelin, was a Royalist supporter and Gentleman of the Privy Chamber to Charles II. He was Lord of Lampeter and came from an ancient and respectable lineage. Helping the King with his toilet was a task that gave Sir Francis power and prestige. His estate was large and he needed to provide an heir but his wife was barren. The solution was simple; he took a mistress.

Bridget was twenty-five years younger than Sir Francis and their union produced two sons, Charles and Lucius. The boys were quickly named as his legal heirs in Sir Francis's will. A regular visitor to the Great House at Maesyfelin was the Vicar of Llandovery. He was an old friend and advisor to Sir Francis. One day, the Vicar brought his son, Samuel, with him to visit. While the older men talked, Samuel, a headstrong, impetuous, youth chatted happily with Bridget in the garden.

Bridget enjoyed the young man's company and encouraged him to call again. Soon Samuel was a regular visitor. Sir Francis watched the affection develop between his mistress and the Vicar's son. Their gay laughter annoyed him and he grew jealous of their private jokes.

One afternoon, when Samuel was walking home from Maesyfelin, three ruffians assailed him. He fought valiantly but was no match for the brutes. They gave the youth a beating. His body was found floating in the River Teifi the following day. The Vicar had no proof that Sir Francis had ordered the murder but in his heart he knew the truth. He cursed Sir Francis for the crime and called on God to avenge the death of his son.

When Sir Francis died, his son Charles inherited the estate but committed suicide a short time later. The second son, Lucius inherited. He was a gambler and wagered the whole estate in a bet with his brother-in-law, on who would die first. He died shortly after and lost the bet. Maesyfelin then passed to the brother-in-law living at nearby Peterwell House. And so, Sir Herbert Lloyd became Lord and Master of two estates.

Sir Herbert was a braggart and a bully who inflicted hardships on his tenants and never paid his debts. As Lord of Lampeter, he controlled the courts and had himself appointed as the Member of Parliament. He had no interest in Maesyfelin and dismantled the house, taking the stone to improve his own home. Money from the Maesyfelin Estate was plundered and squandered. A great roof garden was added to Peterwell.

Looking out from his roof garden, Sir Herbert saw a small patch of land that he did not own. He sent his henchman, Oakley, to buy the land but the peasant who owned it would not sell. When Oakley returned with the news, Sir Herbert flew into a rage. He wanted the land and no peasant was going to stand in his way. They hatched a plan.

The following day Sir Herbert's prize Black Ram went missing and the constable was told to investigate the theft of the animal. Two nights later Oakley and some accomplices lowered the Black Ram down the peasant's chimney while Sir Herbert summoned the Constable.

'Come quickly. I know who the thief is!' cried Sir Herbert. He led the Constable to the peasant's house and banged on the door. The peasant and his wife had just been woken by the Black Ram and were confused when Sir Herbert barged his way in.

'There is your evidence,' he said pointing at the Ram. The peasant was led away in chains. He protested his innocence at the trial but the jury, picked by Sir Herbert, quickly found him guilty of rustling and sentence was passed; death by hanging. Later, after the sentence had been carried out, Sir Herbert produced a bill of sale as evidence that he had bought the land.

Sir Herbert tried a similar trick with another neighbour when he claimed a valuable tapestry was stolen from his house. Once more Oakley and some servants lowered the item down the victim's chimney but the plan went wrong when the tapestry caught fire. As arranged, Sir Herbert burst into the house, expecting to recover his property but the evidence had gone up in smoke.

Sir Herbert and his henchman Oakley were dangerous men. One biographer of Sir Herbert wrote;

'He was regarded by his contemporaries and later generations as the very epitome of evil'.

Chronicler, Elisabeth Inglis-Jones wrote about Oakley;

'infamous agent, whose bastards overran the town, who had his own methods of extorting votes for his master'

Reports show that Oakley had 14 illegitimate children.

Pressure mounted to bring Sir Herbert down and his evil ways began to catch up with him. At the time, M.P.s could not be pursued for debt but, following pressure from local Squires, he lost his Parliamentary seat in 1768. His creditors were, at last, able to pursue Sir Herbert for their money but he had squandered the fortunes of two great families. There was nothing left.

Within a year, Sir Herbert Lloyd killed himself. He left no heir and, because his death was a suicide, his body was buried in the dead of night. Two Great Houses, built using the same stone, had been destroyed. The Vicar's curse had come true.

Chapter 47...Melangell and the Hare

Melangell was an Irish Princess, born in the 7th Century. As a girl she had great beauty and charm. Melangell grew into an intelligent and serene young woman with a calmness that all admired. Her father, the King, chose a noble of high birth for Melangell to marry. When he told the Princess she was to be wed, she refused to accept her suitor. The King persisted. He cajoled and bullied. He ranted and threatened but it made no difference. Melangell did not argue with her father, that was not her way, but her stubbornness made him realise she would never marry the nobleman.

Furious with his daughter for being so selfish, the King banished her from his kingdom forever. The young Princess left Ireland and sailed away, never to return. She crossed the sea and landed in the Kingdom of Powys where she made her way across the mountains to the hidden valley of Pennant, a place so remote and wild that no one would ever find her.

Princess Melangell found a crevice in the rock face with a stone slab on the floor. She fetched bracken to make a bed and the tiny cave became her home. Melangell passed the days wandering the Berwyn Mountains collecting berries, seeds and honey. Her diet was meagre. She gathered wool caught in the hawthorn bushes and wove simple garments to replace her tattered rags.

Her life was hard but Melangell was not alone; she had God as her daily companion. Each morning, before she went foraging, Melangell would pray. She chatted gaily to God like an old friend. Each night before she lay down on her stone slab to rest, she would go down on her knees and beg forgiveness for her sins that day.

This was Melangell's life for fifteen years. She lived alone and forgotten by the world, for no man of woman ever ventured into her hidden valley. One bright spring morning, while Melangell was saying her prayers, she heard the sound of hunting horns echoing along the valley. There was a haunting baying of hunting dogs and the thunder of horse's hooves.

A hare darted across the ground and under Melangell's cloak. The Princess remained on her knees and calmly continued to pray, as the huntsmen appeared. The dogs gathered around the kneeling woman but would not approach. They could see the hare hiding beneath Melangell and in their lust for blood they snapped and snarled at her.

A huntsman lifted his horn to his lips and blew but there was no sound. Melangell went on praying and, slowly, the hounds grew quiet. They sat and waited. The horses stopped prancing and stood still with steam rising from their flanks. The men watched in silence as Melangell finished her devotions, stood up and walked towards them. The hare hopped along beneath her coat. As the woman got closer the dogs and the horses began to back away.

'Who are you? What are you doing on my land?' demanded one of the riders.

'I am Melangell and this is my home,' replied the Princess calmly. The rider, who had spoken, dismounted and took off his gloves. He surveyed the woman. Her clothes were shabby but he saw she was no peasant.

'I am Brochwel, Prince of Powys,' he said.

'You have cowered my horses and silenced my hounds. You are brave Melangell,' added Brochwel.

'It is not bravery to let a frightened animal shelter under my skirts. My Lord, your dogs are fierce and your men outnumber the hare,' said Melangell. The Prince of Powys considered her answer for a moment and then he laughed.

'You are right Melangell. My dogs are fierce and we are many, so I say this. The hare can stay here with you and I give you this valley as a sanctuary for the frightened and the weak.' The Prince remounted and turned his steed.

'Gentlemen, let us find bigger prey to hunt this day,' he cried and spurred his horse forward down the valley. Melangell watched as the hunters disappeared from view while the hare sat quietly nibbling at the grass, by the feet of its protector. As news of Melangell's courage and the Prince's gift of the valley spread, pious women, wanting to live a good life, joined Melangell. They built a chapel in God's honour and, as the Prince had said, tended to the frightened and the weak that arrived seeking help. Melangell lived as the Abbess of her holy community for another thirty-five years. When she died her bones were interred in a shrine within the church.

1300 years after her death, Princess Melangell is still venerated and Pennant Melangell remains a quiet place of retreat for the sick and frightened of this world.

Chapter 48...The Five Saints

Cynyr ap Cunedda and his wife lived in the 6th Century, in the little village of Caio. When his wife told him she was expecting a child Cynyr's heart filled with pride and love for his wife. The day of her confinement arrived and the women of the village gathered to help deliver the baby. But there was not just one child delivered that night; there were five and they were all sons. It was a miracle and the people rejoiced when they heard the news.

The boys were named Ceitho, Gwyn, Gwynno, Gwynnoro and Celynin. Cynyr gave thanks to God for his good fortune and vowed to raise them as devout Christians.

'They will live the lives of saints,' promised the proud Father. There was no school in the village but, as the boys grew, their priest taught them letters and to write their names. One day, a tinker came to the village with news. St. David was coming to preach at Llanddewi Brefi. The priest went to the boy's Father.

'Cynyr, you must send your sons to hear the great man speak,' said the priest. It was agreed and the next day the five young men left Caio to travel north and hear St. David's sermon. Not far from Caio, the road passes the caves of Ogufau, a dank and forbidding place. An evil, jealous wizard lived in the caves. He heard the five brothers chatting happily as they approached. The wizard summoned great storm clouds. A fierce wind howled between the mountains. Darkness smothered the land and rain began to fall in torrents. Thunder boomed across the valley and lightning bolted across the heavens.

The five brothers grew weary as they tried to continue their journey but the rain and the wind were too strong.

'We cannot go on,' cried Ceitho.

'We must stop,' yelled Gwyn. A great weariness had come over the brothers, brought on by the sorcerer's spell.

'Let us rest by that rock,' called Celynin. The five brothers sat down with their backs resting against a giant boulder. They tried to stay awake but the sorcerer's spell was too powerful. Soon all five were asleep. The rain turned to hail that was so violent it pushed the boy's faces deep into the stone. The wicked wizard had trapped the brothers. The wizard emerged from his cave and released the sleeping boys from the rock that was holding them. Then, he dragged them into the caves of Ogufau and down into the bowels of the earth.

After the five brothers vanished, a young woman named Gweno, who was their friend, went looking for them. She went into the caves and slowly made her way through the subterranean passages, passing deeper and deeper into the ground, until she reached a strange chamber. In the middle of the chamber stood a pillar. There was a small opening on the far side of the chamber. Gweno went towards it.

Suddenly, freezing water flooded into the chamber. The force of the water swept her off her feet. She struggled to stand but the water level rose until her head pressed against the roof of the cave. Gweno gulped for air. Something hard and cold gripped her ankles. She kicked out, trying to break free but the hold was too strong. Slowly her tired body was pulled beneath the surface. With one last piercing scream she vanished, down into the depths of the underworld. The people call the cavern where Gweno vanished 'Clochdy Gweno' 'Gwen's Belfry' in English. It lies deep in the ground but the ghost of Gweno still roams the Ogufau caves. Her spirit vapour sometimes appears as a white mist while she moans and wails to be released from her fetid subterranean grave, in the rocks below.

The five brothers were never seen again. They are still slumbering somewhere in the caves, ready to wake when King Arthur returns or, according to Bishop Baldwin's writing in 1188, when a truly apostolic prelate occupies the throne of St. David.

Fifteen Centuries later, the giant boulder where the brothers slept is still there. Look closely. Can you see where their faces were pushed into the rock on that dreadful day?

Part Four South-eastern Wales

Chapter 49...The Blue Knight of Gwent

And Crispin Crispian shall ne'er go by,
From this day to the ending of the world,
But we in it shall be remembered-
We few, we happy few, we band of brothers;
For he to-day that sheds his blood with me
Shall be my brother
Henry V- William Shakespeare

William ap Thomas, born the son of minor Welsh gentry, grew into an ambitious young man, ready to make his way in the world. One way for a Squire to advance was by marriage and shortly after 1406 William ap Thomas married Elizabeth Bloet, the wealthy widow of Sir James Berkley. William's new wife came complete with a dowry and the manor of Raglan including Raglan Castle.

Overnight, the young Squire had become a man of property and status but that was not enough to quench his thirst for wealth and power. He also wanted glory and fame. William ap Thomas joined his King, Henry V and travelled to France. On the morning of the 25th October 1415, he stood and listened to the rousing speech that Henry gave before the Battle of Agincourt. He cheered with the other men as King Henry encouraged his outnumbered soldiers to fight for their country and their lives. He fought alongside his monarch in the thick of battle, slashing and cutting right and left. It was a fierce and bloody day that only ended when King Henry ordered his exhausted men to execute several thousand French prisoners. As they watched the murder of their countrymen, the morale of the French army collapsed and the battle was won.

Following the battle, William returned to Wales but in 1420 his wife died and ownership of the castle passed to William's stepson Lord James Berkley. It was a major setback but William was determined to keep Raglan and, following five years of negotiation, managed to agree a lease with his stepson. The lease allowed William to keep the Castle and live in it for the rest of his life.

William needed money and married for the second time to Gwladus, known by many as Gwladus Ddu or Gwladus the Dark because of her beauty. Gwladus was another heiress and, like William, her Father had fought at Agincourt. Once more William had married well and was quickly becoming a notable figure in Wales. In 1426 Henry VI knighted him for his services to the crown. People referred to him as 'Y marchog glas o Went' (The Blue Knight of Gwent) and he was happy to let others embroider and enrich his colourful reputation as a great warrior who fought with kings.

Sir William now had the desire and the money to make his mark for posterity and he began to rebuild Raglan Castle. The Castle would be his monument. He began by demolishing most of the old structure and, using styles he had seen during his time in France, built a new castle. A great tower known as the Yellow Tower, a fortress in its own right, was constructed within the castle. The Welsh Warrior Poet, Guto'r Glyn, wrote of the great tower 'which stands above all other buildings'.

Sir William began to educate himself in the sciences and in philosophy. He established a fine library of valuable books and manuscripts at the castle where he spent hours reading and making notes of his research, to improve his understanding. The castle and the library were his passions and would, he believed, be his legacy to the world.

As he grew older, Sir William held many positions of high office and influence in South Wales. When he died in London in 1445, his body was returned to Wales and interred in the Benedictine Priory Church of St. Mary at Abergavenny. Sir William's effigy, as a sleeping knight in armour, can still be seen in the church. His wife Gwladus died nine years later and is also buried at St. Mary's.

Sir William's family continued to enlarge Raglan Castle after his death but, in 1646, during the civil war, Parliamentary forces besieged the castle. It was one of the last great sieges of the war. The attackers mined under the walls where they placed gunpowder charges. The great tower was almost destroyed by the explosions and the valuable contents of the library, which had been hidden for safety in the bowels of the castle, were lost forever.

Today, it is said, a ghost wanders the ruins of Raglan Castle and can sometimes be heard moaning near the spot where Sir William's library once stood. As recently as 2001, a schoolgirl emerged from the castle, white faced, having seen a ghostly figure beckoning to her from the dark shadows. Some say it is the heartbroken spirit of Sir William, The Blue Knight of Gwent, returned from his grave to discover that his great tower and library are no more.

Chapter 50...Jack o' Kent and the Devil

One day, the devil was bored. He wanted to cause some mischief and amuse himself.

'Who can I tempt today?' said the devil and looked around. He saw a little man digging in a field. It was Jack o' Kent.

'What are you doing?' asked the devil. Jack o' Kent looked up from his work and saw the devil sitting in a tree.

'I'm planting this field,' he replied casually, pretending he did not recognise the devil.

'Can I help?' said the devil.

'I've nearly finished planting but you can water the field every night and make the sun shine every day if you like,' answered Jack.

'What will you give me for my effort?' asked the devil.

'To be fair, we could share the crop,' suggested Jack. The devil agreed.

'Do you want the top half or the bottom half?' asked Jack. The devil thought about the question for a moment.

'I will take the top half,' he replied thinking of all the lovely bread he would bake with the wheat. Each night, the devil took a watering can and carefully watered the field. Each morning, he moved the clouds and made the sun shine, so that the crop grew tall and strong. One morning Jack returned to his field.

'You have kept your word. Shall I harvest our crop?' he called to the devil.

'Please do and remember our bargain, the top is all mine,' agreed the devil. Jack worked hard. The crop was heavy and it took all day to gather it in. It was nearly dark when he was finished.

'Here is your share,' he said to the devil and pointed at a pile of leaves and stalks.

'The stalks are yours Jack but where is my wheat?' demanded the devil.

'What wheat? I grew no wheat. I grew turnips and as we agreed the bottoms, including the roots, are all mine,' said Jack and locked his beautiful crop of turnips in the barn. The devil knew he had been tricked and was angry.

'I'll be back. You wait and see,' he cried and vanished. The very next year Jack was in his field when the devil returned.

'What are you doing?' smirked the devil.

'I'm planting a crop in this field,' answered Jack.

'Would you like me to water it each night and make the sun shine each day,' enquired the devil.

'I'm not sure. What payment would you want?' said Jack.

'I'll take the bottom of the crop as my share,' answered the devil. Jack stroked his chin and considered the devil's offer.

'Are you sure that is fair?' he replied.

'Of course, let us shake hands on the deal,' said the devil and held out his hand. They shook hands. Each night the devil watered the crop and each morning he made the sun shine until one day the crop was ready for harvest. Jack worked hard that day until the field was bare. It was nearly dark.

'Here is your share,' he called to the devil and pointed at a pile of stalks.

'Where are my turnips?' cried the devil.

'You are a fool. There are no turnips,' laughed Jack and locked the doors to his barn. Its sides were bursting with beautiful golden grain.

'You have tricked me again Jack o' Kent, but I shall have my revenge,' screamed the devil and vanished. Jack was eating a dinner of turnip stew and fresh bread when the devil returned.

'You are clever Jack o' Kent but I have a challenge you will not beat,' said the devil.

'What is your challenge?' asked Jack finishing his stew.

'Meet me tomorrow on the top of Ysgyryd Fawr and I will tell you,' answered the devil. The next day Jack left his bed before the sun was up and climbed to the top of Ysgyryd Fawr. The devil was waiting for him.

'Look east Jack and tell me what mountain you see,' said the devil.

'There are no mountains east of us, only the Malvern Hills,' replied Jack.

'Look west Jack and tell me what mountain you see,' said the devil.

'Sugar Loaf Mountain stands tall and firm. So, what is your challenge?' asked Jack.

'Tell me which is the higher and if you are right I will grant you any wish,' replied the devil.

'What will it cost me if I am wrong?' asked Jack.

'If you are wrong all the turnips and grain in your barn will belong to me,' said the devil. Jack knew the answer was plainly Sugar Loaf Mountain and quickly agreed to the challenge. The devil laughed and before Jack could measure the mountains to prove he was right the devil flew up into the air. Jack watched, horrified, as the wicked demon gathered his apron into a giant sling. The devil swooped down, raked a mountain of earth from the fields and rose up, twirling the apron above his head. Then suddenly, before the devil could fling the earth onto the top of the Malvern Hills and turn them into high mountains, there was a loud crack. His apron strings snapped under the tremendous strain. Earth flew in all directions. Jack laughed as the devil returned to Ysgyryd Fawr. His trick had failed.

'You have lost your bet but when you grant my wish, I will do something to make you smile,' said Jack. Hearing Jack's offer, the devil cheered up.

'What is your wish?' said the devil.

'I have always been rather small. My wish is to be the biggest strongest man on earth,' answered Jack o' Kent.

'That's easy,' replied the devil and, in an instant, turned Jack into a giant.

'I have kept my promise Jack. Now how are you going to make me smile,' said the devil. Jack examined his strong arms and wide, bulging thighs. He took deep breaths and watched his enormous chest rise and fall.

'With one leap, I am going to fly from Sugar Loaf Mountain to the Malvern Hills,' answered Jack. The devil roared with laughter. He knew it was impossible even for a giant.

'This I have got to see,' he chortled.

'Why don't you stay here on Ysgyryd Fawr so you will get a good view as I fly right over your head?' suggested Jack, helpfully.

'Good idea,' said the devil as he made a cup of tea and sat down at a table ready for the spectacle.

Jack stood on Sugar Loaf Mountain and leapt high into the air. Up and up he soared until his body almost vanished into the clouds. The devil watched in amazement as Jack flew east through the air until, suddenly, he started to come down.

'He's not going to make it,' sneered the devil and he was right. Jack o' Kent did not land on the Malvern Hill. He dropped on Ysgyryd Fawr and squashed the devil flat. If you don't believe me, look closely at the side of the mountain. You can still see the table where the devil sat drinking tea and, beside the table, the crater Jack o' Kent's foot gouged out of the mountain as he landed.

Chapter 51...The Ogre of Abergavenny

William de Braose was born in 1049 in Normandy. He fought alongside William the Conqueror at the Battle of Hastings, in 1066, when the Normans invaded Britain and he was rewarded with large estates in Sussex and the Welsh Marches. De Braose was created 1st Lord of Bramber and became one of the most powerful Norman Barons. He quickly consolidated his position, building castles to intimidate the Saxon natives of Sussex and the Celtic people of Wales. The De Braose family prospered, expanding their estates, and by 1175 the Great Grandson of the 1st Lord of Bramber, also called William de Braose, became 4th Lord of Bramber and inherited the family estates in Wales. His lands included the Gower, Abergavenny, Brecon, Builth, Radnor, Kington, Limerick, Glamorgan, Skenfrith, Briouze in Normandy, Grosmont and White Castle.

The 4th Lord was a wealthy, ruthless and ambitious man who mercilessly suppressed the people whose lives he controlled. Not all of the Welshmen, however, accepted Norman rule willingly and there were occasional skirmishes between the Celtic Welsh and their Norman invaders.

It was October and the ground was thick with frost when news reached De Braose that his uncle had been killed in a dispute with an unknown Welshman. It was an insult to the Norman rulers and could not go unpunished. He decided to settle matters with the impudent Celts, once and for all. William de Braose commanded his men to take messages to the Welsh leaders inviting them to visit him.

'My Lord, William de Braose, 4th Lord of Bramber invites you and your retainers to join him on Christmas Day, at Abergavenny Castle, to enjoy Lord Bramber's hospitality and feast together. He wants to celebrate a new friendship so that Norman and Welshman may learn to live together in peace,' announced the messengers.

One prominent Welshman who was invited was Seisyll ap Dyfnwal, Lord of Upper Gwent. Dyfnwal had land and a small castle near Llanover, south of Abergavenny. He was related, by marriage, to the King of Deheubarth (South West Wales) and an influential member of the community. Seisyll ap Dyfnwal called the leaders of the families together.

'I don't trust the Normans,' said one.

'It could be a trap,' warned another.

'My friends, he has invited us on Christmas Day. What better omen could there be that William de Braose wants to end the bad feeling between us? We should show good faith and go to the castle,' said Seisyll. The meeting was divided. Some wanted to trust the Norman baron and others, who were afraid, would not.

'Christmas is a time of goodwill, a time for ending feuds. My men and I will go and offer our hands in friendship. Who will join us?' asked Seisyll. The silence that followed spoke loudly enough.

It was Christmas Day. The ground was frozen and large snowflakes were falling silently as Seisyll ap Dyfnwal led his men through the gate of Abergavenny Castle.

'Come in. You are welcome. Come and warm yourselves by the fires,' cried the castle warden. The men followed the warden across the courtyard towards the inner keep, looking warily to the right and left. They reached the inner keep and the Warden stopped.

'Your weapons please, Gentlemen?' asked the Warden, pointing to a table.

'We keep our swords,' replied Seisyll ap Dyfnwal.

'My Lord. That would be an insult to the Baron. He has invited you into his home on this festive day, in trust and friendship. Please, keep faith with him,' said the Warden. Seisyll ap Dyfnwal looked at his men, unsheathed his sword and placed it on the table.

'Come, my friends. Today is Christmas Day, a day of goodwill to all men. To keep our weapons would mean a lack of trust and is no way to start a friendship. They entered the great hall, unarmed. A hundred candles flooded the hall with light. Flames, from the ash logs which roared in each hearth, filled the hall with warmth and the smell of honest wood fires.

'My Lord Dyfnwal. I welcome you and your men to Abergavenny but where are the rest of your countrymen?' called the Baron, across the great hall.

'I regret that many of my kinsmen are wary and prefer to stay at home with their families this festive day,' replied Seisyll ap Dyfnwal.

'Shame on them for their timidity but I will deal with them another day,' said de Braose. Then, without warning, Norman soldiers burst into the hall with their weapons drawn.

'What foul trickery is this?' cried the Welshmen. They turned and ran for the door and their weapons beyond but it was no use, the door was locked. The Normans fell on them, and struck down every Welshman in the castle. William de Braose walked across the great hall, stepping over the dead bodies.

'Captain of the Guard, your men have done well. Now finish your task,' he cried.

'I will my Lord,' replied the Captain of the Guard. When the Norman soldiers arrived at Seisyll ap Dyfnwal's castle, all was quiet. The women were waiting for their men folk to return from Abergavenny. The sentry opened the gate without challenging the visitors, a mistake which cost him his life. A small boy was playing in the courtyard. It was Cadwaladr, Seisyll ap Dyfnwal's seven-year-old son. He looked up at the men at arms advancing towards him and saw the blood on their weapons. Cadwaladr turned to run but he was too slow. The Captain of the Guard lunged forward and thrust his sword into the boy's back.

'No one is to leave the castle alive,' he cried. The soldiers murdered everyone and returned to their master with the news. The impudent Welsh had been punished.

News of William de Braose's treachery and the massacre of innocents at Abergavenny quickly spread across Wales.

186

Resentment grew and, realising his mistake, de Braose gave generous donations to the priories at Abergavenny and Brecon. The chronicler Gerald of Wales, a Norman sympathiser, recorded the acts of religious piety and exonerated de Braose for his treachery in his writings but it made no difference. William de Braose had earned his place in Welsh history and is remembered to this day as The Ogre of Abergavenny.

Chapter 52...The King's Tax Collector

When the Welshman, Harri Tudor was crowned King Henry VII on the Battlefield at Bosworth, in 1485, the civil war known as the 'War of the Roses' had been raging for over thirty years. During the war thousands died. Intrigue and treachery were common. Noble families changed sides as the ebb and flow of war favoured one side and then the other. Traitors were executed and estates seized to be given as reward to loyal followers. One man, who changed sides more than once, lived to tell the tale. He was John Morton, the King's Tax Collector.

John Morton was born in 1420. He was an intelligent man and trained as a lawyer at Balliol College, Oxford. As a young man, Morton was a committed Lancastrian and was on the battlefield at Towton on the 29th March 1461 when the Lancastrians suffered their bloodiest defeat of the war. Following the battle, Morton was named as a traitor by the Yorkist victors and escaped to France to live in exile with Margaret of Anjou, the Lancastrian Queen. Morton returned to Britain in 1471 and, following the Battle of Tewkesbury, another Lancastrian defeat, he changed his allegiance and supported the cause of the Yorkist King, Edward IV. Edward rewarded Morton by appointing him Ambassador to the French Court and, in 1479, made him Archbishop of Ely.

When Edward died, John Morton intrigued against the new Yorkist King, Richard III. Richard was unpopular and many believed that he had murdered Edward's young sons, the real heirs, in the tower of London, in order to claim the crown for himself. The plot to remove King Richard failed and John Morton was declared a traitor for the second time. Morton, unlike the other plotters who were executed, was sent to Brecon to be the prisoner of Henry Stafford Duke of Buckingham, a Marcher Lord and loyal ally of King Richard.

Marcher Lords had different rights to other nobles. They could make their own laws and were Petty Kings who, provided they did not commit treason, could do as they pleased in their own land. The borderlands were wild and dangerous and King Richard needed strong leaders who would contain the Welsh population who generally supported the Lancastrian cause. Marcher Lords were powerful, dangerous men.

John Morton used all his experience as a lawyer and diplomat to engage his jailer and quickly made friends with the Marcher Lord, Stafford. The Duke installed his prisoner in a tower, outside the castle, where he lived in comfort. The two men talked late into the nights debating what was best for Britain. Morton argued convincingly and after several weeks of debate Lord Stafford agreed to join the Lancastrian cause and help remove the Yorkist usurper Richard.

The Duke raised a Welsh army and advanced towards England but when they reached the River Severn it was in flood and, although Stafford crossed successfully, his army, unsure of the Duke's true loyalty, did not follow. King Richard had been warned about the Welsh army, led by the Duke of Buckingham and had decreed him a traitor. The Marcher Lord went on the run and hid at Lacon Hall, near Wem. The owner, Ralph Bannister, betrayed him for a reward and the Duke, who had been persuaded to change sides by Morton, was executed on Sunday 2nd November 1483.

John Morton escaped from Brecon and made his way to Flanders where he spent the next two years gathering support for Harri Tudor and the Lancastrian cause. Following the death of Richard III at Bosworth, Harri was crowned King and appointed John Morton as Archbishop of Canterbury. In 1487, King Henry VII made Morton his chief advisor and Lord Chancellor.

As Lord Chancellor, John Morton quickly realised there was a serious problem. The new King had no money; the royal treasury was empty. His solution was simple. Morton began to visit the great houses and castles of the land.

'I am the King's Tax Collector,' he would announce as he arrived. Nobles would honour him with a great banquet and house him in a fine bedchamber with roaring fires. They would give

Morton valuable gifts, hoping to bribe him. As he left, the following morning, Morton would beckon the noble.

'You live well my lord. Your table is laden with food and your fires are well fed. I see that you are a wealthy man and can give generously to the King.' He would then levy a hefty tax.

Other nobles adopted a different approach. They would take the King's Tax Collector and give him a frugal supper of bread and cheese then send him to bed in the coldest dampest room in the castle. As he left, the following morning, Morton would beckon his host.

'You live very frugally my lord. You eat very little and waste no money on fires to heat your castle. I see that you save your money and are a wealthy man. You can give generously to the King.' As before, he would levy a hefty tax.

Henry VII united the Kingdom and built a reputation as an able administrator who bought peace to the land. He needed money to run his affairs and it was John Morton, the King's Tax Collector, who working on the principle that everyone should pay tax, successfully filled the King's treasury and made everything possible. Morton died peacefully, on the 15th September 1500, at the age of 80 years and is still remembered as the man who helped the Welshman, Harri Tudor win his throne and secure a dynasty.

The expression 'Morton's Fork', describing his way of collecting tax, is used today to illustrate a position where someone has a dilemma involving two unpleasant alternatives. The ruin of Ely Tower, named after the prisoner Morton, who was then the Archbishop of Ely, still stands opposite the Castle at Brecon.

Chapter 53...Doctor Price of Llantrisant

On the 18th January 1884 history was made in the parish of Llantrisant. Local Doctor William Price who was 83 years old carried the dead body of his five month old son, Jesu Grist Price (Jesus Christ Price) to the top of East Caerlan Hill above the town, placed it in a tin tray of paraffin, covered the vessel with a towel and set it alight. Onlookers from the town saw the flames and ran up the hill to find Doctor Price chanting over the burning body. The crowd, angry at seeing such an evil, pagan act assaulted Doctor Price and handed him over to the police. They had just witnessed the first cremation, an illegal act at that time.

A court case followed at Cardiff Crown Court during which Doctor Price conducted his own defence. Price was a brilliant orator and argued, 'It was wrong to allow a body to decompose, since it polluted land and was a constant danger to all living things'. He was acquitted amid international interest, the Cremation Act of 1902 followed shortly thereafter making cremation legal in the United Kingdom.

This was not the first time that Doctor Price had attracted attention for his unusual behaviour. From his early days he stood out from his contemporaries. Within a year of starting his training in London he had passed the Royal College of Surgeons Examinations. Once established as a doctor near Pontypridd he refused to treat patients who smoked, claiming that the way people lived was the principle cause of sickness and that powerful drugs were not the solution to illness. He preferred to use herbal remedies wherever possible.

Doctor Price declared that he was an Archdruid and was often seen wandering on the mountains late at night dressed in a fox skin hat, green trousers and a scarlet waistcoat chanting strange laments while carrying a crescent moon and a burning torch – both druidic symbols. He scoffed at conventional religion, became a vegetarian and supported the ideas of nudism and free love, a principle he practiced until the end of his life. His housekeeper,

191

Gwenllian Llywelyn, who was 60 years younger than Price, gave birth to two further children fathered by Price while he was in his late 80's.

Despite being recognised as a gifted doctor, the establishment was often at odds with his weird and wonderful ideas and he was frequently called upon to defend himself in the courts.

On the 23rd January 1893, aged 93, Dr. Price slipped and fell off a chair. He called for Gwenllian to bring him some champagne and promptly died. According to his written instructions his body was carried up East Caerlan Hill to the same spot where he had cremated his son. He was laid on two tons of coal and the funeral pyre lit. Tickets were sold for the event and a crowd of over 20,000 people stood on Caerlan Hill to watch the first legal cremation in the United Kingdom.

Regarded by many as an eccentric crank and others as an enlightened radical man Dr. Price was certainly a revolutionary figure. Today, over 100 years later, many of his views are now quite acceptable

Chapter 54...The Maid of Sker

Elizabeth Williams lived with her father, Isaac. They lived at Sker House. It was a big house that stood barren and alone on the coast near Sker Point. On some days the sun would shine and Elizabeth would stroll along the beach at Kenfig, watching gulls diving into the sky blue water. On others, when cold winter winds blew from the west and storm clouds filled the sky, she would stay indoors, glad of the log fire that roared in the grate. Her father was a wealthy man. He was respected in the community, a Constable of the Hundred and a Magistrate. It was a lonely, solitary life for a young woman, particularly for one as outgoing as Elizabeth. But there was one occasion each year when she could really enjoy herself.

Elizabeth Williams loved to dance. She looked forward to the annual 'Gwyl Mabsant', a dance to celebrate the local saint. The dance, a rather boisterous affair, took place in the old town hall at Kenfig. The hall was cleared for the dance. A harpist sat on a table at the end of the room and played. Older people would gather in groups around the sides of the hall to gossip and drink while younger revellers stamped their feet and danced with gay abandon.

The dance had already started when Elizabeth and her father arrived. She hurried into the hall and hung her cloak with others near the door. Shrieks of laughter and music filled the air. She looked at the harpist as his fingers plucked and strummed the strings. His feet jiggled with the beat. He looked towards her and smiled as he played. It was a warm friendly smile. She smiled back.

'Who is that man playing the harp so beautifully?' she asked a girl.

'He's Thomas Evans from Newton Nottage,' replied the girl. Elizabeth listened, enchanted with his playing. Before long she was reeling around the dance floor with the others. At the interval the harpist came over to her.

'What's your name?' he asked.

'Elizabeth,' she replied. They talked happily, as if they had known each other for years. It was love at first sight.

'Who was the young man you were talking to?' inquired her father on the way home.

'Thomas Evans. He was the harp player. He has asked to call for me tomorrow,' replied Elizabeth.

'What is his occupation?' asked her father.

'He is a carpenter,' answered Elizabeth.

'A carpenter! No common tradesman is coming courting at my house,' thundered Elizabeth's father. The next morning, when Elizabeth tried to leave her bedroom, she found that the door was locked. She called but no one came. Later, when Thomas arrived her father received him in the drawing room.

'Can I ask your permission to call on Elizabeth?' said the young man.

'She refuses to see you,' lied the father and showed the distraught young man out. Thomas called every day but he never got to see Elizabeth. He did not know her father was keeping her a prisoner in the house. Finally, the heartbroken boy gave up and stopped coming to the house but he never forgot the beautiful girl he met at the dance.

It was only when Elizabeth promised to marry one of her father's friends that he released her from her prison. The marriage took place the very next day. Her new husband was a sour, taciturn man. He never smiled and never took Elizabeth dancing. Elizabeth was cleaning her house one day when a neighbour arrived.

'Have you heard the news?' called the neighbour.

'A French ship has been wrecked at Sker Point. Ruffians are looting the cargo. The militia are coming from Swansea,' said the neighbour gleefully. Later she returned with more news.

'Seventeen men have been taken for thieving the cargo,' she said.

'Serves them right for being so dishonest,' replied Elizabeth.

'There's more. One of them was your husband and your father has been accused,' added the neighbour.

194

That night, with her husband away, Elizabeth put on her cloak and went out. It was the night of the 'Gwyl Mabsant' and she wanted to dance: to escape her unhappy life for a few precious hours. She heard the music from the harp as she entered the hall. It was a melancholy tune. She looked at the harp player. It was Thomas. He was singing softly.

> *Mab wyf i sy'n byw dan benyd*
> *Am f'anwylyd fawr ei bri*
> *Gwaith fwy'n ei charu'n fwy na digon*
> *Curio wnaeth fy nghalon i*
> *Gwell yw dangos beth yw'r achos*
> *Nag ymaros dan fy nghur*
> *Dere'r seren atai'n llawen*
> *Ti gei barch a chariad pur.*

> *I am a young man living in sorrow*
> *'Tis for a lady known for her charms*
> *Too well I love her and every morrow*
> *Ever I pine and long for her arms.*
> *Better it is to show my passion*
> *Than to endure this restless pain*
> *Come bright star, beam kindly on me*
> *Then shall my pure love be near me again.*

Elizabeth slipped quietly out of the hall and walked home with tears running down her cheeks. She opened the door and went into the dark house. Her father and husband were in the kitchen.

'Where have you been?' they demanded. She would not answer.

Perhaps because of his influence, Isaac Williams and Elizabeth's husband were never prosecuted but the other thieves were and one of the looters was hanged for the crime. On the 6th January 1776, just ten years after her marriage, Elizabeth was buried in Llansamlet churchyard. Some say, she never recovered from her broken heart.

Thomas Evans sang his love song regularly over the years but he recovered from his heartbreak and, when he was fifty years old, he married a girl of nineteen. They went on to have eleven children. Thomas died on the 30th October 1819 and is buried at Newton Church, Porthcawl.

Chapter 55...The Iron Masters of Merthyr

'Eccentricity, genius and such a strict feeling of honour that it is common, saying that their word is as good as another's bond.'
George Borrow, Writer 1803 - 1881

The town of Merthyr Tydfil takes its name from Saint Tydfil, another daughter of King Brychan of Brycheiniog, who, because of her Christian beliefs, was murdered by pagan Saxons. There is, however, a more interesting family from Merthyr Tydfil whose vision and energy made Merthyr Tydfil one of the greatest industrial centres of the world. The Crawshay family built the largest iron foundry in the world and left a mock gothic castle in the town as a monument to their exploits. The story began, in 1755 in Yorkshire when 16-year-old Richard Crawshay argued with his father.

'You're a fool and a dreamer. You don't know the meaning of work,' yelled his father. Richard did not answer. Instead, he took a horse and left. It took the penniless youth twenty days to travel to London where he took a job working in an ironmonger's shop. The owner of the business took a liking to young Richard and, in time, he allowed Richard to marry his daughter. When the owner died, Richard Crawshay inherited the business and some money.

In the 18th Century the sleepy village of Merthyr Tydfil found itself at the centre of the industrial revolution. Limestone, coal and iron ore were all available locally and the rivers Taff Fechan and Taff Fawr ran swiftly enough to provide power. In 1765, Anthony Bacon established a small iron foundry at Cyfarthfa, Merthyr Tydfil using water from the rivers to power his blast furnace. News of the town in South Wales where a man could make his fortune reached Richard and he travelled to Wales to find a way to get involved.

'My foundry is too far from its customer in Cardiff. I can't pay the men's wages. We are going broke,' admitted Bacon to Crawshay.

'You're transporting heavy cast iron by horse and cart! That's mad,' said Richard.

'There is no other way,' replied Bacon.

'Here is money for the wages. Make me your partner,' said Richard. The two men became partners.

'We need to reduce our transport costs. We'll build a canal,' announced Richard.

'It can't be done. We don't have the money,' replied Bacon.

'I'll borrow it. We can use the foundry as security,' said Richard. Richard gambled everything and mortgaged everything he had. The Merthyr and Cardiff canal opened in 1794, slashing the cost of moving the cast iron being produced at Cyfarthfa. Crawshay's gamble had paid off. He summoned Bacon to his office.

'Here is the rest of your money,' said Richard and handed a banker's draft to Bacon.

'What's this for?' asked Bacon.

'I've dissolved our partnership and bought you out,' replied Richard Crawshay.

'It's Nelson. Cheer you buggers!' cried Richard when the Admiral visited Cyfarthfa in 1802. The men responded with three hearty cheers and the band played Rule Britannia.

'The war with Napoleon will be good for us. The Navy will need lots of cannons,' forecast Richard. He was right and valuable orders for urgently needed ordnance soon began to arrive from the admiralty. Cannons manufactured by Crawshay were fitted in HMS Victory and helped win the Battle of Trafalgar.

Merthyr quickly became a boomtown. Workers from across Britain flocked to the town, eager to work in the new foundry. The valley filled with the stench of burning coal. Soot covered everything. The air was full of sulphur and the night sky glowed red with molten iron from furnaces that never cooled. By 1804 Crawshay's Cyfartha works employed over 1500 men and was still growing.

Other foundry owners watched Richard with envy. They needed to bring down their costs and wanted to compete with him. The owner of Penydarren foundry contracted a Cornishman; Richard Trevithick to build a steam powered tram system to move cast iron from Penydarren.

'I bet you 500 guineas that your steam engine will not pull ten tons of iron from Merthyr to Abercynon,' sneered Richard and the bet was agreed. On the 24th February 1804, his challenge was met when trucks loaded with ten tons of iron plus a gang of 70 men were hauled the full nine miles, without stopping. Constructed 26 years before the rocket, it was the first practical steam locomotive. Richard Crawshay had lost his bet but he did not care. Cyfarthfa Works was the largest iron foundry in the world.

In 1810, Richard Crawshay fell ill.

'You are the Iron Master now,' he whispered to his son, William, and died.

'I hate Merthyr, it stinks,' said William and moved to London, leaving his young son, also named William, to run the foundry.

Guided by his father, young William did a good job and Cyfarthfa foundry continued to prosper. The development of the railway system brought huge new orders for iron tracks and the business expanded again. The Tsar sent negotiators from Russia to buy thousands of miles of track. Money was pouring in and young William began to buy out his competitors.

By 1819, Cyfarthfa foundry had six furnaces and was capable of producing 23,000 tons of iron a year.

'I need a new house, one that shows my importance,' stated William Crawshay junior and started to build a new family home, overlooking the works. The house, built in 1825 was named Cyfarthfa Castle and cost £30,000 to build, equal to £3m in today's money. It sat in 158 acres of parkland and dominated the valley. It was an unambiguous statement of wealth.

William Crawshay junior died in 1867 and a new Iron Master ruled Merthyr, his son, Robert Thompson-Crawshay.

Robert quickly tired of the business. Music, horticulture and photography were his passions and he had little time left to run a noisy foundry.

'I will employ managers to run my company,' he said and returned to his hobbies.

'You must modernise the foundry so we can produce steel,' pleaded his managers.

'Why should I waste my money?' he replied.

'No one wants to buy our iron products. Your foundry is losing money,' said the managers.

'Losing money, you say. Then we will close it,' answered Robert. He closed the foundry that had been built up over 100 years and threw 500 men out of work, making their families destitute. The people of Merthyr shunned Robert in the street and he retreated to his castle. Ostracised by everyone, he became a hated, reclusive figure. Only then did he realise what he had done and the shock affected him badly. His health deteriorated and he had a stroke.

'God forgive me,' were the last words he uttered when he died four years later. A ten-ton slab of pink rock, surrounded by iron railing covers his grave. The inscription simply says; -

Robert Thompson-Crawshay. Died May 10th 1879.
'God forgive me.'

The family moved out of Cyfarthfa Castle in 1889 and the house was sold in 1909 for £19,700. It opened as a school in 1913 and today, the house and park are open to the public as a museum and art centre. On the 16th June 2003 Robert Thompson-Crawshay's gravestone at Vaynor was made a Grade II listed monument, ensuring that his foolishness and regret will be remembered forever.

Chapter 56...The Green Lady of Caerphilly

The 13th Century was a turbulent time in Wales. War was common and powerful barons fought constantly. Gilbert de Clare, Earl of Gloucester was such a baron. War was his passion and delight. He took pleasure in killing and plundering his neighbours. Other barons hated and feared him. Aware that they might join together and attack him, de Clare built a great castle in Caerphilly. It was the biggest and most formidable castle in all of Wales. Thick stone ramparts surrounded the keep and a vast lake protected the castle from attack. The Earl was pleased with his castle but there was something missing.

'You should take a wife, my Lord,' suggested his squire.

'What do I want a wife for?' replied the Earl, arrogantly.

'A wife would fill the castle with gay laughter and make you happy,' said the squire. The Earl considered his servant's suggestion and decided that he would marry. He searched the land for a beautiful woman to become his bride but none were pretty enough. Then the Earl inherited an estate in France and decided to inspect his new lands. As he arrived, a beautiful girl greeted him. Her long hair glistened in the sun and her smile entranced him.

'Tell me girl, what's your name?' asked the Earl.

'I am Alice of Angouleme,' she replied.

'Come Alice. Let us walk together,' commanded the Earl. Alice chatted gaily as they strolled and Gilbert de Clare resolved at once that he would take this girl and marry her. Within days, they were married and the triumphant Earl returned to his castle with his new bride. It was not a happy union. As soon as the Earl returned to Wales, he left to fight his enemies. Alice was left alone in the castle for weeks and months while her husband was at war. She wandered through the great halls, alone and sad.

One day a visitor arrived at the castle.

'Who are you?' asked Alice, looking at the handsome young man.

'I'm Gruffudd the Fair, Prince of Brithdir,' he replied and smiled at her. She shuddered at the power of the attraction between them. Soon Alice and the fair prince were lovers. Aware of the dangers of such an affair, they met furtively and told no one of their love. But like most secrets, theirs would soon be revealed. One day Gruffudd the Fair was chatting to a monk.

'I am in love,' he blurted out, without thinking.

'Who is the lucky girl?' enquired the monk.

'Promise you will tell no one?' said the prince.

'Have no fear. I am a man of God. Your secret is safe with me,' replied the monk.

'Alice has stolen my heart,' said the prince. He had given his word but it meant nothing to the monk. When he heard of Alice's adultery he wrote at once to the Earl to tell him the news.

'What's this? We will return to Caerphilly at once,' roared the Earl when he read the letter. His skin turned green with envy and his face contorted with rage.

'Find Gruffudd the Fair and hang him from the nearest tree,' he ordered. Hearing that he was a wanted man, Gruffudd fled, before the soldiers arrived. The demented Earl returned to Caerphilly seeking vengeance on his unfaithful wife.

'I will not kill you, Alice. That would be too easy. You will return to Angouleme where you will remain a prisoner for the rest of your days,' said the Earl. His men dragged the sobbing Alice away.

When Gruffudd heard that his beloved Alice had gone forever, he sought out the friar that had betrayed him. He caught the wicked monk and hung him from a tree. Before long, Gilbert de Clare captured Gruffudd the Fair and he too was left dangling at the end of a rope.

'You will take a message to my wife, immediately. Tell her that her young lover hangs from a tall ash tree outside the castle and his putrid, rotting body will remain there as a reminder to others of her adultery,' ordered the Earl.

On hearing of her lover's death, Alice of Angouleme collapsed and died. Her heart had burst with grief. Since that day, the ghost of a woman dressed in fine clothing has wandered the halls of Caerphilly Castle, searching for her lost love. The spectre never speaks a word but a green mist, which some say is her husband's envy, follows in her footsteps.

Chapter 57...The Rise of Sir Gawain

'For it was located in a delightful spot in Glamorgan on the River Usk not far from the Severn Sea. Abounding in wealth more than other cities, it was suited for such a ceremony. For the noble river I have named flows along it on one side, upon which the kings and princes who would be coming from overseas could be carried by ship. But on the other side, protected by meadow and woods, it was remarkable for royal palaces, so that it imitated Rome in the golden roofs of its buildings. Famous for so many pleasant features, Caerleon was made ready for the announced feast.'

'History of the Kings of Britain'
Geoffrey of Monmouth - (1100 – 1155).

Geoffrey of Monmouth tells us how Uther Pendragon united the people to fight the Saxons and became King of Britain. He sired two children Arthur and Anna. As a young woman Anna fell in love with Lot, King of Orkney and Lothian and had a son by him. She was unmarried and concealed the birth from her family. She named the boy Gwalchmei, which translates as Gawain and sent him away with a trusted merchant.

'Promise me you will tell no one his real identity, not even Gawain himself, until he is full grown,' she said. The merchant agreed and swore a binding oath.

'Here is a gold ring and a letter to prove who he is and a chest of gold. Give them to him when he is a man,' commanded Anna. When King Lot discovered the child was gone he flew into a rage. His love turned to hate. He made Anna a prisoner and locked her in the tallest tower of his castle.

The merchant took the infant and travelled abroad but their ship floundered. A fisherman discovered the wreckage. He searched and found the baby. It was alive. Nearby was the chest. The fisherman opened the chest and read the letter. He saw the ring tied around the infant's neck. He gave the baby to his barren wife to nurse and the three of them travelled to Rome. Now wealthy, the fisherman lived like royalty and when the boy reached the age of

15 he was sent for military training. The child had grown into a powerful man and learned the skills of war quickly. He was slow to anger but quick to attack, chivalrous to women, courteous to men but merciless in battle. The young warrior was a brave soldier and was knighted for his valour.

'What name?' asked the Emperor as he placed a crimson tunic over the youth's armour.

'I have no name,' replied the youth.

'Then you shall be known as the 'Knight of the Surcoat',' said the Emperor and pointed to the tunic. One day the fisherman, who was now old, told the young knight how he had been discovered in the wreckage.

'Here is the ring and letter I found with you,' he said.

'You have kept this secret for all these years! I will go to Britannia and discover my true identity,' announced the Knight of the Surcoat and set out to find his past.

By now Arthur was King and his royal palace was at Caerleon, near the mouth of the River Usk. One evening Arthur was chatting with Gwendolena, his wife, who some called Guinevere, when suddenly a strange look came into her face. She grinned at her husband.

'Why do you grin?' he asked.

'A stranger is coming from Rome, one who is strong enough to humiliate a King. He crosses the River Usk tonight.' She replied.

'That's not possible. The river is in flood,' replied Arthur.

'Look upstream where the water is shallower,' she replied and retired to bed. King Arthur summoned his retainer Sir Kay.

'Saddle two horses and put on your armour,' he commanded.

'But Sire, it is late. Where are we going?' asked Sir Kay.

'We ride north along the river to find a stranger,' said the King. The King and his Knight followed the river for many miles looking for a likely crossing place. They reached the ford at Usk.

'The water runs deep and fast, Sire. No one can cross here,' said Sir Kay.

'Then we will go on, further upstream,' ordered the King and spurred his horse on. Later, they came to a stone cross, near a bend in the river.

'What place is this?' asked the King.

'That's the preaching cross of Llanover,' answered Sir Kay, pointing to the cross.

'Let us rest here for a moment,' said the King. He stepped down from his mount and sat wearily on the base of the cross. As they rested, a mounted figure wearing a crimson tunic appeared on the far side of the river.

'Is the water shallow enough to cross here?' called the figure.

'Go back and cross when it is light,' replied King Arthur.

'No man tells me what to do,' replied the figure. He threw back his cloak and lowered his lance. His armour shone in the moonlight.

'He means to fight,' said Sir Kay and advanced to protect his King.

'Stand fast. I will deal with this impudent lout myself,' said Arthur. Quickly he mounted his horse and charged across the river. The King never got to the other side. With a deft flick of his lance the Knight of the Surcoat pitched Arthur, ungraciously into the River. Sir Kay dashed after the King, intent on avenging his master's fall. But with another deft flick, he too was tossed into the freezing water. When Arthur and Sir Kay reached the riverbank their attacker had vanished.

'Where are the horses?' demanded the King.

'They galloped away Sire,' replied Sir Kay. It took the bedraggled men several hours to walk back to Camelot.

'Why are you soaking wet and covered in mud?' asked Guinevere with a grin.

'It's raining and some of the men were fighting in the yard. I went to stop them,' fibbed the embarrassed King and fell into bed without removing his tunic. Within moments he was fast asleep.

Guinevere dressed and went to the great hall. Suddenly, a page entered the hall.

'Your majesty, the King's horse has returned. It's caked with mud and sweating hard,' said the page.

'But the King has not ridden his horse tonight. He told me so,' said the queen. The page said nothing.

'Take the King's horse to his bed chamber and leave it there. They can dry off together,' laughed Guinevere. The King was woken early when his horse sat on the bed. His cries echoed around the palace. Later that morning, the Knight of the Surcoat entered the palace. He bowed before King Arthur.

'I am the Knight of the Surcoat. I come from Rome to offer my services,' said the Knight.

'You!' cried the king.

'I beg your humble pardon Your Majesty. In the dark, I thought I was being challenged by ruffians. I did not know my attacker was a King,' said the Knight.

'Never mind that. What do you want at Caerleon?' demanded Arthur, changing the subject.

'I have come to join your Round Table and to discover my true identity. I have a ring and a letter which I believe will reveal my past,' replied the Knight.

'No Knight can join the Round Table without first proving himself. As for finding your true identity, I wish you luck,' said the King.

'I will prove myself. Who is your worst enemy?' asked the Knight of the Surcoat.

'A pagan King of the North who keeps a Lady prisoner in his castle against her will. The Lady is my sister Anna,' replied Arthur.

'If I rescue Lady Anna will you help me find out who I am?' said the Knight.

'To rescue the Lady from such an impregnable fortress would indeed prove your valour. I agree to your request,' replied the King.

When the Knight of the Surcoat returned with the Lady Anna and the head of the pagan King Lot on his lance Arthur kept his pledge. The courtiers gathered in the great hall.

'Show me your ring and the letter,' he commanded. The Knight of the Surcoat undid his tunic to reveal a ring, hanging from a gold chain around his neck. He offered the ring to King Arthur. Then, he removed a crumpled letter from a small pouch and handed it to the King. The King studied them both carefully. He looked confused as he held the ring up to the light.

'Let me see them,' cried Anna and pushed herself forward. She seized the ring and recognised it at once. She shrieked and threw her arms around the Knight.

'My son!' she cried.

'What is my name?' asked the Knight of the Surcoat.

'You are Gawain. You are my Son and King Arthur is your uncle,' she replied. Tears of joy ran down her face. The courtiers cheered as Gawain knelt humbly before Lady Anna, the mother he had rescued and returned safely to Caerleon.

'Arise Sir Gawain. I dub you a Knight of the Round Table,' commanded King Arthur and the young Knight rose up and stood proudly with his family.

Chapter 58...King Tewdrig's Return

Dear as remembered kisses after death,
And sweet as those by hopeless fancy feign'd
On lips that are for others; deep as love,
Deep as first love, and wild with all regret;
O Death in Life, the days that are no more!
    'Tears, Idle Tears' – Alfred Lord Tennyson.

The ancient Book of Llandaff tells of the 6th Century when King Tewdrig was the ruler of Gwent. Tewdrig was a pious man and a good King. His people loved and respected him. He reigned for many years. Tewdrig had a son named Meurig. Prince Meurig enjoyed being a loyal prince but, like others since, he coveted the throne for himself. One day Meurig went to his father.

'Father, do you like being the king?' he asked.

'Yes. I do like being the king. Besides, it's my job. Why do you ask such a question?' replied his father.

'It must be very tiring having to look regal and give orders all the time,' said Meurig.

'I don't mind,' replied the king.

'Why don't you retire? Then you could spend more time enjoying yourself, doing things you want to do instead of working all the time. I would be happy to do the job for you,' suggested Meurig helpfully.

'I'll think about what you have said,' replied King Tewdrig. A few days later King Tewdrig summoned his son.

'I have carefully considered what you said and have decided to renounce the throne. Here is the royal crown. I give it to you,' said Tewdrig and handed the crown to his son. A royal coronation was arranged and Meurig was formally crowned as the new King of Gwent.

'What are you going to do now that you are retired?' King Meurig asked his father.

'I am going to live in a little place I know by the River Wye called Tyndyrn. It's a calm place where I will meditate and the fishing is quite good,' replied Tewdrig. He left the royal court quietly the following day and made his way to his new home. Tewdrig soon found that he liked not being king anymore and was glad. He spent his days happily fishing, praying and resting.

'Life is good,' he said to himself. At first, King Meurig found his royal duties quite easy. The people obeyed their new king and everything went well until one day a messenger arrived.

'I bring dire news, Majesty. A Saxon army is approaching from the east. It will be here in three days,' announced the messenger.

'Why does a Saxon army come here?' asked the King.

'They mean to seize your kingdom, Sire,' replied the messenger. King Meurig summoned his advisors.

'What are we to do?' he cried.

'You are the king. You must lead our army into battle and drive the Saxons away,' replied the advisors. Suddenly, King Meurig did not want to be king any more.

'I abdicate,' he wailed and snatched the crown from his head.

'You cannot abdicate. There is no one else to do the job,' replied the advisors. King Meurig knew they were right. Then an idea came to him. He travelled to Tyndyrn and found his father sitting by the river.

'Father, I have come to ask you to return. I am not ready to be king,' said Meurig and handed the crown to his father. Tewdrig looked up at his son and saw fear in his eyes.

'What is wrong?' he asked.

'A Saxon horde is approaching. The heathens mean to steal the kingdom from us,' said Meurig. Tewdrig stood up.

'I will return. Gather our army and meet me at Pont-y-Saeson as the sun comes up tomorrow. We will stand and fight together,' said Tewdrig and placed the crown on his head.

'I will do as you command, Sire,' replied Meurig and bowed to his father. King Tewdrig slept badly that night and dreamed of the coming battle. He saw himself lying injured on the ground then

210

being carried to safety on a cart. He watched as men at arms bathed his bleeding head. Then, he saw himself laid in a bed with clean blankets. Outside the sun was shining and birds were singing. King Tewdrig woke with a start. The room was dark and his bed was wet; soaked with perspiration.

The army was ready when King Tewdrig arrived. The men cheered as Tewdrig and his son rode forward, towards the enemy. The battle was fierce and the army of Gwent, led by King Tewdrig, won the day but they did not celebrate. Their king had fallen. A Saxon axe had split his skull and he lay mortally wounded on the ground. Meurig tenderly lifted his father onto a cart.

The men hitched oxen to the cart and slowly took the wounded king away. King Tewdrig cried in pain with every jolt of the wagon. Hearing his terrible cries the men stopped repeatedly and lifted the stricken king from the cart to rest. Each time his body touched the ground, a spring appeared and fresh water bubbled up. The men used the water to wash the blood from the gaping wound. They travelled for three days until they reached the village of Mathern, the place of King Tewdrig's birth.

When King Tewdrig woke he was in a bed. His head lay on a pillow filled with goose feathers and fine woollen blankets covered his body. Outside birds sang in the sunshine. King Tewdrig smiled. He was content. He had returned. Then, with a quiet sigh, he died.

Meurig honoured his father's memory by giving the land at Tyndyrn to the church and today, 1500 years later, visitors flock to view the ruin of the great abbey that is known as Tintern, unaware of how King Tewdrig returned from there, to save his kingdom.

Chapter 59...The Legend of Llyn Syfaddan (Langorse Lake)

Brychan, King of Brycheiniog, ruled in the 9th Century. His kingdom lay in the lands of the Black Mountains. King Brychan ruled his subjects from a regal palace, a strange place that many who saw it said, floated on a vast lake. But it did not float. Brychan, like his Irish ancestors before him, lived on an island in the middle of a lake. The palace sat high above the water surrounded by great wooden piles, like huge sentinels standing guard. The people called the lake Brecknock Mere, in honour of their king, and marvelled at his fine palace on the water.

The king was a wealthy man. His palace was filled with beautiful objects. Gold and silver coins filled his treasury. He had enough riches for any king but he was not satisfied. King Brychan was a greedy man. Avarice was his obsession and a desire for money the demon that drove him. King Brychan had a beautiful daughter. She was in love with one of the king's subjects: a youth of low status. One day the boy, encouraged by the king's daughter, paddled out to the palace in his dugout canoe.

'Why have you come to my palace?' demanded the king.

'I have come to ask for your daughter's hand in marriage,' replied the lovesick young man.

'Do you have any money to keep her?' inquired the king.

'Not one penny to my name, your Majesty, but we are in love,' answered the youth. King Brychan laughed at the young man.

'Love will not feed her boy, and it will not buy her for your bride. If you are serious in your desire, leave here and make your fortune. Return rich, pay me well and you will have her hand,' said the king. The youth paddled away from the palace broken hearted but a determination burned like a hot flame in his chest.

'Somehow, I will win her!' he whispered to himself.

'But how?' a voice in his head enquired. As he reached the shore a desperate plan began to form in his furtive mind. Abbot Ecgberht was a Saxon emissary who travelled the land visiting the different rulers and keeping the peace but that was not his only occupation. He was also a merchant who used his position to increase his wealth. One day the Abbot arrived at the king's palace. King Brychan welcomed his visitor.

'Come and sit down, Abbot. Let us talk business,' invited the king. It was dark when the Abbot returned to the shore. The youth was waiting. He leapt out of the shadows and struck the Abbot's head with a cudgel. The single blow killed Abbot Ecgberht instantly. Then the youth took the Abbots heavy bag and opened it. The bag was full of gold. The youth took the lifeless body and dragged it into his canoe. He paddled across the lake and pushed the corpse into water so deep it would never be found. When the youth returned to the palace, he was dressed in fine robes.

'I have come to claim my bride,' announced the youth.

'Do you have money to buy her?' demanded the king. The young man took out a silk purse and threw it on the table.

'Come. We will agree a price,' said the king and smiled at the youth. After the wedding, the married couple left on honeymoon and the king retired to count his money. In the moonlight a strange form floated on the lake. That night Saxon soldiers arrived at Brecknock Mere. They were looking for the missing Abbot. His body was found the following morning.

'What evil has happened here?' yelled the soldiers.

'Burn the palace,' cried the Saxon leader. The soldiers wanted revenge for the death of Abbot Ecgberht. They killed all the men, set fire to the palace and carried off the women. When the young man and his bride returned there was nothing left of the great palace but a smouldering ruin. They found a small island near the shore and built a crude shelter. That night they shivered and huddled together as a cold wind blew from the north. Then, there was a tremendous roar. A huge wave swept across the lake. In the morning the lake was calm. The sun shone down on the blue water. Birds waded in the shallows. Fish broke the still surface of the lake but the great palace; the little island with its crude shelter, the young man and his bride had all vanished.

Chapter 60...Y Bugail Unig (The Lonely Shepherd)

The shepherd spent his days on the mountains of Llangattock. It was a solitary life, wet and cold in winter, hot and dry in summer. Each season was different but all meant hard work for the shepherd. In winter his back strained as he carried fodder over the mountain to the pens so his sheep would not starve. In spring he worked through the nights to help them lamb. Before the hot days when the sun would be high in the sky he sheared the sheep and carried the heavy fleeces to market. In summer he would walk miles over the mountains searching for stray lambs. All year long he protected his flock from wolves and robbers. He didn't mind. His sheep were his living. This was his life. But a shepherd's life is lonely and a man that is alone grows sad.

One day the shepherd sat and looked around. His cottage was neglected and cold. His hearth un-swept and his clothes were un-mended. 'I need a wife,' muttered the shepherd. 'One who will look after me, mend my coat, keep a warming fire in the grate and put a hot supper on the table.'

The next day the shepherd went to town in search of a wife. He found a widow, a quiet, comely woman, in need of a home. He courted her and she agreed to be his wife. They married and she moved into his cottage. At first, the shepherd was pleased with the changes his new wife made. She cleaned the cottage and polished the grate. She scrubbed the table and repaired the curtains. She mended his coat and chopped wood for the fire. Each night they ate a hot supper and his wife would sew while he smoked. The shepherd was content.

One evening the shepherd came home after a long hard day on the mountain. He opened the door and went into the cottage.

'Get outside with those muddy boots. Can't you see, I've just cleaned the floor,' yelled his wife. The shepherd was shocked. His wife had never yelled at him before. He took off his boots and put them outside the door. The shepherd and his wife sat in silence as they ate supper. The following night the shepherd returned home from the mountain and found the cottage blazing with light. Laughter was coming from the open doorway and gay music filled the air. The shepherd went into the cottage and found it full of people.

'Who are these people in my house?' he cried.

'These are my friends, husband,' answered his wife and laughed. The shepherd was angry and threw the people out of the house.

'How dare you treat my friends, visiting me in my house, so badly,' cried his wife and threw the shepherd's supper into the fire. The shepherd went to bed in silence. The next day the shepherd got up early and roused his wife.

'Come, wife. There is work to do,' he said. He marched his wife up the mountain and made her help him gather the sheep. It was dark when they arrived home.

'Light the fire and get my supper,' ordered the shepherd in a loud voice. His wife was afraid of her husband's mood and did as she was told. Once more they ate in silence. In the morning the shepherd woke his wife before the sun had risen.

'Get dressed. We have sheep to shear today,' commanded the shepherd. The shepherd made his wife work all day long shearing the sheep and moving them from pen to pen. It was dark when they returned to the cottage.

'Why is there no firewood by the grate? Where is my supper?' demanded the shepherd.

'I am tired, husband. I have been working all day with you,' replied his wife.

Hearing his wife's answer, the shepherd flew into a rage.

'You lazy woman,' he yelled. Each day the shepherd made his wife work on the mountain until she was exhausted. Each night he scolded her for not doing her chores.

'The house is dirty,' he snapped.

'My clothes are not washed,' he sneered.

'You bake no bread and make no cheese. How do you expect us to eat?' he yelled. The husband's cruelty grew worse as the months passed. The shepherd's wife grew weary and sadness filled her heart. One evening, when they returned from the mountain and her husband began to rant and rage once more, the shepherd's wife ran from the house. Tears filled her eyes. She could take no more of her husband's browbeating. The poor woman ran to the River Usk, threw herself into the water and drowned.

Later, when she did not return, the shepherd began to look for his wife but she was nowhere to be found. The shepherd was alone once more and grew sad. He missed his wife and knew that he had behaved badly towards her.

'If only I could find my wife and take back my hurtful words,' he thought. Every day he searched for his wife. Then, one day, he did not return. His sheep grew wild on the mountain and his cottage fell into ruin.

The people found the lonely shepherd high on the mountain. Because of his cruelty, the shepherd had been turned into a pillar of rock and stood like a silent sentinel looking down on the valley where his wife had vanished. The people named the rock Y Bugail Unig or, in English, the Lonely Shepherd.

Each Midsummer's Eve, in the light of the moon, the rock returns to human form and the lonely shepherd once more roams the land, calling for his lost wife. For many years after his cruel acts the women of the valley, fearful of meeting the lonely shepherd, would whitewash Y Bugail Unig to be sure of seeing him approaching through the darkness.

Chapter 61...Dafydd Gam (The Cross Eyed Knight)

Fluellen: 'If your Majesty is remembered of it, the Welshmen did good service in a garden where leeks did grow, wearing leeks in their Monmouth caps, which your Majesty knows, to this hour is an honourable badge of the service, and I do believe, your Majesty takes no scorn to wear the leek upon Saint Tavy's day'.
King Henry: 'I wear it for a memorable honour; for I am Welsh, you know, good countryman'.
Henry V- William Shakespeare

Dafydd ap Llewelyn ap Hywel Fychan ap Hywel ap Einion Sais, which in English means David, son of Llewelyn, son of Hywel Fychan, son of Hywel, son of Einion Sais was from a Breconshire family that could trace its line back to the ancient Welsh kings. By the 14th Century the family was prospering under English rule. Dafydd was a short, stocky youth with powerful shoulders and stout legs but his eyes were so crossed that they stared at each other across his nose. Because of this, he was known as Dafydd Gam; gam being a Welsh word for lame or deformed from which the English word 'gammy' is taken.

As a boy, he was teased for his gammy eyes until one day when he was walking through Brecon, a man approached him and laughed at his crossed eyes. It was the final insult. Dafydd Gam lost his temper and struck the man so hard that he killed him.

'You must go away from here,' said his father.

'But where should I go, father?' asked Dafydd Gam.

'The army is a safe place to hide,' replied his father. Dafydd Gam did as his father said and enlisted in the service of Henry of Monmouth, Prince of Wales. Dafydd was a courageous fighter and his bravery was soon recognised by the young Henry. Promotion followed and Dafydd's brothers joined him in the army.

'My father, the King, has commanded me to crush Owain Glyndwr and end his rebellion. Are you with me?' said Prince Henry.

'We are your sworn liege men and will do as you command,' replied Dafydd and his brothers. When Owain Glyndwr heard that Dafydd Gam and his brothers had sided with the English he was furious.

'Dafydd Gam is a crooked man and his brothers are traitors to their own people,' cried Glyndwr. From that day on Glyndwr and Dafydd Gam were enemies. As the civil war raged, Dafydd Gam played a major role against Glyndwr and on 5th May 1405 he defeated Glyndwr at a battle near Usk, capturing Glyndwr's son and 300 men.

'Execute all the prisoners except Glyndwr's son,' he ordered after the battle. Despite the defeat, Glyndwr's rebellion continued and in 1412 his men captured Dafydd Gam.

'You spared my son at Usk. In return, if you swear an oath never again to bear arms against any Welshman I will ransom you for release to the English,' offered Glyndwr. Dafydd Gam swore the oath and, with the ransom paid, was released.

Then his master, Henry Prince of Wales was crowned Henry V.

'Come with me. Let us find and destroy Glyndwr together,' ordered the King.

'I cannot, for I have sworn a sacred oath,' replied Dafydd. 'But your majesty, I can tell you where he is,' he added.

'Burn Dafydd Gam's house and barns to the ground,' cried Glyndwr when he heard of the treachery.

'You are still my liege man and I have work for you, Dafydd Gam. We are at war with France. Bring your archers,' said the king. Dafydd gathered stout men from the valleys of South Wales. Men came from Penderyn and Bryn Mawr, from Carmarthen in the west and Caer Llan in the east. They cut branches from yew trees to make war bows and felled birch trees to fill their quivers with arrows. Dafydd Gam and his archers joined King Henry V in a muddy field in Northern France on the 25th October 1415.

'Your archers look spirited and ready for a fight. You have done well Dafydd,' said the King and drew his sword.

'Kneel before me,' he commanded. Dafydd dropped to his knees and bowed his head.

'Arise Sir Llewelyn,' said the King and laid the sword on Dafydd's shoulders.

'Now, my friends, we are outnumbered six to one but the day shall be ours.' The king and his knights rode towards the French and dismounted, ready to fight on foot in the mud with their men. A great roar went up from the English army and it advanced towards the French. The archers let fly. Arrows cut down the French in swathes. Wounded and dead covered the ground. Then, the archers threw down their bows and ran forward with swords and axes. King Henry was in the centre of the battle, surrounded by Frenchmen and in mortal danger.

'Protect the King,' cried Dafydd Gam and leapt to his defence. A French knight slashed a plume from the Kings helmet. Dafydd cut him down. Another lunged at the King with a pike. Dafydd ran him through with his sword. As the battle raged, French soldiers and knights threw down their arms and surrendered.

'Sire. We are being attacked from the rear,' cried a knight.

'Kill the prisoners,' ordered the King. It was a pitiful sight as the cream of French nobility was butchered in cold blood. Seeing their friends being killed so callously, the attacking French turned and fled. The battle was won.

'Bring Dafydd Gam to me. He saved my life,' said the King.

'He is dead your Majesty,' replied his men.

'A more loyal man I never knew. He was closer than a brother to me,' said the King.

Today, Dafydd Gam is remembered with a stained glass window in the north wall of Llantilio Crossenny church. The Latin inscription reads 'David Gam, golden haired knight, Lord of the manor of Llantilio Crossenny, killed on the field of Agincourt 1415'.

Chapter 62...The Love of Gwladus and Einion

Brychan of Brycheiniog was a 5th century King. He had 24 daughters. All of them were beautiful but the most beautiful of his daughters was Gwladus. Her hair shimmered in the sunlight, her skin glowed with health and her innocent smile melted the hearts of all who saw her. Each day Gwladus and her sisters would walk to the river where they would bathe. As they walked they would talk of love and romance, of brave knights in shining armour and noble deeds of chivalry. They laughed and teased each other as they washed.

'I will marry a handsome prince with delicate hands and fine manners,' cried one.

'You will marry a blacksmith with huge black hands who eats like a peasant,' answered another.

'My husband will be rich and I will live in a grand palace,' laughed the next.

'Your husband will be fat and bald and you will live in a cave,' taunted another. As her sisters chatted and giggled, Gwladus sat quietly by the river.

'Gwladus, what kind of husband do you want to marry?' asked a sister.

Gwladus stroked the water. It felt cold and clean, refreshing and thrilling. She felt awake and happy.

'What kind of husband you ask? He may be fat or thin, tall or short, rich or poor. It doesn't matter to me,' she answered and smiled at her sisters.

'But what if he is bald? Would you marry him then?' asked a sister.

'Possibly,' replied Gwladus.

'Would you marry him if he was ugly,' asked another.

'Probably,' replied Gwladus.

'If he only had one leg, one arm and one ear, would you marry him then?' asked another.

'Perhaps,' replied Gwladus. The sisters crowded around Gwladus.

'Tell us,' they cried, 'What kind of man would you refuse to wed?'

'There is one kind of man that I would never marry,' answered Gwladus.

'One kind. What kind is that?' asked the sisters together.

'The kind of man I will not wed is any man without true love in his heart,' said Gwladus. At hearing her answer the sisters fell quiet, each considering what she had said. One by one the sisters left their father's home. One married a prince with fine hands, another a blacksmith with horny black hands, one a rich merchant and another a farmer. One, named Dwynwen, went to live the pious life of a nun. (Her story is told in 'Walking with Welsh Legends, north Wales'.) Like her other sisters, Gwladus had many suitors. Some were wealthy, others great warriors. A King travelled from a distant land to win the beautiful Gwladus.

'They would all make good husbands and every one asks me for your hand. Which of these fine suitors do you chose?' demanded her Father, King Brychan.

'None, father. They are the wrong kind,' replied Gwladus.

'The wrong kind. What nonsense is this?' said her Father.

'These are men that just want me for my beauty, to possess me. Not one has true love in his heart,' said the princess. Brychan pleaded with his daughter but she was resolute and refused all offers of marriage.

Alone now, Gwladus still went to the river each day to bathe. One day, as she sat watching the water cascade over the rocks, a man appeared. He was walking through the wood collecting kindling. A large bundle of twigs was tied to his back. The man saw Gwladus and smiled. He walked towards her.

'Good day, my Lady. My load is heavy. May I sit with you and rest a while?' asked the man.

Without waiting for her reply the man untied his bundle and sat down beside Gwladus.

'I am Einion. I live in a cottage further down the valley. What is your name?' said the man.

'I am Gwladus. I live with my Father Brychan,' replied Gwladus. She felt strange, somehow excited but not afraid. The princess, Gwladus and the peasant, Einion sat and talked as if they were old friends. The hours passed and the sun began to sink behind the mountain.

'It will be dark soon. I must go,' said Gwladus.

'Will you come again tomorrow?' asked Einion.

'I come to the river every day,' replied Gwladus. Each day Gwladus returned to the river and each day Einion would meet her. The young couple would talk for hours. Gwladus enjoyed Einion's company. They were kindred spirits with no secrets and there was no pretence between them. Talking was easy and, as the days passed, affection grew between the happy pair. Gwladus was in love. She had found the right man to share her life, a man with true love in his heart.

'I will ask your Father for your hand,' said Einion and approached the King to ask for his permission to marry Gwladus.

'Will you consent and bless our union?' he asked.

'I will not. You will never marry my daughter,' replied the King.

'But my lord, we are in love,' pleaded Einion.

'Love! What use is love? Love will not keep my daughter. You have no land. You have no position and you have no prospects. I will never permit such a foolish marriage,' said the King. The King would not listen to the forlorn lovers as they begged him to change his mind. He would not be swayed. The decision was final. Gwladus ran from the palace with tears in her eyes. Einion stayed behind to try once more and change the King's mind.

'My lord. If I can earn wealth and position would you then reconsider?' he asked.

'Einion. You are an honest boy but you have nothing. If an Einion of status and property came to woo my daughter things would be very different. But that will never be,' replied the King.

'Thank you my lord. Now, I understand what I must do to win your daughter's hand,' said Einion. He left the palace to find Gwladus and tell her the good news. Gwladus was sat by the river, weeping. She felt as if her heart had been stabbed with a shard of ice. Suddenly, she jumped up and threw herself into the fast running water, unwilling to live without her one true love by her side. Einion ran to the river but he was too late. The ground shook and the trees swayed. The river roared and swept the princess away. When she was gone, the water calmed and Einion saw that a beautiful waterfall had appeared where Gwladus had entered the river.

The love struck youth was distraught with anguish. He paced the riverbank calling her name but there was no answer except the sound of the water cascading across the rocks. Gwladus had vanished into the river, forever. Einion's heart broke. He could stand the grief no longer and, in a final act of love, he threw himself into the icy water. Once more, the earth shuddered and the trees shook and then all was calm. Einion was gone but now there was a second waterfall above the first.

The two lovers were never seen again but, to this day, their spirits have been together in the magical water of the Afon Pyrddin and can never be parted. Today the waterfalls created by their sad deaths are known as Sgwd Gwladus and Sgwd Einion Gam. The waterfalls are beautiful features of the landscape and a fitting monument to the couples' young, impetuous love.

Chapter 63...The Hermits of Llanthony Priory

In the deep vale of Ewyas, which is about an arrow-shot broad, encircled on all sides by lofty mountains, stands the church of Saint John the Baptist, covered with lead, and built of wrought stone; and, considering the nature of the place, not unhandsomely constructed, on the very spot where the humble chapel of Dewi, the bishop, had formerly stood decorated only with moss and ivy.
Gerald Cambrensis – Gerald of Wales 1146 - 1223

There was once a secluded valley hidden from view in the east of Wales. The south end of the valley was boggy and impassable. There were high mountains to the west, the north and the east. The only way into the valley was over the mountain along a narrow pass. The people called it the Gospel Pass because it was the route that holy men took searching for solitude. It was along this path that St. David walked as he entered the valley. The saint was looking for somewhere to rest, to meditate and to pray. He stopped at a grassy spot near the river and knew it was the place he was seeking. He built a small cell to shelter from the rain and there he lived, in communion with God, waiting for his calling.

Years later, in 1108, another man entered the valley. He was a knight, William de Lacy. He came from a noble Norman family. His ancestors had arrived in Britain with William the Conqueror. They had fought at the battle of Hastings and were rewarded for their loyalty with vast estates in Ireland, Wales and England. William de Lacy was a man of pleasure. He enjoyed the good things in life and spent his days hunting, riding and any other forms of entertainment he could think of.

The days hunting had been good. Sir William had seen a big stag on the mountain and galloped after it. His squire and friend, Erinisius struggled to keep up as they chased the majestic animal through the trees.

'Have you ever seen such a magnificent beast? Where is he?' cried Erinisius.

'Come on. He's heading down into the valley,' replied Sir William. The two men spurred on their horses. When they got to the valley floor, the stag had vanished. The horses were covered with sweat and blowing hard.

'We will rest the horses here, by the river,' said Sir William. The two men dismounted and allowed the horses to drink.

'What's that strange little hut over there?' asked Erinisius. He had seen the cell which St. David had built years before. Sir William and his companion walked over to the hut.

'This is a strange, tranquil place. I feel joyful, relaxed and somehow at peace with the world,' said Sir William. The two men sat on the soft grass and looked at the mountains that surrounded them. They did not speak. Hours later Sir William stirred.

'Can you feel it? There is a presence. Something is here in this valley with us,' he said quietly. Sir William and Erinisius were enchanted. That very afternoon, the two men decided to stay in the valley and build a church where the little hut was standing. Day and night they laboured. They carried rocks to build the walls. They carved heavy beams and rafters to support the ceiling. They cut and split slates to make a roof.

Hearing news of their work in the valley, curious people visited. They wanted to see why a nobleman was toiling with his hands like a serf. The beauty of the valley was captivating and many men stayed to help. Before long, an Abbey was built and forty canons filled the pews.

'Sir William, will you lead us and be our Abbot?' asked the canons.

'Not I. You need someone with a purer heart than mine. Erinisius is a good man. He used to be the Queen's chaplain. He shall be Abbot,' replied the knight. At first, life at the Abbey was hard but, before long, rich patrons, seeking absolution for their sins, donated land and made gifts of money. The Abbey prospered. The canons worked the land growing wheat and brewing beer. They took fish from nearby lakes and feasted on venison and wild boar.

The hungry peasants watched the canons grow fat and their good living created jealousy and resentment. There were violent attacks and, by 1160, only 52 years after it had been built, the Abbey at Llanthony was abandoned. The canons had been driven out. They took all the valuables and retreated to a new house in Gloucester. Fifteen years later a message arrived at the holy order in Gloucester.

'I command you to return to the ruined Abbey at Llanthony and build a new Priory. I will pay for the work to be done,' said the message.

'Who dares give us this bold command,' sneered the canons. They read the seal: Sir Hugh de Lacy. It was Sir William's heir.

'How can we refuse? We must return and complete our work,' said the canons. Never in their lives had the canons worked so hard. Their bodies grew thin and their sinews strengthened. Their skin turned brown as they toiled under the hot sun. Their cassocks grew ragged as they laboured. Slowly, a beautiful Priory grew from the Abbey ruin. Fine pillars soared high above the chancel. Coloured light flooded the aisle through stained glass windows. Music filled the vaulted Priory. They had created one of the most beautiful gothic buildings in the land.

But, when the building work was finished, the canons grew idle and slowly they returned to their old ways. They ate and drank and grew fat. Once again, the people resented their lazy existence and turned against them. Fearing attack, many of the canons ran away.

There were only four canons left at Llanthony Priory when, in 1538, news of a royal decree arrived.

'By command of his Majesty King Henry VIII all monasteries are hereby dissolved and all church property now belongs to the crown.' The four canons were given a pension of £8 and sent on their way. It was the end of Llanthony Priory as a house of God. Today, its ruin stands as a monument to the power of wealthy men and the destructive folly in their hearts.

Chapter 64...Sir Harry's Revenge

'The fate proclaimed – Sir Harry rose
To name the pirates parting time,'
The final hour that here should close
His dark career of crime.'
Taken from a poem by Taliesin Williams, published in 1837.

'Don't go. Your voyage will end in tears,' cried Lady
Elizabeth Stradling as her husband climbed down the ladder into
the boat, his faithful servant Dewryn following close behind.

'Don't be foolish, woman. You can't see the future. It was
just a dream. Nothing is going to happen,' called her husband as the
crew untied the mooring ropes. It was a bright summer morning, in
1449, when Sir Harry Stradling left Somerset. The voyage across
the Bristol Channel, to visit his Castle and Estate at St. Donats,
Wales, was one he regularly undertook. The wind was fair and the
tide was turning as the St. Barbe left the harbour at Minehead and
sailed slowly across the shimmering blue water of the channel.
Seagulls circled overhead, shrieking and diving in the wake of the
boat. Sir Harry did not pay any attention to the barque further
offshore. He did not see the spyglass watching him or notice the
ship turn towards them and tighten its sheets to catch the wind. He
did not know the Sea Swallow was a pirate ship.

The pirate Captain, Colyn Dolphyn, a Breton brute and a
bloody villain had found his next prize. His ship was fast and his
crew were cutthroats. They quickly came alongside the St. Barbe
and boarded her. Colyn Dolphyn was first aboard with his cutlass at
the ready.

'Throw the crew into the sea, they can swim for shore. We
have our prize. Now search the ship. What cargo does she carry?
Wait who's this; a gentleman I see?' cried the pirate chief. They
seized Sir Harry and his man and bound them hand and foot.

'Come Dewryn. Do not fret. We shall soon escape,'
whispered Sir Harry to his squire.

'Tell me where your money is or I will seal your fate,' ordered the evil pirate, grinning as he spoke.

'I am Sir Harry Stradling. You cannot threaten me. My money is safe at home out of reach of thee,' replied Sir Harry, defiantly.

'If that is so then you will stay and we shall send a note. Your money for your life, a simple, open trade.' They took Sir Harry and his man aboard the pirate ship.

'Where are you taking us?' asked the Knight.

'To Lundy Island, our pirate lair, where you will live until your ransom's paid,' answered Dolphyn. The pirates set Dewryn free to deliver their ransom demand. Dolphyn wanted 2200 marks. It was a huge amount but Sir Harry was a wealthy man. When Lady Elizabeth read the ransom note tears came to her eyes. Her dream of disaster had come true.

'There is no cash to send,' wailed Elizabeth.

'My Lady, Sir Harry said to sell his land to pay the evil rogue,' said Dewryn. It took Lady Elizabeth two years to raise the money by selling her husband's estates in Bassaleg and Rogerstone. Dewryn delivered the ransom to the Pirate Dolphyn and Sir Harry was eventually released. He returned to St. Donats, a vengeful and bitter man. Colyn Dolphyn and his pirate crew continued their evil ways: seizing ships and striking terror into the hearts of honest sailors.

Sir Harry built a lookout tower and men stood watch day and night. They scanned the sea and waited while Sir Harry made his plan to trap the evil pirate and kill him.

'Dewryn. I want you to go to Bristol and visit taverns there. Tell all that I am mad and have taken all my treasure to be hidden in the sand, to hide it from the pirates and the robbers that abound,' said Sir Harry with a smile.

'But you have no money left to hide,' replied Dewryn.

'I know that but our story is a sneaky lure to tempt Dolphyn here,' said Sir Harry with a wink. News of the hidden treasure soon reached the pirates lair and days later the lookouts watched the pirate ship appear. They came ashore to search for gold but got a big surprise when Sir Harry and his men at arms sprang out and seized them all. The trial was brief and brutal. The sentence quickly passed, while they stood there on the beach.

'Hang the crew this morning and bury them right here but not the Captain of the crew. Colyn Dolphyn and his ship belongs to me,' said Sir. Harry. They took the evil pirates and hung them in a line while Dolphyn stared and pondered on his doom.

'But what of me?' cried Colyn Dolphyn, no longer looking brave.

'You will come with me, my evil friend, and soon shall know your fate,' said Sir Harry with a sneer. They dragged the captured pirate chief to a cave in Tresillian Bay and made him dig a hole, below the high tide mark.

'Now bury him, up to his neck and leave him in the dark. A fitting end for a wicked man,' said Sir Harry, as they left. The screams were heard for miles around until the tide came in and drowned Colyn Dolphyn, which finally finished him. The sound of his screams still haunts Tresillian. Sir Harry had taken his revenge.

Following the summary and illegal execution of Colyn Dolphyn, King Henry VI pursued Sir Harry Stradling for murder. Sir Harry left Britain and travelled, as a pilgrim, to Jerusalem. He died on the Island of Cyprus, in 1453, during the return journey and is buried in Famagusta.

Part Five North eastern Wales

Chapter 65..Saint Winefride's Well

Tyfid ap Eiludd was a 7th Century Welsh nobleman who had a daughter named Winefride. In modern English her name would be Winifred. Winefride was an attractive girl and, as she grew to womanhood, potential suitors began to court her. One attentive admirer was Caradoc. Caradoc was the son of a prince and, being of royal blood, was used to having what he wanted. At first he wooed her with gifts and soft words of love, confident that his blandishments would win her heart. When Winefride did not yield to his charms, Caradoc's longing grew stronger. Her rejection fanned the flames of his desire and he grew more determined to pluck the fruits of passion which Winefride declined to share.

The intensity of Caradoc's pursuit grew. He followed Winefride about like a love sick puppy. He commissioned scribes to write passionate sonnets, to gain her affection and wrote endless letters protesting his love for her. Still, for she was a virtuous woman, Winefride refused his advances.

Caradoc did not give up. No woman was going to refuse him. He turned to her father with promises of marriage for this was a time when these things were arranged and young women were mere chattels. Tyfid ap Eiludd listened to Caradoc's offer carefully. A union with a royal household would make a valuable alliance.

When Winefride learned that her father was negotiating dowry terms with Caradoc she was distraught. She knew that, as a daughter, she could not refuse her father if he commanded her to marry the prince. It was her duty to obey her father.

'I do not love him, Father,' said Winefride, when her father told her the news that she was pledged to marry Prince Caradoc.

'It's a good match. You will be a dutiful wife and, who knows, one day you may grow to love him,' replied her father. The idea of marriage to Prince Caradoc frightened Winefride, for the prince was a conceited man with the manners of a peasant and a violent temper. Winefride was repelled by his coarse behaviour and knew that she could never be happy with such a brute. But what could she do? Her father had given his word and now she was betrothed.

Then, an idea came to Winefride. She would visit her Great Aunt Tenoi, the Abbess at Gwytherin. Aunt Tenoi was a wise woman. She would know what Winefride must do.

'You poor girl! To escape your fate, you must pledge your life to another; one that is more regal than any prince,' said the Abbess, when she heard Winefride's sorry tale. Winefride listened carefully while her aunt explained what needed to be done. When Winefride returned home her father was horrified.

'What have you done?' He demanded, staring at her new clothes.

'Father, I cannot marry Prince Caradoc for another, higher, deity has chosen me,' answered Winefride. Tyfid ap Eiludd looked at the nun's habit his daughter was wearing and realised that she would never submit to be Caradoc's wife. Instead, she had accepted a greater calling and had married Almighty God.

'By your action you have broken my promise to a prince and brought shame on our house but if what you have done makes you happy I am content,' said her father. Tears of joy ran down Winefride's face as she ran from the hall. Her father had forgiven her and the bonds of marriage to Prince Caradoc were no longer tightening around her heart. She saw Caradoc coming towards her. His face was dark with anger and contorted with rage. He had already heard the news.

'Great Prince, do not be angry. I cannot marry you for I have been called by God and cannot refuse his plea,' said Winefride. Hearing Winefride confirming, beyond doubt, that his love had been thwarted, Caradoc lost control of himself. He drew his sword and, with one blow, struck Winefride's head from her shoulder.

'If you will not have me, then you will have no one, not even God Almighty.' He cried and gloated as Winefride's severed

232

head rolled down a grassy bank. Then, realising the evil he had done, all anger drained away leaving only remorse and pity for the woman he had slain so cruelly. Caradoc threw down his blood stained sword and fell to the ground sobbing. His sorrow and anguish was disturbed by a strange gurgling noise. A spring gushed up from beneath the lifeless head and a pool of water appeared where none had been before.

When Winefride's corpse was brought before her father he wept and could not be consoled. A great funeral was arranged for family and friends to pay their respects to a life so brutally cut short. Beuno, Winefride's maternal uncle was one of the mourners. On seeing the body of his niece, Beuno, had a vision and demanded that the body be returned to the place where she was murdered.

'Trust me, cousin,' he said to her father as the bier was carried, shoulder high, to the spring. The assembled mourners watched, curiously, as Beuno gently lowered the body into the water. He took the head and placed it where it belonged. All present witnessed what happened next. Winefride's body and head were rejoined and life returned to the body of the pious virgin who had pledged herself to God.

The miracle that Beuno performed that day was recounted across the land and Beuno was recognised as a saint. Hearing about the miracle, a generous benefactor gave to 'God and Saint Beuno' the town of Clynnog Fawr on the Llyn Peninsula where he built a great abbey.

Caradoc did not live long. Winefride's brother, Owain, hunted and slew the villain in revenge for his evil deed. Winefride honoured her solemn vows and lived the life of a nun for the rest of her life. She retreated to the Abbey at Gwytherin and eventually replaced her aunt as the abbess.

The spring that appeared when she was murdered has become a shrine, been recognised as having healing powers and been called the 'Lourdes of Wales'. For centuries it has been an important destination for pilgrims. In 1189, Richard I visited the shrine to pray for a successful crusade. Henry V is said to have walked there from Shrewsbury in 1416 and a chapel was built over the spring during the 15th Century. More recent visitors have included James II, whose barren wife became pregnant shortly after the visit, those involved in the gunpowder plot and, in 1829, by Princess Victoria.

Today, visitors travel from all over the world to visit the shrine and are still allowed to bathe in its sacred water. Although the Vatican never formally canonised Winefride, it recognised her as a person who lived an exemplary religious life and she is known as Saint Winefride by popular acclaim.

Chapter 66..Pwll-yr-Wrach (The Witches Pool).

There is a cold, dank, forbidding place on Flint Mountain known a 'Pwll-yr-Wrach' or 'The Witch's Pool.' Its reputation as a place of evil is well known. Strange creatures lurk in its deep, slimy waters. Close grown trees guard the pool and the sun rarely warms the putrid air that lingers above the quiet surface. It was not always thus. Once, the pond had been a meeting place for people. Young couples would visit to enjoy the sun, sparkling on the dappled water and make promises of eternal love. Timid animals would come to drink and nesting birds would sing with joy. But that was long ago. Few people venture to the pool now. The birds have flown and even the animals know better than to visit the 'Pwll-yr-Wrach.'

More than five hundred years ago King Henry VII or Harri Tudor, as he was known, often hunted on Flint Mountain. Wild boar and deer were plentiful. The sport was good and the king loved to test his skills with bow and lance. Harri Tudor was popular with the people for he was a Welshman and had seized the crown from the Plantagenet Richard III, with the support of Welsh archers, at the battle of Bosworth in 1485.

One day, the king's soldiers came across an old woman, named Malid Malwod, gathering firewood. Malid lived alone in a small hut on the mountain. She kept a few chickens and grew corn to supplement the wild berries and nuts she collected. It was a meagre existence. Once, Malid had been young and beautiful. She had loved but disease had contorted her features and driven her love away. Few could look at her without shuddering. Loneliness and disfigurement had crippled her mind and the old woman would roam the mountain shouting obscenities in a strange tongue and cackling.

When the king's soldiers saw Malid they recoiled at seeing her ugly face and were frightened by her shouting.

'She's a witch!' cried one.

'Keep away, you old hag,' ordered another.

Malid laughed at the soldiers and cursed them with evil words. Fearing the old woman would put a magic spell on them the soldiers grabbed and bound Malid. They stuffed her mouth with rags to stifle her cries and covered her face to hide her piercing eyes. They dragged Malid to a pond, tossed her frail body into the water and jeered as she writhed in the cold water. The soldiers threw stones at the old woman and taunted her. A rock hit her head and Malid stopped struggling. Her motionless body floated on the now still water. The soldiers stopped laughing and watched silently as the old woman sank slowly beneath the surface. As she vanished the sun disappeared and the soldiers shuddered. A cold feeling gripped their hearts and they hurried away. Malid Malwod was dead but, deep in the pool, something evil stirred in the mud.

Today, the pond is a forbidding gloomy place. People tell tales about strange deaths and flowers are sometimes left by a great oak tree that has grown by the pond. According to one story, in 1852 Thomas Roberts, a farm labourer, was seized by an apparition and held with his face inches from the water.

'When the cuckoo sings its first note on Flint Mountain I shall come again to fetch you,' said the spirit, and vanished. John Roberts was killed at Pen y Glyn Hall the following May when a wall he was repairing collapsed. A cuckoo was singing in a nearby tree as the accident happened.

Chapter 67..The Church of the White Stag.

Some say that the construction of Llan Garw Gwyn (The Church of the White Stag) was started in the 13th Century. Others claim that it was built earlier, in the 11th Century, when a suitable site for a church was chosen near the bridge over the river Dee at Cynwyd. Plans were drawn and stones gathered, ready to build the church. Stonemasons prepared their tools to build the walls. Trees were felled and dragged to the site. Carpenters split the trees to fashioned the heavy frames and rafters needed to support the roof.

But, when the workmen returned next morning the stones had gone, the heavy timber frames which the carpenters had crafted were twisted and the rafters were split and useless. More stones were gathered, fresh trees were sent for and work began again. The next day, the stonemasons returned to find that once more the stones had vanished. The carpenters had toiled in vain and their work was all undone.

The following night, a watchman stood guard to catch the thieves who stole the rocks and damaged the wood. It was a dark moonless night, cold and silent as the grave. The solitary night watchman huddled closer to the fire and peered nervously into the darkness that surrounded him. He built the fire high to give more light but nothing would penetrate the gloom that surrounded him. In the morning, despite the watchman's vigilance, the stones were gone and the timbers again destroyed.

'You saw nothing? You heard nothing? You were asleep,' sneered the workmen when they returned.

The next night more men stayed to guard the site. Once more, it was a dark cold night and the men shivered as they waited for hour after hour. They saw nothing and heard not a sound but the next day the site was bare. All the building materials had been removed and the foundations destroyed.

The workmen went to a holy man. 'What is the meaning of these strange events?' they asked.

'No mortal is stealing your stones. You are trying to build your church in the wrong place. The divine powers do not want it there,' explained the holy man.

'What should we do?' asked the men.

'You must look for a white stag. The place where you see him is where you should build the church. Follow the stag for his track will mark the bounds of the parish. But there is more; to build the church you must kill the stag and mix his blood with the mortar,' replied the holy man.

The workmen gathered weapons and went in search of the white stag. They found the animal in a thicket by the River Dee. It was a fine beast and did not fear the approaching men. The workmen let fly with arrows and spears but they were not hunters and their aim was poor. The white stag escaped across the river and vanished into the forest.

Hunters were summoned to chase and kill the stag. They followed the stag's tracks as the poor animal ran for his life. Eventually, the exhausted beast stopped on a hill, west of the village. It turned to face the hunters and waited. They ran up to the beast and killed it with a spear. Afterwards, the hunters examined the stag and were staggered by its beauty and majesty. All felt sad at having killed such a wonderful creature. From that day on hill where the stag was killed was known as Moel y Lladdfa (Hill of Slaughter).

The site by the bridge was abandoned and, remembering the words of the holy man, blood from the butchered stag was mixed with the mortar used to build a church which they named Llan Garw Gwyn (The Church of The White Stag), where the white stag had first been seen. The culprits who stole the stone and destroyed the foundations of the original church were never caught. Some blamed a spirit or fairies, others the Devil and some said God himself had intervened.

Years later, when the workmen were bent with age and curious visitors would ask about the white stag's brutal death they would shake their heads and remain silent, unwilling to discuss the affair. Were they ashamed of what they had done or frightened of invoking something more powerful than they understood? We shall never know. The legacy that the legend of the white stag leaves behind is Llangar Church, as it is now known, a beautiful building standing alone in an enchanting location by the River Dee.

Chapter 68..The Lonely Lighthouse Keeper.

From early times the River Dee has been a major trade route. The Roman garrison at Chester was supplied by seagoing vessels. Ships carrying goods from Ireland, Spain and Germany used the Dee Estuary to shelter from unfavourable winds. During the Industrial Revolution traffic along the river increased dramatically. In 1737 a new channel was cut to improve navigation and in 1777 a lighthouse was built at the Point of Ayr to guide ships into the estuary. Situated on the most northerly point of the Welsh mainland, Point of Ayr was the earliest lighthouse to be built in Wales. Records show that Edward Price, the first lighthouse keeper, was paid an annual salary of sixteen guineas for his duties.

The original lighthouse fell into the sea and was replaced in 1819 by the structure that stands, like a sentinel, on Talacre Beach today. It no longer operates as a lighthouse and the lamp has not been lit for over 160 years. The tower that rises out of the sand is 18 metres (58 feet) tall and, when it operated, the light could be seen from 19 miles away. Census records show that many of the keepers lived in the lighthouse with their wives and children. In 1841, the keeper, Samuel Brooks, his wife and three children lived there, together with keeper Richard Hughes. At the time of the next census in 1851, ten years later, both men were still stationed at the Point of Ayr lighthouse.

Other lighthouse keepers at Talacre were single men and, for them, the life of a keeper could a lonely one. In 1844, while Samuel Brook was the keeper, a new lighthouse, built offshore on piles sunk into the seabed, replaced the Talacre beach lighthouse making it redundant. Not long after it was closed, strange things began to happen. Visitors to the beach would report seeing a man dressed in a frock coat cleaning the lighthouse lantern. But, when the lighthouse was searched no one was there and the door leading to the tower was secured with stout chains and padlocks. There were more sightings of the ghostly lighthouse keeper. People who approached the lighthouse complained of feeling ill and uneasy as if an evil spirit was watching them. Whole families were struck down with sickness. Dogs walking with their owners ran away and cowered, refusing to approach the lighthouse.

As the paranormal reputation of Talacre lighthouse spread, ghost hunters arrived to search for phantom spirits. Some said the ghost of a long dead lighthouse keeper, unable to light the lamp to warn passing ships, kept a lonely vigil at the top of the tower. Others, more sceptical, scoffed at such nonsense and said the apparitions were a reflection through the lens and nothing more than a trick of the light.

During the Second World War, Talacre lighthouse was used as an observation post and reports of the ghostly keeper stopped. But, at the end of the war, with the lookout post no longer needed, the lighthouse was abandoned and sealed once more. Not long after, sightings began again of a strange man, dressed in old fashioned clothes, at the top of the lighthouse. A couple on holiday watched the man for some time. A family from Hereford started to take photographs by the lighthouse and started to feel unwell. Four of their five children became ill with a fever. In 1966 Jeffrey Moses tried to buy the lighthouse. He had spent many summer holidays at Talacre as a boy and fallen in love with the place. Immediately after he made an offer to purchase the tower he fell ill and died a short while later. He was an apparently healthy 38 years old.

On the 22nd April 2006 a team of eight paranormal investigators, using modern techniques, examined Talacre lighthouse, searching for evidence that would explain the sightings. They set up night vision cameras on every floor and placed motion sensors, sound detectors, electromagnetic sensors and digital cameras throughout the lighthouse. During the night they heard strange sounds and their monitors went crazy. While this was going on, Mary White, a respected medium, was conducting a séance during which she made contact with four spirits. One of the spirits told her he was Raymond, a lighthouse keeper who had died of fever, possibly typhoid, and a broken heart.

One medium claimed that the spirit of one of the lighthouse keepers has returned to his duties and that his name is either Daniel or Samuel. No record exists of a keeper at Talacre named Daniel. Has the ghost of Samuel Brooks, the lighthouse keeper who lived there with his wife until 1844, come back? We can speculate but no one really knows.

Today, if you visit Talacre beach and look up at the lighthouse you will see the figure of a man near the lantern but it isn't the ghost of the lighthouse keeper, Raymond or any other spectre. The seven foot tall figure is a sculpture, named 'The Keeper' that was placed on the balcony of the lighthouse in 2010. Said to represent the ghost, the artwork is made of 120 pieces of stainless steel designed to let the wind blow through it and, according to the artist, make an unsettling moaning noise.

Chapter 69..The Grey Lady of Ruthin.

Anchetil de Greye was a Norman knight and a vassal of William the Conqueror. Following William's success in 1066, defeating the Saxon King Harold, De Greye was rewarded with estates in Kent. During the next 200 years, his family grew more powerful and spread across Britain. By the 13th Century, the De Grey family, as they were now known, had become one of the wealthiest land owners in the country. In 1265, Reginald De Gray became Constable of Nottingham Castle. Reginald was also High Sheriff of Nottinghamshire, Derbyshire and the Royal Forests.

In 1270 he became High Sheriff of Chester and with his new position came a difficult challenge. Llywelyn the Great's Grandson, Llywelyn ap Gruffydd, Prince of Wales, sometimes called Llywelyn the Last, had taken arms against the English and been declared a traitor by King Edward I. Reginald De Gray was made an army commander in the campaign to defeat Llywelyn. Llywelyn was killed on the 11th December 1282. It was a bitter defeat for the Welsh. In recognition of his services to the English crown, De Grey was given the estates of Dyffryn Clwyd which included Ruthin Castle. Reginald De Grey was now a Marcher Lord with the title 1st Baron Grey De Wilton.

The death of Llywelyn deprived the Welsh people of their figurehead and with no one to lead them there was a period of relative quiet. It would be another 120 years before Owain Glyndwr would rise up and challenge the yoke of English rule. De Grey enjoyed being Baron Grey De Wilton and, like other feudal lords, took what he wanted. Marcher Lords were charged with suppressing the Welsh. They had special powers to confiscate land, tax the people, outlaw individuals, raise armies and wage war against the Welsh without referring to the king.

Using his new powers, De Grey grew richer. He scorned any weakness and ruthlessly destroyed anyone who dared to stand in his way. The dungeons, whipping pit and drowning pool at Ruthin Castle struck fear into the hearts of the peasants. Like their master, his men were cruel and took what they wanted. When De Grey learned that King Edward was to visit with his entourage, the castle was prepared for feasting. It was important to entertain the king and make a good impression.

Peasant's animals were seized and slaughtered. The town granary raided to make sweet pastries and breads. Ale was brewed and fine wines fetched from France. Serving wenches were summoned from the town and told to wait on the king and his men. Musicians ordered to play lively music to amuse the guests. During the banquet to welcome the king, a young woman, waiting at table, caught the eye of one of the king's lieutenants. He admired her beauty and asked De Grey who the girl was.

'Some local girl. If you want her, take her,' replied De Grey with a sneer, seeing the lust in the lieutenant's eyes. The girl was the daughter of a free man but that meant nothing to De Grey or his guest. The lieutenant's wife, another member of the king's party and a vengeful woman with a pallid sickly complexion overheard what had been said. She listened carefully but pretended not to hear.

Later that night, once he thought his wife was asleep, the lieutenant crept away to claim the girl and have his evil way. But after he left, his wife got up and followed silently. She watched him go into the girl's room and shut the door. There was a scream as the girl woke to find a strange man in her room. As the girl's protests grew louder, the wife picked up an axe and ran into the room. Her eyes were red with fury as she spied the struggling pair. She raised the axe up high and bought it down with force, slicing off the head of the poor girl her husband had attacked. It was a bloody sight.

'Now you will not have her,' sobbed the wife as her anger ebbed away.

De Grey was not bothered that a young girl had been slain.

'There are plenty more where she came from,' he laughed.

A trial was held quite quickly to test the case in court. The lieutenant's wife admitted her guilt without remorse and was found guilty of so brutally killing the girl by cutting off her head - afoul

244

and wicked deed. They took the jealous wife to a wooden block and carried out a sentence that, all agreed, was an appropriate punishment for the crime. The convicted woman was beheaded, some say, with the very same axe that she had used.

The body of a murderer could not be laid to rest in consecrated ground. Instead, it was buried beside the castle wall. The lieutenant, who despite his infidelity, mourned the loss of his vengeful wife, built a tiny chapel around the grave and placed a stone to mark the spot where the executed woman was buried. The chapel walls have long since crumbled but the tombstone remains to this day.

In the centuries since the execution of the soldier's wife, the ghost of a 'Grey Lady' with a pale complexion has been seen roaming the castle, searching, it is said, for her unfaithful husband.

Chapter 70..Saint Chwyfan's Cross.

In 793, a band of heavily armed men landed from boats and destroyed the great abbey at Lindisfarne, killing most of the monks. The Viking invasion of Britain had begun. More attacks followed as the Viking longboats travelled around the coast looking for plunder. Medieval chroniclers described the hoards of violent men, roaming and killing, as rapacious 'wolves among sheep'. Before long, the strange looking craft appeared in the Dee estuary; the Vikings had come to Wales.

'We have no one to protect us. What can we do?' cried the people. They went to St. Chwyfan and asked him to intercede.

'We are Christian people. Surely god will help us,' they said. The saint, who was their spiritual leader, retreated to a quiet field and prayed to God for guidance. Chwyfan believed in divine miracles but he was also a practical man. When he returned, he called the people together.

'When the Vikings come we must be ready,' said the saint.

'How can we be ready? We don't know when they will come. We cannot fight them. They will rape our women, kill us all and plunder everything we possess,' replied the frightened people. St. Chwyfan listened for a while and when the crowd had fallen silent he spoke again.

'We must build a lookout tower high on a hill and keep a watch on the sea. That is where the Vikings will come from,' said the saint. The people went to Garreg Hill and built a stone tower that gave good views of any approaching ships. They cut wood and stacked it into a giant warning beacon, to be lit when the Vikings were seen. Sentries stood watch day and night, ready to warn of attack.

'Keep men in church steeples to watch for the blaze and ring the bells in alarm,' ordered St. Chwyfan.

'Our women and children, what shall we do to protect them?' asked the people.

246

'On seeing the beacon alight and hearing the church bells ringing everyone must run and hide. The forest will conceal us all and keep us safe until the Vikings depart,' replied the saint.

'What of our treasures, our gold our silver and our pewter?' asked the people.

'Bring me your treasure and together we'll hide it where no Viking dare look,' answered St. Chwyfan. The people from the villages gathered together their valuables and loaded them on carts. There was so much gold, silver and pewter that it took six oxen to pull each load.

'Follow me,' commanded the saint and led the people to the quiet field where he had prayed for guidance.

'Dig here,' said the saint and pointed to a spot. The men dug a great hole and buried the treasure. As they covered the treasure, they took a large stone and stood it upright to mark where the fortune was buried.

'No one must ever speak of this place,' said Saint Chwyfan and led the group in solemn prayer.

'What if the Vikings find the treasure?' asked a troubled man as they were walking home.

'Have no fear and keep your faith with God,' replied the saint and smiled knowingly.

Late one afternoon, the Vikings came. They rushed ashore with fearful yells and weapons at the ready, but there was no one to be found. The warning beacon had been lit, the church bells rung and, as they had been told, all the people had run deep into the forest and hidden. The Vikings couldn't find anyone. They ran from village to village searching for victims but the houses were deserted. When no one could be found, the Vikings shouted angrily. The Vikings searched for treasure to steal but nothing was to be found.

'Where is the gold and silver?' yelled the Vikings to each other. The Vikings searched in vain until they found an upright stone that had recently been moved.

'What's underneath this rock?' they wondered and began to dig. Big, black clouds began to gather while the Vikings dug and then there was a clap of thunder, so close and loud, it startled the Viking raiders. Heavy rain began to fall turning the ground to mud.

'Ignore the noise. It's just a storm,' cried the Viking leader. A bolt of lightning hit the earth, near the standing stone. A second followed and a third. With each lightning bolt, the ground shook violently throwing the Vikings off their feet. Fearing for their lives, the Vikings threw down their spades, ran back to their ships and set sail in search of easier treasure to steal.

Once the Viking raiders had gone and the coast was clear, the people emerged and went to thank the saint. They went back to the standing stone and carved a beautiful cross on it as an offering, thanking God for the strange storm that had saved their treasure.

Years later, when the threat of Viking raiders was long gone, the people returned to dig up their treasure. As they approached the stone cross with shovels, black storm clouds began to gather above their heads. Heavy rain started to fall. Then, there was a clap of thunder and a bolt of lightning struck the ground just near the standing stone, followed by a second and a third. The people threw down their spades and ran away, all thoughts of treasure gone. No one dared go back to claim their share.

It is said, that the treasure buried underneath Maen Achwyfaen is still there today, protected by the thunderbolts that St. Chwyfan invoked more than 1200 years ago.

Chapter 71..The Princess of Rhuddlan.

Rhuddlan castle was once a fine palace. Inside the castle there were great state rooms where a petty king and his family lived, protected by men at arms. The king had fought countless battles and was tired of war. No matter how many enemies he killed more appeared to challenge him.

'How can I end the fighting and live a peaceful life?' he asked himself. The question was a vexing one and he could find no simple answer. One afternoon, a stranger approached the castle gates with a flag of truce and asked to speak with the king.

'Let him enter. We will hear what he wants,' ordered the king. The drawbridge lowered and the stranger was led to the great hall where he made an offer that interested the king.

'I come to offer peace and, to sanctify the peace; my master offers his hand in marriage to your daughter. A union between our peoples would help end the bitterness,' said the emissary. The king was delighted to hear the proposal. It was a chance to end the wars, just as he had prayed.

'Bring wine and food for our visitor. We will refresh you before you depart and you can take a letter to your master agreeing to the arrangement,' said the king. After the stranger had left, the king sent for his daughter and told her of the plan but the princess did not want to marry a strange man she did not know.

'I will choose who I marry, when and if I please,' replied the headstrong girl and stormed out of the great hall. The princess was determined to thwart her father's plan and decided to run away. She packed a bag and crept out of the castle. Outside the castle, she stopped; unsure which path to take. Then, she ran along the riverbank, heading north towards the sea. At first, the ground was hard but, as she went further, her feet began to slip in the mud that the tide had left behind. Soon, she found it hard to run. Her legs were sinking into the mud. The princess struggled on. She grew hot with effort and angry for being such a fool.

'Why didn't I go the other way?' She asked herself. Finally, exhausted she stopped. She could go no further. Thick foul smelling ooze now gripped her legs. She was stuck fast in the mud. She heaved with all her strength but it was no use. With each tug of her legs she sank further into the mire. Realising it was hopeless; the princess stopped struggling and began to sob. The cold mud chilled her and she began to shiver.

After a while, the princess saw that the water in the river was getting closer. The tide was coming in. The princess began to shout and scream. She didn't want to drown. Luckily, a knight was passing nearby and heard her plaintive cries. He took a rope, made a loop and threw it towards the stranded girl.

'Take hold of the rope and tie it around your middle. I will pull you out,' yelled the knight. The princess did as she was told. The knight tied the end of the rope to his saddle. The horse pulled, with all its might and, like a cork leaving a bottle, the princess popped out of the mud. She looked a bedraggled mess. Her clothes were torn and she was covered in mud from head to foot.

'Thank you, kind sir. You have saved my life. You are my knight in shining armour,' the princess said and smiled coyly. She kissed the knight to reward him for the deed and, in that moment, fell in love with her rescuer. The princess told the knight of her father's plan and why she had run away.

'Come with me,' said the knight and sat her on his horse. As they rode away together, the princess laughed with joy. She felt safe and secure with her love to protect and provide for her. They set up house in a distant place where no one knew the princess. To begin with, the princess was happy but her bliss did not last long. Her knight in shining armour had a dark and evil side. He was a jealous man and quick to lose his temper. He would shout at the princess and make her cry for the silliest little thing. The princess grew unhappier with each passing day until, at last, she realised that she had made a terrible mistake.

'I wish that I had listened to my father and done as I was told,' said the princess and vowed to return and beg his forgiveness for being such a fool.

The princess waited until the knight was out and set off to her father's castle. When the knight came home and found that she was gone, he flew into a terrible rage and swore to drag her back. The princess was nearly at the castle when she heard a galloping horse coming from behind. She looked back and saw the knight. He thrashed his mount and urged it on, intent to overtake her. The princess ran on but stood no chance and was quickly overhauled.

'Please, let me go,' pleaded the princess as she struggled with the knight. Then she saw the knight had changed and had become a demon. His eyes were red. His hands were claws and there were horns above his ears. The princess screamed in terror at seeing such a ghoul.

Hearing her plaintiff cry, the demon took the princess and threw her in the river. The tide was ebbing fast. The princess, who had disobeyed her father, floating out to sea and was never seen again. Without a daughter to give in marriage, the king was called a cheat; his broken pledge proving he was unworthy of his crown. He lost his head in battle and his kingdom passed into history. The castle, once so grand, was left to rot and crumble.

Even today, if you listen when the tide goes out, you'll hear a plaintiff cry; it's the princess floating by, to meet her watery grave.

Chapter 72..The Spirit of Llandegla.

It was Sunday morning and Llandegla Parish Church was full. The congregation waited, patiently at first and then with increasing agitation when the rector did not appear to conduct the service. A boy was sent to the rectory to find the missing clergyman.

'The house is empty. There's no one there,' said the boy, when he returned. The disappearance of the rector did not surprise everyone. He had recently seemed absent minded and confused. Villagers had seen the cleric wandering around the village muttering in a foreign tongue and chalking strange symbols on walls. Superstitious folk said,

'The devil had stolen his mind;' other, more kindly people, 'That the rector must be ill.'

A search was made of the countryside but there was no trace of the clergyman. The rector's clothes were hanging in his bedroom and all of his possessions were still at the rectory. Hearing of the disappearance, the bishop sent a canon to care for the spiritual needs of the parish and find out what had happened to the missing priest.

The canon moved into the rectory and unpacked his things. The rooms felt cold and dank. Strange satanic symbols were scrawled on the walls. He lit a fire to warm the house and opened some windows to air it. That night, while going up the stairs to bed, his candle flickered and went out. The canon felt his way slowly across the landing in the dark. Then, he heard a creaking noise. A door was opening but how could that be? He was alone in the house. Something pushed past him. Footsteps clattered down the stairs, the kitchen door slammed shut and then there was silence.

Once he reached his bedroom, the canon shut and locked the door. He lit a lamp and waited for another sound but the house stayed silent. It was in the early hours and the canon was asleep when a crash awoke him. He sat up in the darkness and stared into the gloom. There was another bang and cries of pain on the stairs.

The screams of anguish continued until the morning sun peeped through the windows, then the house went quiet.

The canon searched the house from the attic to the cellar but found nothing untoward. The next night the canon heard more strange sounds but again, the following morning, the house fell silent.

'The house is cursed,' the people said.

'Fetch my prayer-book and bible from the church,' said the canon and held a service in the rectory to exorcise the spirit.

The next night a group of stout hearted parishioners stayed in the rectory. As it got dark the noises started again, much louder than before. The spirit was still in the house and seemed angry as it banged and thumped and shouted. The exorcism had not worked.

'Send for the conjuror Mr. Griffiths from Graianrhyd. He will know what to do. He will catch the devil,' said the postmaster, when he heard the news. They fetched Mr. Griffiths to the rectory to lay the demon to rest. He walked from room to room, placing charms and chanting spells. He waited through the night until the spirit started to bang and yell. It was a fearful sound that made his heart turn cold. In the morning all was silent but Mr. Griffiths knew the demon was still residing in the house.

The next night, when the spirit went to work, the sounds were different. The banging was quieter and there were no screams of pain. Instead, there was a growling noise as if a huge dog had got into the rectory. Mr. Griffiths returned the following evening with more amulets and spells. Again, that night, there were strange sounds but instead of a dog's growl he heard a cat spitting and hissing in the dark. Mr. Griffiths returned night after night. Each night the sounds were quieter and the animals he heard were smaller. One night Mr. Griffiths saw a rat. It ran across the landing and vanished. The next night a bat flew past his head.

'We will have the demon tonight,' said Mr. Griffiths the next evening. He opened a small wooden casket, put it on the landing floor and waited. Downstairs, something stirred in the darkness. A quiet hum reverberated though the house. The noise was growing louder. Mr. Griffiths could hear the frantic flapping of tiny wings. Something was flying up the stairs. The hum became a shrill buzz. Two glowing red eyes appeared. They were coming towards Mr. Griffiths. Suddenly a huge fly hit the ghost hunter in the face. Instinctively, he hit the insect with his hand, swatting it into the wooden box. He flicked the lid shut and turned the key in the lock. The angry fly repeatedly banged against the sides of the box but it could not escape its wooden prison.

In the morning, curious villagers watched as Mr. Griffiths carried the wooden box containing the spirit down to the river. The demon was still buzzing loudly as Mr. Griffiths buried the box in the river bed, near the bridge. The villagers helped him place a large stone over the box.

'If a tree grows from beneath this rock do not kill it. If you do, the spirit will be free to return and haunt again,' said Mr. Griffiths.

The following spring a strange sapling sprouted from the water. The people debated what to do with it.

'Poison it,' said one.

'Dig it up and burn it,' answered another.

'Remember Griffith's words. The spirit would be free to return and haunt again,' reminded the sensible postmaster. They sent for Mr. Griffiths and asked for his advice.

'Let the strange tree live but its branches must never reach the parapet of the bridge. If it does, the demon will climb up from his watery prison and escape,' explained the ghost hunter.

Not wishing to have a demon in their village again, the people made a pledge to prune the tree each year. No one ever discovered what happened to the unfortunate missing clergyman. Had he been foolish enough to play with mysterious things that are best left alone? Is it the rector's spirit that is locked beneath the rock at the bottom of the river? We shall never know but, even today, village children still snip branches off the tree to make sure the demon buried in the riverbed is kept secure inside his wooden prison.

Chapter 73..The Dancing Innkeeper.

The magician, Dick Spot was going to Llanrwst and had been walking all day. It was getting late and he was tired, thirsty and hungry when he reached the village of Henllan. Dick trudged through the village looking for somewhere to stop for the night. The Llindir Inn, opposite the church, looked inviting.

'Here will do,' said Dick and in he went. The landlord, a miserable man, showed Dick a room.

'We're busy so this is all we have available,' said the innkeeper and pointed to a straw mattress on the floor. It was a shabby resting place but Dick was tired and past arguing. He dropped his bundle on the mattress and followed the landlord downstairs.

The innkeeper's wife was as disagreeable as her husband. She poured a tankard of ale and handed it to Dick without speaking.

'I'm starving and could eat a side of beef. What food are you serving tonight?' asked Dick. He sipped the beer and shuddered. It was sour.

'We have cheese and bread,' replied the landlady.

'Surely you have some succulent meat, simmering in a pot and potatoes to fill a hungry man that has travelled far?' said Dick.

'I've no time to cook for the likes of you. Cheese and bread is what you'll have. That or nothing,' answered the woman. The supper, when it came, was a morsel on a plate. The crust was stale and mouldy. The tiny piece of stinking cheese wouldn't even fill a mouse. Dick called the landlord over to remonstrate with him.

'Your beer is flat and sour. Your cheese stinks and is bad. This really will not do,' said Dick. The innkeeper picked up the tankard and swallowed a mouthful. Then he snatched the cheese and took a bite.

'My beer is sweet and our cheese is tasty fare. You are just a moaning traveller, like many we get here,' said the landlord and demanded to be paid.

'Six pence, for your meal and four more for the beer. Six and four make ten. Ten pence is what you owe,' he said. The price was outrageous but Dick Spot had little choice. He opened his purse and counted out ten pennies. Knowing he was being swindled, Dick decided to teach the unpleasant publican and his wife a lesson.

'Six and four make ten. Landlord, will you count it o'er again?' asked Dick, to make sure. Then, he summoned the landlord's wife and bid her do the same.

'Six and four make ten. Will you count it o'er again?' To be doubly sure they called the servant girl to do the same. Then Dick took a scrap of paper, scribbled a short rhyme on it, hid it under the table and went upstairs to bed.

Dick Spot slept badly that night. The mattress was hard and filled with bugs that bit him everywhere. His stomach churned and gurgled, upset by the sour beer and putrid cheese. He left early in the morning glad to be on his way. After he had gone, the servant girl arose and started to clear up. But as she worked she began to dance and sing a merry song.

'Six and four are ten. Count it o'er again,' she sang and danced frantically around the kitchen. The landlord, on hearing the commotion, got up and went to investigate. As he entered the kitchen his legs began to twitch and he too started to dance.

'Six and four are ten. Count it o'er again,' he sang and skipped uncontrollably around the kitchen. By now everyone in the tavern was awake and the landlady went to see what all the noise was about. She stood in the kitchen doorway and watched, amazed, as her husband danced furiously with the servant girl.

'Six and four are ten. Count it o'er again,' they sang as they danced. Tears ran down their faces but they could not stop.

The landlady was angry to see her husband dancing and enjoying himself with another woman. She went to separate them and stop their cavorting. As she entered the kitchen she also started to jiggle about.

'Six and four are ten. Count it o'er again,' the three of them sang as they danced.

Hearing the laughter and singing, villagers rushed to the tavern and soon a crowd of people had collected to watch the dancing landlord and his wife. Realising what had happened, one of the villagers ran after Dick Spot to ask for his help.

'How do we stop the dancing?' he asked, when he caught up with the magician.

'Take the spell from under the table and burn it. Only when the paper is consumed, will the dance end,' answered the magician and went on his way. The villager returned to the tavern and found the slip of paper hidden under the table. He read the spell and then threw it into the fire. As he did so the three exhausted dancers collapsed in a heap.

'What did the spell say?' asked an onlooker.

'Six and four are ten. Count it o'er again,' replied the villager.

Despite Dick Spot's dancing lesson, miserable publicans continued to run the Llindir Inn. Some years later, an equally unhappy landlord, reputedly, murdered his wife after discovering her with another man. The unfortunate woman now haunts the premises and her ghostly antics have been featured on national television. In more recent times a different publican at the Llindir Inn, with a particularly unpleasant disposition, was referred to, by customers, as 'Happy Al' and described as the most miserable landlord in North Wales.

Chapter 74..The Devil Dogs of Marchwiel.

'Like one that on a lonesome road doth walk in fear and dread...
because he knows a frightful fiend doth close behind him tread.'
The Rhyme of the Ancient Mariner - Samuel Taylor Coleridge

It was late when the farmer left the tavern in Marchwiel. Gusts of icy wind chilled his bones and stung his eyes. A fine spray of rain, like a mist, soaked his face and ran down his neck. He was tempted to turn back to the tavern with its roaring log fire where his friends were still drinking but he kept on.

'This is no night to be walking two miles home,' he muttered and pulled his collar up around his neck. The farmer hurried past the churchyard in the darkness. Gravestones, leaning like drunken sailors, beckoned but he dare not turn and look. By the time he reached the gate his eyes had grown accustomed to the dim light. He knew that going home across the fields was shorter but he hesitated; the path went past the hanging hill. He'd used the path across the fields hundreds of time before and wondered why he felt so reluctant tonight.

'It's been raining hard all day so the fields will be sodden,' he reasoned. 'The bottom field may even be underwater,' he said to himself to settle the argument. Deciding that he didn't want to wade through mud or land on his face in the slime, the farmer turned away from the gate and set off along the road. He walked quickly and hummed to keep his spirits up. After a while, the rain stopped and the farmer began to feel more confident.

'It won't take that long and there's a bottle of brandy in the dresser,' he whispered, as an inducement to himself. Someone coughed in the darkness, startling the farmer. He stopped and peered along the road. There was another cough and something large moved by the hedge. The farmer stood still and braced himself.

258

'Who's there?' he cried as whoever had coughed came closer. If he was going to be robbed he would defend himself. Then he saw his attacker. It was a cow. The farmer laughed at himself for being so nervous. Cows can cough like humans. He had heard the sound many times before. The farmer walked on, past the cow and wondered how far he had gone. Soon he would need to turn along the lane that led to his farm.

'We don't want to miss the turn. That would not be good,' he said to himself. There were more noises in the dark. Small animals scurried in the hedge. A patrolling fox, hunting for his supper, crossed the road ahead and vanished into a field. Clouds began to fill the sky, like a great weight above the land, so low that the farmer imagined he could reach up and touch them.

'Only a mile left now,' said the farmer, when he reached the lane. The first part of the lane, along Cock Bank, was clear and the farmer made good progress but, when he reached Pentre Mailyn and began to walk down the hill, something happened. The trees that grew over the lane made it impossible to see. Something moved behind the farmer. It was snuffling and disturbing the fallen leaves.

'It's a badger rooting for worms,' the farmer told himself and, comforted by the explanation, hurried on. The gusts of wind were stronger now and shook the trees that shrouded the lane. Branches crashed together adding to the din but another noise reached the farmer's ears. A howl so carnal and loathsome, that the farmer shuddered with fear. It was a Devil Dog, an animal that few people ever saw and lived to tell the tale. The Welsh called them the 'Gwyllgi' or 'Dogs of Darkness'.

The farmer began to run. He passed the old clay pit, now filled with water and the clouds cleared for a moment. There, in the moonlight, stood a huge dog. It turned to look at the running man and the farmer saw its eyes. They were bright red. More Devil Dogs appeared. They began to follow the farmer, their paws pounding along the lane and their breath rasping with effort.

'Any moment now and they will have me,' thought the farmer and strained with every sinew to run like the wind. His legs ached and his chest pounded as he ran. He could hear the pack of dogs getting closer but dared not look back in case he tripped and fell. The dogs were almost on him when he reached the farmyard. The farmer charged across the yard and through the kitchen door. His wife was reading when, without warning, the door burst open and the farmer staggered in. He bolted the door and collapsed on the floor. His face was ashen and his eyes wide with terror.

At first no one believed the farmer's story. Some said it was the drink. Others, that the moonlight had played tricks on the unfortunate fellow and the more unkind villagers said the farmer was a madman. They were, of course, right because the poor man had gone mad that night and never recovered his sanity. It was only when others, brave enough to venture along the lane on dark nights, heard and saw strange things that the farmer's account of the Devil Dogs was believed.

Today the lane that the farmer had run along, is called 'Lon Bwgan Ddu' (Black Phantom Lane) to warn the unwary that terrible dark creatures lurk there, late at night, waiting for their next victim.

Chapter 75..The Mad King's Monument.

King George III, the first Hanoverian king of Britain who spoke English as his main language, had been on the throne for nearly forty years. Unlike his German father, he was born in Britain and had never been to Hanover. Some called him mad George because he suffered periods of insanity. American colonists resented paying taxes on tea and newspapers that his government levied. They rebelled and, following a bloody war, gained their independence.

'George has lost us America,' cried the people. Unkind commentators called him Farmer George because he preferred gardening and growing vegetables to matters of state. But, as George got older the people grew to admire the pious and modest man he had become.

'We must do something to celebrate the king's golden jubilee,' announced the splendidly named Reverend Whitehall-Whitehall Davies. The reverend, a local squire, wrote to his friend Lord Kenyon and they formed a committee to decide what to do.

'Let's erect a giant tower,' they said and sent for a famous architect. The architect, Thomas Harrison, got to work and produced a design for a 115 foot tall tower that would look like an Egyptian temple.

'We need to put the tower somewhere high, so it can be seen from miles away. Moel Famau would be perfect,' suggested the Reverend and the committee agreed. Moel Famau or 'Mother Mountain' was the highest Moel in the Clwydian Range and the planned monument would be visible for miles.

On the 24th October 1810, the year of the king's jubilee, Lord Kenyon laid the foundation stone. Special sermons, to commemorate the event, were preached in Mold and Ruthin. Then, dignitaries rode horses to the top of Moel Famau, accompanied by a band of musicians and beautiful female attendants. More than 5000 people climbed to the top of Moel Famau to witness the great occasion. Pits were dug and filled with wood to roast oxen and 'cwru da' - 'good beer' was served to aid the day long festivities.

Following the laying of the foundation stone, things began to go wrong. The Wrexham surveyor Thomas Penson had calculated the cost of building the tower to be £3235. A public fund had been started to pay for the work but it only raised £1129. The people of Denbighshire and Flintshire loved their king, so it seemed, but not quite enough to pay for such an extravagant monument. Lord Kenyon added £650 to bolster the fund and building work began. From the start, there were problems. Lack of money and constant bickering between the architect and the surveyor resulted in the project slowing to a snail's pace. By 1815 Penson and Harrison were no longer cooperating and it was clear that the original design was unaffordable. Things dragged on until, in 1817, a more modest and less costly design was agreed. Construction progressed for a while until the money ran out and work on the half finished jubilee tower stopped.

The monument remained as it was for the next 29 years. The residents of Denbighshire and Flintshire had lost interest in their celebratory jubilee tower. In 1846, one corner of the tower collapsed. Poorly constructed foundations and shoddy workmanship had left the structure unsafe; urgent repairs were needed. Another fund was started and, with the £500 that it raised, limited repairs could be made to the tower.

In October 1862, following two days of storms, the half built jubilee tower collapsed. All that remained was the plinth and a pile of rubble. Local people pilfered material to build stone walls and the remains of the tower became an eyesore visible for miles.

King George III died in 1820, after almost sixty years on the throne. By then he was blind, deaf and permanently insane with what we now call dementia. He was, at the time, the longest serving British monarch. Later Queens, Victoria and Elizabeth II would reign longer. In 1970 the site of the jubilee tower was tidied up to look as it does today and it is now part of a country park. From a distance, the plinth, which is all that remains of the tower, looks more like a mausoleum than the base of an Egyptian tower, built to celebrate the reign of mad King George, who lost us America.

Chapter 76..The Bishop and the Ring.

Maelgwyn Gwynedd, King of Gwynedd, who some called Maelgwyn Hir - 'Maelgwyn the Tall', reigned in the 6th Century. Of the five kings of the 'Old North' which the Welsh called 'Yr Hen Ogledd', Maelgwyn Gwynedd was the senior and most pre-eminent. The other kings, who ruled in what we now call Scotland and the North of England, paid him homage.

Maelgwyn was, at times during his life, a devout Christian. He gave generously to the church and was a patron of several Welsh saints. He had not always been so pious and had gained the throne by killing and overthrowing his uncle. Once he had become king, he was overcome with remorse and became a monk, turning his back on worldly pleasures. The monastic life did not suit Maelgwyn: he soon renounced his vows and returned to continue his life as a king. As well as being tall, Maelgwyn was a strong and powerful warrior with a violent temper.

Having resumed the life of a king, Maelgwyn decided to take a wife and chose Nest, the most beautiful woman in the land. They were married and Maelgwyn placed the royal 'Wedding Ring of the North,' on Nest's finger. The sacred ring, made from dark Welsh gold, had been handed down for generations and could only be worn by Queens of North Wales.

'Never, let this ring slip from your finger,' warned Maelgwyn.

Later, while accompanying Maelgwyn on a visit to the Bishop Kentigern of Asaph, Nest went for a walk along the bank of the River Elwy. It was a hot day and the water looked cool and inviting. Nest decided to bathe. As she swam in the clear water Nest felt refreshed and happy. She got out of the water and began to dry herself when, to her horror, she noticed that the sacred ring had gone from her finger. Fearful of Maelgwyn's temper and remembering his warning on their wedding day, she went to the bishop for help. Bishop Kentigern was a maker of miracles. As a boy, he had brought back to life a little robin that had been killed

264

by other boys and he had once used his sacred powers to start a fire so that freezing monks would stay warm.

'The ring must have slipped from my finger in the cold water. What am I to do?' She cried. Knowing of the king's violent temper, Bishop Kentigern reassured Nest and offered to help break the news to Maelgwyn that the royal ring was lost. They waited until the evening when the three of them were alone and the king was more relaxed. The bishop started to explain to the king what had happened but, before he could finish, Maelgwyn flew into a rage.

'That ring has been in my family for generations. How dare you be so stupid and lose it,' he shouted at Nest. Slowly, and with great tact the bishop calmed the king's temper. He talked of the importance of love transcending all else and the meaningless worth of mere trinkets. Eventually, the king grew more composed and, seeing his wife in tears, he went to her and comforted her.

'Let us say grace together and enjoy our supper,' said Kentigern and they all thanked God for his bounty. The meal, a fine fresh salmon was bought to the table.

'Leave it, I will serve the king and queen,' commanded the bishop to his servant and sliced large portions for his guests. Feeling better, now the king was calm, Nest began to eat her fish. Then, in the candlelight, something caught her eye. Glinting on the plate was a band of gold. The ring was back, returned by the salmon that had been caught that very same day. She pushed the ring back onto her finger and promised never to lose it again.

Although the ring was recovered, thanks to the intersession of Bishop Kentigern, there was, sadly, no happy ending to the story. A few years later, King Maelgwyn lusted after another man's beautiful young wife and, when she refused his advances, he killed the husband and took the woman by force. Queen Nest objected to the young woman in Maelgwyn's arms and, in a fit of temper, Maelgwyn slaughtered Nest as well. From then on Maelgwyn lived a life of depravity until a terrible plague swept the land. Fearing for his life, Maelgwyn locked himself, alone, in a church with orders not to be disturbed until the plague had passed. Later, when his soldiers entered the church, they found his rotting body bloated with yellow fever.

Today, if you visit St. Aspah's Cathedral, you can see a beautiful stained glass window showing Saint Kentigern holding the salmon and the ring that was returned to Queen Nest.

Chapter 77..Tylwyth Teg (The Fairies) of Pentrefoelas.

It has been a well known fact for hundreds of years that there is another world alongside our own. The underworld, or Annwn as it is known in Welsh, is close to the surface, near the village of Pentrefoelas and it is here that the two worlds sometimes cross each other's paths. The Tylwyth Teg, for that is the name of the inhabitants of Annwn, are a fair haired race with blue eyes who are neither good nor bad. Sometimes they are kind, leaving small gifts to people they meet, and sometimes full of mischief. Tylwyth Teg have been known to steal a child and leave a changeling - the offspring of a Tylwth Teg - in its place. They are afraid of iron and wise mothers who love their children have always placed a poker over the crib to keep the Tylwyth Teg away.

One day Gwyn, the shepherd boy who lived at Hafod y Garreg Farm, was high on the Cefnen Wen with his father's sheep when he heard a strange sound. Someone was crying. Gwyn went in search of the sound. After searching for the noise for some time, he found a girl sitting in the heather. She was sobbing quietly to herself. The girl was slim with fair hair and she had blue eyes. Gwyn was a shy young man but he felt sorry for the crying girl and, throwing all inhibitions aside, he approached her and tried to comfort her. Not sure what to say, he simply sat with his arm around the girl but as he did so a queer feeling came over him. His heart started to beat quickly and he felt light headed. He was falling in love. There was a cough behind the seated pair. Turning to look, Gwyn saw a little old man standing behind them. The man was dressed in a strange frock coat and wore stockings.

'What's this, my girl?' demanded the man.

'Father,' exclaimed the girl but, before she could say another word, the old man took her by the arm and led her away. They vanished in a cloud of mist.

The next day Gwyn returned to the same place on Cefnen Wen to look for the girl but she was nowhere to be found. Broken hearted, he returned each day, desperate to find his love. Gwyn was unaware that the girl of his desire had been affected by their meeting in the same way and was in love with him. Each day she tried in vain to find a way back to Gwyn's world.

The weeks passed. Autumn turned to winter and when spring came there was extra work to do. Lambing on a hill farm is always busy and Gwyn had no time for wandering on the mountain. When at last the grass began to grow on the mountain and the sheep returned to Cefnen Wen, Gwyn started to search once more.

'I will never stop looking,' vowed Gwyn as he hunted for his love. His persistence was rewarded when the girl appeared one day. She had found a way to join him. They laughed and kissed and cried with joy. They hugged and promised never to be parted. Their happiness was however short lived because the girl's father had followed her and suddenly appeared.

He took the girl's arm and tried to lead her away but Gwyn grabbed her other arm and begged him, 'let her stay.' Seeing that the young couple were deeply in love, the little old man relented and let go of her arm.

'You may wed my daughter with my blessing but if you ever touch her with anything made of iron I will return and lead her back to Annwn,' said the old man and produced a sack full of gold coins.

'No daughter of mine will marry without a dowry,' said her father. He handing the sack of gold to Gwyn and vanished.

The couple married and lived happily together for many years.

'There are some fine ponies on the mountain this year. I'm going to catch one,' said Gwyn one day. He took a bridle from the barn and set off on his journey. Gwyn chased the ponies for hours but they were fast and he could not catch them. When he did not return for lunch, his wife packed a hamper and followed, planning to surprise him with a picnic. As she turned a corner by some pens, the ponies galloped past. She heard an angry cry. Gwyn was cross; once more he had failed to catch the horses. She didn't notice the bridle which Gwyn had thrown in anger after seeing them escape.

The iron bridle hit her on the arm and caused a tiny wound. In a flash, the little old man appeared and, taking Gwyn's wife by the arm, led her back to the underworld. Gwyn never saw her again.

Chapter 78..Robert Llwyd Hari's Card Game.

Robert Llwyd Hari was a farm servant at Gilar Farm, near the village of Rhydlydan. His hobby was playing cards. Each evening, after he had finished his work on the farm Bob, as people called him, would walk down to the village and meet his friends for a game. Sometimes they would play in the tavern. On Sunday nights, when the tavern was shut, he would go to Aunty Ann's house and spend the evening playing cards there. Some villagers frowned at Bob's hobby. They called his card playing wicked and the work of the devil. The minister had tried to stop Bob playing cards on Sundays but his sermons fell on deaf ears. Bob's ability with a deck of cards was well known across the county and he was a champion card player.

Late one Sunday evening, Bob was walking along the lane, on his way home from Aunty Ann's when he saw a strange looking man coming towards him. It was a warm night but the man was dressed in a long, tightly buttoned coat. He wore a tall hat and a long scarf was tied around his neck.

'Good evening,' said the stranger, as he approached. The men stopped on a small bridge.

'Good evening to you,' replied Bob, not wishing to be rude to the stranger.

'I believe you are a card player,' said the stranger. Bob wondered how the stranger knew he played cards. He had never met the man before.

'I enjoy a hand of cards myself. Come with me to Plas Lolyn and we will have a game or two,' suggested the stranger.

'Why would I go to a deserted farmhouse to play cards at this late hour?' replied Bob.

'I have just moved into Plas Lolyn. The house is warm and there is plenty of light to play,' said the stranger. Bob considered the offer for a moment. It might be fun to pit his skill against the stranger but he had to be up early in the morning, to milk the cows.

'Thank you for the invitation but it is late and I need my bed,' said Bob and bid the stranger goodnight.

'Wait,' said the stranger, 'The moon is bright. We can have our game here on the bridge'.

'I have no playing cards with me,' said Bob.

'Yes you have. There are two packs in your jacket pocket,' replied the stranger. Bob laughed and produced a deck of cards from his pocket.

'Just a quick game. I have to be up with the sun in the morning,' said Bob. The two men sat astride the bridge parapet and began their game. The stranger was a good player but Bob was better. Robert Llwyd Hari was winning every hand and enjoying himself. The competition got fiercer. Now, the men were playing as if their lives were at stake. Bob was playing with all his concentration. Any thought of getting up early to milk the cows had been pushed from his mind.

The stranger dealt a hand and one of the cards fell, from the parapet, into the water below. Bob looked down. He could see his reflection and the stranger's reflection in the moonlight. Then he saw the stranger's reflected foot, or was it? He looked again. It was no foot…but a hoof. Bob threw down his cards and jumped up.

'I'll not play cards with you any longer,' he cried and marched quickly away from the bridge. On seeing that the match was over, the stranger became a wheel of fire and rolled up the hill in the direction of Plas Lolyn.

Next day, when Bob enquired, no one had heard of the stranger from Plas Lolyn. The farm was still derelict when he went to look. The following Sunday, the minister was pleased to see Bob in his congregation and overjoyed when he learnt that Bob had pledged to never again play with cards on the Sabbath.

Chapter 79..The Angelystor of Llangernyw.

'When the bell begins to toll,
Lord, have mercy on the soul.'
The Venerable Bede, 672-735.

In days past, when good and evil were known to be two sides of the same coin, people feared the devil. They understood that Satan and his followers congregated around churches, hoping to steal souls. Devils and demons, it was believed, were afraid of the sound of bells. In Ireland, evil spirits were driven away by the ringing of church bells. The same is true in Scotland. In Wales, the mournful toll of a church bell, known as the passing bell, would start when a person was on their death bed. During the funeral, the church bell was often accompanied by the ringing of a second, smaller, hand bell. This corpse bell, as it was known, would be carried in front of the body, as it was carried to its final resting place, to protect the soul of the dead person from Satan.

Many Welsh churches were built with north and south facing doors. Before a funeral or christening, the north door would be opened but then the priest would enter through the south door. The north door, commonly known as the devil's door, would remain open during the service so that evil spirits in the church could flee from the ringing bells they hated so much.

Despite these and other precautions, evil spirits were still a problem in churches. One church with a particularly unpleasant kind of demon was St. Dygain's in the village of Llangernyw. The demon was an Angelystor or 'Recording Angel' so named because, at the stroke of midnight each All-Hallows Eve, the demon would whisper the names of those who would pass away in the coming year.

When a new tailor named Shon Ap Robert moved into the village he was amused to learn about the messenger of death that haunted the church. Shon was a strong, confident young fellow, full of life and always ready for some fun.

'An Angelystor you call it, who can foretell the future. What nonsense. I don't believe in spirits,' he said one evening in the tavern.

'Don't scoff at things you don't understand,' warned his drinking companions. As the evening passed and more ale flowed, Shon grew bolder.

'I'll prove there's no such thing, this very Halloween, by waiting in the church until the clock strikes twelve,' said Shon.

'Don't be a fool,' replied the landlord.

'Leave the Angelystor in peace if you value your soul,' said another.

'How much do you wager that I will hear no names?' challenged Shon with a swagger.

'I will stake five shillings that you will hear the names and those people will be dead within the year,' said a drinker by the bar.

'I accept your wager,' cried Shon.

Every day the villagers tried to dissuade the tailor from his quest. The priest warned him it was a mistake. The doctor told Shon he was a fool and the tavern keeper, frightened for the young man's sanity, tried to stop him.

'A bet has been made and, as a man of principle, I am obliged to honour it,' replied the confident tailor and would not be swayed.

October passed quickly and late on All-Hallows Eve he entered the church alone. His solitary candle flickered, casting strange dancing shadows on the walls. Shon ap Robert sat quietly on a pew, near the altar and waited. Outside, the great yew that grew in the churchyard was being buffeted by the wind. Shon held his pocket watch up to the candle. It was ten minutes to twelve. Slowly, the minutes ticked past. The cold church air was chilling Shon to his very marrow and he felt less confident than he had done that convivial evening in the tavern.

'Even if I hear a name, it cannot harm me,' said Shon to himself and waited nervously in the gloom. There was a bang and the door of the church burst open. A gust of wind blew out Shon's candle. Then, the door slammed shut, leaving Shon in darkness.

'Who's there,' shouted Shon but there was no reply. Instead, he heard something shuffling across the floor. Shon wanted to jump up and flee but the church was dark as ink and he had no idea where the door was. He sat as if riveted to the pew.

'Shon Ap Robert, Shon Ap Robert,' whispered a voice, close by. Shon could feel putrid breath near his face.

'Hold. Hold. I'm not ready,' cried the tailor and fumbled for a match.

'Shon Ap Robert,' whispered the voice again. He struck the match. There was no one there. He was alone in the church. Shon looked at his watch. It was one minute past twelve.

The people were shocked the following morning, when they saw the tailor. His hair had turned white and his face was wrinkled with age.

'Did you see the Angelystor?' asked the villagers.

'I saw nothing,' replied Shon.

'Tell us. Did he whisper the names?' asked the priest.

'Just one,' replied Shon and wearily handed over the five shillings he had wagered.

Shon Ap Robert never told the people of Llangernyw who the messenger of death had named that fearful night but, when he died within the year, they knew. The little parish church was packed for the funeral of Shon Ap Robert and, as he was laid to rest, the corpse bell was rung loudly to protect the soul of the unfortunate tailor who had so rashly dared to challenge the Angelystor.

Chapter 80...The Goblin Tower.

Ask residents of Denbigh about the Goblin Tower and some will turn and shuffle away without answering. Others may mumble about evil spirits that lurk around that huge rampart and warn you to keep away when the moon is high in the night sky. To understand their dread of that dark place we must look back seven hundred years, to a time of war when barons ruled the land and life was cheap.

Denbigh and the surrounding lands once belonged to Llywelyn the Great. He built a castle there. Later, it became the stronghold of Dafydd ap Gruffydd, brother of Llywelyn the Last. Following Prince Llywelyn's death and the defeat of the Welsh, the unfortunate Dafydd ap Gruffydd was hung, drawn and quartered for his part in the rebellion. Then, King Edward I gave the lordship of Denbigh to Henry de Lacy 3rd Earl of Lincoln. Intent on suppressing the Welsh after Llywelyn's rebellion, King Edward ordered the building of castles across Wales to dominate the country and project the power of the English crown.

In 1282, Henry de Lacy began work by destroying all traces of the Welsh castle that was on the site. Denbigh, or 'Dinbych,' is Welsh for 'little fort' and there had been a fort on the site since the iron ages, but there was nothing little about the design of the new castle Henry de Lacy proposed.

'Who is the best castle builder in Europe?' demanded de Lacy.

'Master James of Saint George from Savoy,' replied his squire.

'Get him,' ordered de Lacy. Master James was the king's architect and master mason, brought from France to design and build a ring of castles around Wales described as a 'ring of steel fortresses' which would subdue the Welsh. The architect set to work and designed a magnificent fortification for Denbigh. Stonemasons were ordered to work on the castle, building huge curtain walls and defensive towers. A long wall was built around the town to protect it from attack by the Welsh. Inside the castle, a deep well was dug to provide water for the garrison in case of a siege. As the town grew, more water was needed and a second well was dug below the castle. To protect the town water supply from attack a huge tower was built over it and linked to the town walls. A stonemason was given the job of lining the well, helped by his teenage son. As they worked, Edmond de Lacy, the Earl's son came to have a look.

'Don't go near the edge,' shouted the stonemason but Edward was an arrogant youth and ignored the warning. Peering over the edge of the open well, he slipped, fell head first down the shaft and was killed. When the Earl heard of the death of his son, he flew into a rage.

'Fetch the stonemason and his boy to me,' he ordered.

'It was an accident, my Lord. If you punish the stonemason the other masons will stop work and the castle will never be finished,' warned his squires. Henry de Lacy knew his men were right. He could not punish the stonemason if he wanted to keep the goodwill of the workers but he was a vengeful man.

'I'll deal with them later in my own way,' he told himself.

Days later, one of the Earl's landowners came to the castle asking for an audience.

'My Lord, I come to you seeking justice for a great crime has been done to my family honour,' said the landowner.

'Tell me all and I will consider what is to be done,' answered the Earl.

'My daughter, a beautiful childlike young girl, has been violated by one of the workmen from the castle,' explained the distressed landowner.

'Can you identify the villain? If you can, he will be suitably punished,' said the Earl. The landowner went with men at arms to find the perpetrator of the crime. They returned, a short while later, with the stonemason's son.

'I deny the charge,' cried the fearful youth.

'Don't hurt my boy. He's done nothing wrong,' pleaded the stonemason.

'Take the scoundrel to the highest tower and throw him from the top. That will be his fate,' commanded the Earl and grinned, his plan was working well. The soldiers dragged the crying youth up the tower steps to the highest point and waited for the signal. The Earl nodded and his men pushed the stonemason's son from the half finished battlements. He screamed until he hit the ground with a sickening thud. The tragedy of the young man's death was that his pleas were true. He was innocent, the victim of a pack of lies. The guiltless boy had been condemned for something he did not do.

Following the murder of the unfortunate stonemason's son, building work progressed very slowly on the castle. The Earl's brutish behaviour continued to antagonise the Welsh people and, in 1294, during another revolt led by Madog ap Llywelyn, Denbigh was occupied by a Welsh army.

After the English retook the castle, construction continued with an improved and stronger design that would ensure it never again fell into Welsh hands. The new design included massive towers on each side of the gatehouse, a prison and a gate passage filled with murder holes, arrow slits, portcullises and stout wooden doors. Henry de Lacy did not live to see his huge citadel completed. He died in 1311 twenty nine years after starting work on Denbigh castle.

In 1400, a Welsh army, led by Owain Glyndwr, besieged Denbigh but, despite repeated attempts, failed to take the castle. Sixty years later, during the Wars of the Roses, there were two more failed attempts to capture the castle and it was not until the English civil war in 1646 that royalist forces, defending the castle, surrendered to a parliamentary army after a six month siege.

Today, Denbigh castle is a ruin but look carefully at the shattered walls if you pass beneath the Goblin Tower. The Earl's dead son, it is said, gazes sadly from within. If you hear a piercing scream, beware; a strange, formless shape may be falling from above.

Ty-Hyll - The Ugly House

Ty-Hyll is a small cottage 3 miles west of Betws y Coed. Its crude construction using massive boulders makes the building rather quaint but to explore its possible origin we need to look back more than 1000 years in time to well before the cottage was built.

Hywel Dda, which in English means Hywel the Good, was a 10th Century Welsh King. Hywel was an intelligent man with a good knowledge of Welsh, English and Latin. During his reign, Hywel studied the laws of different lands, looking for guidance showing him how to manage his kingdom. The search led to a pilgrimage to Rome and a study of Islamic law. The result was a book known as 'The Laws of Hywel the Good'. The manuscript, which codified Welsh law for the first time, was kept at Dinefwr Castle and its contents were referred to as Hywel's Laws.

The historian David Jenkins describes the laws as, 'compassionate and full of common sense'; they even recognised the rights of women. One law, attributed to Hywel Dda, was the law of 'Ty Un Nos' which translates as 'One Night House.' According to Ty Un Nos, a squatter who built a house on unclaimed land between sunset and sunrise could declare themselves the owner and keep the house. For the claim to be legal the house had to have walls, a roof and smoke rising from its chimney before the sun came up.

During the 17th Century, agriculture was undergoing dramatic changes. Large estates were enclosing common land to farm sheep. Sheep farming required very little labour and provided larger incomes than the rents being paid by tenant farmers. Wanting more land for sheep, tenants were dispossessed and their farms converted to pasture. More than 5000 enclosure acts were passed in what was a massive land grab by the rich. Families were evicted from homes they had lived in for generations and left destitute. Squatting where they could on odd bits of land was the only choice and the law of

Ty Un Nos, created 900 years earlier, offered a legal way to make a new home.

Families and friends would secretly gather materials together ready for the frantic nights work. The dwelling built in a few hours would be extremely basic, little more than a shelter. Improvements such as doors, windows, a weatherproof roof and a floor could be added later. According to some, once the house was successfully built the squatters had the right to any land within the distance of an axe throw. Examples of Ty Un Nos houses exist across Wales but one of the most notable is Ty-Hyll.

Wales is a land of legends and Ty-Hyll is no exception. According to one story the ugly house was built much earlier, in 1475, by two brothers who were brigands. They used Ty-Hyll as their hideout. These were the dark ages. North Wales was a remote and dangerous place where travellers stayed together for safety; cut throats and robbers were a common problem. There is no evidence that the two brothers existed but it is a romantic story and easy to imagine the house, hidden deep in the forest, as a secret lair.

In 1815, a new road was being driven through Wales, linking London to Holyhead and Thomas Telford was the engineer in charge of the project. What he built was a marvel of design which included great bridges and overcame major obstructions. When Telford arrived at Betws y Coed, he chose a route past Ty-Hyll that would take the road through the Ogwen Valley and the now empty cottage became temporary accommodation for his workmen.

The new road brought stagecoaches containing curious passengers and, before long, Ty-Hyll was being described as a 'picturesque cottage'; tourism had arrived in Wales. In 1853, a "Tourist Guide to North Wales" said, "Walking from Capel Curig to Betws-y-Coed and near to the two-mile stone is one of the most picturesque cottages imaginable, placed on the side of the hill above the bridge that crosses the River Llugwy and gives additional beauty to this romantic dell."

In 1929, Edward and Lilian Riley, who lived locally, bought Ty-Hyll and Edward, who was a colourful man, would entertain passers-by with stories. After the couple died the cottage was used as a tea room and antique shop until it closed in the 1980s. In 1988, the empty building was purchased by the Snowdonia Society, a charity working to enhance and protect Snowdonia, who refurbished the cottage together with surrounding woodland and opened them to the public.

Ty-Hyll - The Ugly House is now a tea room

The true origin of Ty-Hyll has been lost with the passing to time. Although the practice of laying claim to land by building a house in one night existed in other European countries, it was never enshrined in English law and no mention of Ty Un Nos appears in Hywel Dda's book of laws. Despite the lack of a written law, squatters used the practice and it was accepted as legitimate. Was Ty-Hyll built in one night? It's very unlikely that it was. The most probable explanation is that Ty-Hyll was thrown together as a temporary shelter by Telford's navvies and later improved when tourists started to take an interest. The boulders, haphazardly stacked to create makeshift walls, were turned into a 19th Century folly and stories invented to explain its existence.

Despite lacking reference to Ty Un Nos, Hywel Dda's book of laws was significant and in recognition of his work part of the building containing the National Assembly of Wales was named Ty Hywel (Hywel's House). The Government act of Wales, passed in 2006, created the National Assembly and started to return the power to Welsh people to make their own laws, as Hywel Dda had done centuries before.

===

This short extract is from 'Welsh Follies - *The Secrets, Stories and Scandals of 60 Welsh Follies*.' Available as an ebook and paperpack from Amazon.

Other books by Graham Watkins include;

'The Iron Masters'
'Birth of a Salesman'
'Exit Strategy'
'How to sell Ice to Eskimos'
'A White Man's War'
'The Sicilian Defence'
Plus a series of walking book entitled 'Walking with Welsh Legends.'

Details of all his works are available at;
www.grahamwatkins.info/

Printed in Great Britain
by Amazon

67564040R00160